PERGAMON INTERNATIONAL LIBRARY
of Science, Technology, Engineering and Social Studies

The 1000-volume original paperback library in aid of education,
industrial training and the enjoyment of leisure

Publisher: Robert Maxwell, M.C.

Contemporary Constitutional Lawmaking

Pergamon Government and Politics Series
Series Editors

Richard A. Brody
Stanford University

Norman J. Ornstein
America Enterprise Institute for Public Policy Research

Paul Peterson
Brookings Institution

Nelson Polsby
University of California, Berkeley

Martin Shapiro
University of California, Berkeley

Pergamon Government & Politics Series

Contemporary Constitutional Lawmaking

The Supreme Court and the Art of Politics

Lief H. Carter
University of Georgia

PERGAMON PRESS
New York Oxford Toronto Sydney Paris Frankfurt

Pergamon Press Offices:

U.S.A.	Pergamon Press Inc., Maxwell House, Fairview Park, Elmsford, New York 10523, U.S.A.
U.K.	Pergamon Press Ltd., Headington Hill Hall, Oxford OX3 0BW, England
CANADA	Pergamon Press Canada Ltd., Suite 104, 150 Consumers Road, Willowdale, Ontario M2J 1P9, Canada
AUSTRALIA	Pergamon Press (Aust.) Pty. Ltd., P.O. Box 544, Potts Point, NSW 2011, Australia
FRANCE	Pergamon Press SARL, 24 rue des Ecoles, 75240 Paris, Cedex 05, France
FEDERAL REPUBLIC OF GERMANY	Pergamon Press GmbH, Hammerweg 6, D-6242 Kronberg-Taunus, Federal Republic of Germany

Copyright © 1985 Pergamon Press Inc.

Library of Congress Cataloging in Publication Data

Carter, Lief H.
    Contemporary constitutional lawmaking.

    (Pergamon government and politics series)
    Includes index.
    1. United States--Constitutional law. 2. United
States. Supreme Court. 3. Political questions and
judicial power--United States. I. Title. II. Series.
KF4550.C37 1985   342.73   84-26524
ISBN 0-08-030970-4   347.302
ISBN 0-08-030969-0 (pbk.)

Printed in the United States of America

FOR DELIGHT

The power of art is now clear. It introduces value into the world by creating in the hearts of men the experience of order and meaning. To assert the existence of order, meaning, and value, whether natural, divine, or transcendent, is an illusion; to experience them is essential to maintaining life. Art is the source of that experience.   —MORSE PECKHAM

 # CONTENTS

 PREFACE

COOK: Were you ever a cook?
POET: A Cook? No surely.
COOK: Then you can be no good poet: for a good poet differs nothing at all
from a master-cook. Either's art is in the wisdom of the mind.

—Ben Jonson

If a play is any good, any act of it, any scene of it, any character of it, can be
interpreted fifteen different ways, each one as good as the other. . . . The script
itself is merely the raw material on which a group of collaborators have got to
work. It is not the finished article. That idea is merely the invention, for the most
basely materialistic reasons, of literary professors.

—Tyrone Guthrie

Modern jurisprudence is in a bind. The century of Western social philosophy
that has included American pragmatism, German hermeneutics, and French
deconstructionism has severely weakened the building blocks of jurisprudence. The determinateness of legal texts, the intelligibility of the intent or the
goals of lawgivers, and the attainability of a national consensus about fundamental political values all appear as naïve pipedreams. Judges with differing
political goals and values may use the same legal rules and reasoning techniques to justify different outcomes in a case, but neither is necessarily wrong.
Yet in the same century we have learned that groups both small and large exist
and function over time only as long as their members believe the group and
their participation in it serves some normative "good." Slavery and other
forms of subjugation by brute force and economic coercion are the only
exceptions.

In the United States the Constitution and the meanings the Supreme Court
imputes to it, play, judging from the prominent treatment educators and
journalists give it, a major role in maintaining beliefs in the goodness of the
polity. We read judicial opinions in constitutional cases, not just their legal
outcomes, because the opinion, not the outcome, persuades us that we experience political goodness together. Indeed, people who resist the exercise of
power in purely private matters defend their resistance by appealing to their
"constitutional rights." My children have made this claim against me more
than once. A constitution is for them a metaphor, though hardly the only one,
for goodness in relationships.

The tension caused by the collapse of conventional constitutional jurisprudence, on one hand, and the necessary maintenance of faith in the normative
goodness of our participation in the polity, on the other, frame the central
problem for contemporary legal philosophy, but the tension reveals itself in
public affairs, not just in the pages of academic journals. The collapse of
conventional jurisprudence underlines virtually every hour of the 1984 public
television series, "The Constitution: That Delicate Balance." The program's
format, like that of a law school class, deliberately exposes legal uncertainty
and openendedness. Many of the issues discussed—the insanity defense in
criminal trials, for example—raise no conventional constitutional issues at all.
This delicate balance merges legal questions into questions about the goodness of the polity itself. Yet public events also reveal how threatening this
uncertainty is. For some reason evidence of journalistic fictionalizing makes
front page news. In 1984 the *New York Times* and the *Wall Street Journal*
featured on their front pages the confession of a *New Yorker* writer that he
had synthesized from various experiences a composite story (many years earlier) about Spanish politics. We must believe we live in a knowable world, and
we condemn events that shake our faith in such a world.

The jurisprudential bind has, perhaps in conjunction with the increasingly
obvious political agendas of the Burger Court justices, provoked a virtual
explosion of constitutional jurisprudence scholarship in the last 10 years. This
book reviews that explosion and offers one exit from this bind. I assume
without extended argument that the modern philosophical consensus is so
broad and, within current frames of reference, so powerful, that nothing can
be gained by ignoring it or challenging it. Yet normative evaluation of the
opinions of the Supreme Court shows every sign of health within, not in spite
of, this philosophical mandate. The reason is that the normative rightness on
which groups depend does not aspire to final proofs or demonstrably "correct" answers to common questions. People desire the sustained conviction
that group norms are not so much final as intelligible and powerful, capable,
in other words, of generating significant conversations about political goodness.

Norms are of course abstractions, and faith in their power and intelligibility
depends on public rituals, dramas, and performances that recreate the linkage
between abstractions and behavior. The Constitution in this view commands
us to engage in certain political dramas that sustain this conviction. More
specifically, it commands the courts, and primarily the Supreme Court, to
"perform" acts that link norms and action. The standard for evaluating the
Court is thus not the intellectual proof of the rightness of one answer as
against all others. There may be fifteen different right ways to perform *Hamlet*
and the equal protection clause as well. The search for the one proper answer
has brought jurisprudence to its present dead end. Rather, we should evaluate
the quality of a legal performance, using the same aesthetic guides we use to
judge theatrical performances and other artistic acts.

To the charge that this exit from the bind merely jumps from a postrelativistic frying pan into an aesthetic-theory fire that has consumed all meaning—art is anything one chooses to call art—I have two answers. The first is experiential. We have all, I trust, been moved by a good performance. Good performances create a temporary order out of chaos. They give us confidence that we can identify goodness and converse about it. The experience that performances achieve goodness is, I believe, widespread and real. An audience that breaks spontaneously into an ovation at the end of a play or during a jazz or rock concert does not engage in an act of mass psychology. The performance has moved people individually and collectively to a common appreciation that goodness has been achieved. Second, I believe that the nature of this reaction is not nearly as mystical or non-rational as people, with perhaps literary and other professors at their lead, might suppose. I draw on the work of Nelson Goodman and Michael Oakeshott to show that, within the frame of experience of audiences, the "fittedness" of the elements of the performance and the coherence of the thinking the performance conveys explain reactions to paintings, concerts, poems, television shows, and judicial opinions.

Aesthetics examines not objects of art but the relationships between performers and audiences. Aesthetics is, in other words, a version of communications theory wherein the audience matters as much as the performer. In constitutional law the audience is not restricted to professionals: scholars, lawyers, and judges. By definition the process of constituting the polity must speak to laymen, and particularly to students and litigants, actual and potential. Nothing better explains the failure of modern jurisprudence than its failure to appreciate the proper constitutional audience.

The art of politics, as Sheldon Wolin (1960) puts it, "has to do with the reconciliation of a wide range of valid claims" (p. 64). It can achieve only temporary stabilities and syntheses. It makes the incomplete appear momentarily complete, which is what performance accomplishes. But modern constitutional theory has "relied on rules and procedures to the virtual exclusion of the art of politics" (Wolin, p. 390). The exit from the bind seeks to recover this art, and the central questions are, for what audience does the Court in a given case perform, and how may it perform effectively for it?

And who, then, is my audience? Who do I think you are? I have written this book for two kinds of audiences. First, if you are an experienced constitutional scholar, I shall try to persuade you that aesthetic theory has not yet found the central place it deserves in jurisprudence. I review here all the familiar branches of current doctrine: Dworkin and modern positivism, utilitarianism, the Critical Legal Studies movement, and even the last gasps of strict, "back to the Constitution," interpretivism. The Critical movement and philosophers like Rorty and MacIntyre push us toward an aesthetic jurisprudence, and I hope to span the remaining distance here. I think this approach can give us a clearer and more consistent picture of the Court's political role for nearly two centuries. The Court's good performances have helped sustain the conviction of political goodness.

I also write for students who, having read some quantity of Court opinions, know that these opinions do not routinely follow conventional rules of legal logic, do not routinely state normatively appealing public policy, and do not routinely honor a "proper" political place for the courts relative to other centers of political power. Your exposure to opinions presumably shook your faith in the conventional criteria for evaluating the rightness or goodness of an opinion, and this book exposes you to many other more systematic attempts to evaluate constitutional decisions. I hope by the end of this book you will appreciate why there is so much disagreement about how to evaluate the Court, and I hope that you will at least feel some confidence in defending what *you* mean when you argue that one opinion is good and another bad, even if you and I mean different things. If the Constitution is what the Court says it is, we may still agree that some opinions are better than others, even if we do not agree on which ones. That much agreement will sustain our belief that we share a normatively meaningful political community.

I have one additional prefatory message for each of these audiences. I want to caution students that, as Walter Bagehot once wrote, "One of the greatest pains to human nature is the pain of a new idea." You will encounter new ideas that will hurt because they will contradict what you probably take for granted about law, science, religion, knowledge, truth and fiction. Kenneth Boulding once wrote that science is an "organized fantasy about the real world." So is law, and so is religion. The trick is to find ways of fantasizing about experiences whose accuracy we trust in spite of the deeper knowledge that we fantasize.

Many political science scholars, particularly those of a behavioral bent whose reading does not encompass Richard Rorty and Alasdair MacIntyre, will wrestle at their students' sides with these new ideas. To those who have already ventured into post-relativist philosophy I need to caution against expecting closure on one fundamental issue. The model of constitutional lawmaking I offer will seem at some points in my analysis very much a product of post-industrial American political culture. It will seem to claim no more than D. H. Lawrence claimed in asserting, in "Studies of Classic American Literature," linkages between culture and the writings of Franklin or Poe. Similarly, Edward Rothstein has recently asserted that in American music Liberace is the cultural analog to Franz Liszt. The Critical scholar Mark Tushnet urges us to see the work of courts in just this light, and much of what follows will appear to endorse such cultural relativism. However, I also believe, with Sheldon Wolin, that the aesthetic element in politics is imbedded in political experience itself, across time and across culture. I would like to argue that both Rorty and MacIntyre lead us to an aesthetic doorstep, and that it is time to enter (or reenter) an aesthetic home. I hint at this idea more than once in what follows, but the full exposition belongs in another volume.

Let me now offer a few guides to the structure of the argument, chapter by chapter. Chapter one develops the problem abstractly, and chapter two reviews recent and classic constitutional cases, primarily to make the point that the Supreme Court has never seriously or consistently conformed to any conventional theory of constitutional jurisprudence. Chapter three describes and explains the persistence of conventional interpretive theory in some quarters. I say more about modern hermeneutics and the Critical Legal Studies movement by way of criticizing the interpretivists, and readers looking for quick access to that material will find it in the last part of chapter three. I next canvass the well-known non-interpretive alternatives, political alternatives (like Wechsler, Bickel, Ely, and so forth) in chapter four, and normative approaches (Dworkin, Rawls, and Walter Murphy, for example) in chapter five. Chapters five and six describe in more detail post-relativist philosophy, e.g., hermeneutics, Rorty, and Stanley Fish's critique of Dworkin. Chapters six and seven together state the aesthetic theory and apply it to constitutional legal materials. Readers familiar with my legal reasoning book (*Reason in Law*, Little, Brown, 1979 and 1984) will find that the aesthetic argument here takes up where that book stopped. I said in that book's last chapter that the task of the opinion-writing judge is to harmonize the legal, factual and normative elements in the case. I hope I explain here what that statement might mean.

Finally a word about my method. You would not expect a book that tries to explain two hundred years of constitutional history at the same time it reviews the philosophical contributions of Rawls, Dworkin, Gadamer, Habermas, Rorty and Nelson Goodman and describes the full range of constitutional jurisprudence (from Robert Bork to the Critical movement), to provide comprehensive dissections and analyses of the works of each of these scholars. I certainly do not attempt that here. However, I do not touch so many points of view only briefly merely to survey the field for undergraduates. I hope many will benefit from the survey, but I intend this survey to support an important step in my argument. "Schools of thought" are academic polities. The persistence of discredited belief systems within academic communities confirms, I think, the assertion that group life depends on maintaining conversations more than it depends on proofs of ultimate truth.

"Good scholarship" is that which an audience of fellow scholars finds appealing within its own frame of reference. To outsiders the frame of reference may look like a silly fantasy, but the audience within defends the goodness of conversations about the fantasy. We can and regularly do admire the scholarship of those whose fantasy we do not share. I believe the aesthetic properties of a good scholarly performance attract us apart from its conclusion, and I think it helpful to evaluate judicial opinions in the same light.

You may well object that this framework is so value-neutral that it justifies Hitler's demagoguery and other atrocities revealed in political history. I would dispute vigorously the charge that I justify demagoguery, but I do hope to explain it. History so frequently confirms the political effectiveness of the performances of demagogues that we cannot afford to rest comfortable with the observation that the consequences of good performances may be morally repugnant.

I feel fortunate to be able to speak in one voice to two audiences. The aesthetic approach I endorse here allows us to assess the strengths and weaknesses of the efforts of both judges and scholars to communicate their visions. I hope, in applying it at some length to scholarly writing, that this framework will broaden the experienced scholar's sense of philosophical possibilities for the very same reason the framework and its applications narrow, by focusing and ordering, the jumbled mass that for students constitutional law so often resembles. Hence, I am particularly grateful to Martin Shapiro and Pergamon's series editors for endorsing and promoting scholarly work of this sort. Thanks also to Pergamon's Jerry Frank and Lynn Rosen, who have supported the project with a mix of quiet patience and well-vocalized pressures for results, each at the proper time.

I have gained immeasurably from the direct help of Robert Grafstein, John Tietz, Bernard Dauenhauer, and Milner Ball. Each has educated me about crucial elements in my argument. However, since each belongs to a different school of thought, I trust there is little danger that my views will be wrongly ascribed to them. My thanks also to Tom Austin and Emily Cofield for thorough and conscientious research assistance and to that multitude of scholars to whom my ties are deep but indirect.

Oh yes. To avoid confusion or false expectations, you should know that I have dedicated this book to my well-named sister, Delight Carter Willing, of Bainbridge Island, Washington.

Chapter 1 THE CONSTITUTIONAL DILEMMA Judicial Interpretation or Judicial Creation?

Even before the Eighteenth Amendment books about the United States Constitution were apt to be pretty dry. They usually tell what the Supreme Court says in a lot of cases and try to show how what it says in one case will jibe all right with what it says in the other cases. After the writers tell what happens in each case, they then try to forget it and to put all the cases together and make up a set of rules to show what the Supreme Court has been up to and what it is going to do next. This is a very hard thing to do and it is very hard to read after it has been done. You have to think very hard all the time and even then you get all mixed up. This kind of book makes you tired because you have to try so hard to think, and so you usually stop trying to read it.

—Thomas Reed Powell

INTRODUCTION[1]

The epigraphic starting point for this book's constitutional passage appeared in a 1925 review essay for *The New Republic* titled "Constitutional Metaphors." I resort to it in part to assure you that this book does not try to put all the cases together and predict what the Supreme Court will do next. You *can* get through this book without getting "all mixed up." This book offers a straightforward explanation for why the conventional criteria of legal analysis—stare decisis, consistency with canons of legal reasoning, discovery of the intent of those who adopt legal rules, judicial self-restraint, and so forth—mix the reader up: The Supreme Court has never paid much attention to them.

I suggest here that we can more satisfactorily describe and evaluate the quality of the Court's constitutional opinions if we abandon the familiar criteria of legal analysis and employ instead aesthetic criteria of good performances. Courts are, after all, performing bodies. The litigated case abstracts, distills, rearranges, simplifies and thus fictionalizes life's raw materials. The judicial opinion which resolves the case, like a play, puts before an audience a vision of the deeper meaning of the material it has reshaped.

---

[1] Readers who normally skip prefaces are urged to make an exception in this book's case. My introduction really begins there.

1

I shall argue that Supreme Court opinions have performed in this way throughout our history and that the fundamental questions for constitutional jurisprudence are therefore aesthetic questions. But this unconventional way of assessing constitutional law may also threaten to mix you up, so you deserve an illustration. Under the conventional approach we might conclude that *Brown v. Board of Education*, the 1954 school desegregation case, was good because it applies a universal moral truth built into the normative fabric of the Constitution. Or we might hold it good because it was consistent with such recent equal protection precedents as *Sweatt v. Painter* (1950). But we could also criticize it for failing to demonstrate that the result conformed to the expressed intent of those who ratified the Fourteenth Amendment (Berger, 1977), or for failing to dispose unequivocally of the previously declared principle permitting separate but equal facilities. The aesthetic approach, on the other hand, examines how persuasively the Court fit together or harmonized the fundamental elements at issue in the case. I believe the opinion persuasively harmonized the basic principle of equality of opportunity with the evidence that racial segregation unequalizes the opportunities of racial minorities, but my point is that goodness depends not on the rightness of the principle of equality of opportunity or the scientific accuracy of the factual evidence but on the nature of the fit the opinion claimed to create.

This view of constitutional lawmaking will require some readers to break an habitual way of thinking about law, one to which Thomas Reed Powell also alludes. This is the habit of legalistic thinking: law must be mechanistic, determinate, and, like a mathematical proof, demonstrate the singular correctness of its results. All public policymaking dramatizes, simplifies, idealizes and hence falsifies the chaos of raw political experience. (See especially Gusfield, 1981.) I fear that much of the routine academic pontificating occasioned by the bicentennial celebration of the Constitution's founding will reinforce legalistic constitutional models. We have already seen titles like "An Acceptable Meaning of the Constitution" (Leedes, 1984), and "On What the Constitution Means" (Barber, 1984). It is tempting to think that if we have one nation and one supreme law, the Constitution can mean only one thing, but it doesn't. This is the dilemma addressed in this chapter's title. How can we have a legally constituted polity if there is nothing fixed and stable to interpret and apply?

This chapter outlines the aesthetic solution to this dilemma. I don't expect this introduction alone to shake the faith of mechanistic thinkers. I do wish here to offer one clue, however. It is usually not meaningful to identify "the" meaning of any relationship between or among people. What matters in constituting a relationship, including a political relationship, is not some static bargain or agreement. These agreements change continuously, sometimes deliberately, sometimes subconsciously. The phrase "to make love" tells the story. Relationships of all kinds, sexual and otherwise, persist only as the parties regularly remake them. Continuous judicial lawmaking remakes the Constitution in this fashion and thus preserves the political relationship. The bicentennial should celebrate not the document preserved in Washington, D.C., but the dramatic political performances that created it and that have continuously recreated it since its adoption.

POLITICAL JURISPRUDENCE

Another kind of useful book has appeared in the last three decades that also does not try "to put the cases together." These works of "political jurisprudence" describe the Court and its decisions in the same terms that political scientists use to describe and analyze other political institutions, for example, the House Armed Services Committee, the Office of Management and Budget, and state legislatures. The questions common to all politics ask how people in groups make decisions, what the consequences of their decisions have been or might be, and so on.

Political jurisprudence has earned a venerable spot in the political science literature. Its classics include Jack Peltason's description of the political impediments to the implementation of school desegregation (1961), Martin Shapiro's analysis of the effects of the Court's many political environments on its work (1964), and Walter Murphy's revelations of the strategies the justices use to seek their political objectives (1964). This work treats the announced decisions of the Court as no more or less intrinsically interesting than those of any other body. We tend to conclude from it that when nine people holding strong legal and political philosophies create constitutional decisions collectively, they are not likely to produce major philosophical discoveries. After all, how many great philosophical treatises were coauthored? As Benjamin Barber (1982) put it, "[A]ll philosophical solutions . . . are decisive, neat, coherent, and altogether incompatible with real life and the intuitive moral convictions we bring to it. . . . Politics begins where philosophy ends."

The knowledge and theory generated by these explicitly political studies of the Court have undoubtedly improved the state of the discipline. It seems to me thoroughly defensible to read opinions not as truth statements but as works produced by committees, as examples of political compromises at different points in history. And it is defensible to teach the logic of public policy or the foundations of normative political philosophy using the Court's policy and philosophical failures as a foil.

Yet, political jurisprudence lacks something jurisprudential. Scholars, students, journalists, and some "ordinary citizens," as the old "Impeach Earl Warren" billboards once signaled, take quite seriously the normative character of what the Court says and does. It is a peculiar state of affairs, for if the Court is no more or less morally informed or politically significant than any of hundreds of other political institutions, why do both college and law professors treat it as the prima donna subject in all of legal scholarship? Why, given the findings of political jurisprudence, do people persist in seeking rightness and fearing wrongness in constitutional decisions? Why do we celebrate a constitutional bicentennial at all? How is it even possible to state that any constitutional judgment is good or bad, right or wrong, unless we merely assert our personal political ideologies and preferences? The persistent demand for goodness in law is, in other words, a political phenomenon in its own right, and this book examines that phenomenon.

EVALUATING CONSTITUTIONAL DECISIONS

This book offers an answer to a persistent question, one that lawyers, judges, constitutional scholars, political philosophers, students, and the occasionally attentive citizen ask when they read, or read about, a constitutional decision: "By what standards shall I, the evaluator of the decision before me, judge its quality, its rightness, or its goodness?"

To the question, "How good is something?", academicians have a safe, conventional answer: "Well, it all depends on your point of view." Lawyers will read a case as a potential aid or obstacle to prevailing on a similar issue for their client. If the "right side" (the client's side) won, the lawyer will seek in the opinion reinforcement of his client's position. He will believe the court decided rightly. If the other side won, the lawyer may read the facts and the opinion more carefully in hopes of distinguishing his client's problem from the decision before him, or revealing in the decision a fatal flaw. It is presumptively wrong.

The judge or the judge's clerk also evaluates a past judicial decision with reference to the case before him, but with the important additional obligation that he must choose and justify a ruling in the present case. He may already have "hunched" his way to the conclusion, but he must either reconcile the conclusion with what has gone before or pretend the past away. "Good cases" simplify the task of justification. "Bad cases" complicate it.

Scholars, students, and the occasional citizen read a judicial opinion differently. They don't relate it to a professional decision they must make affecting the fortunes of others. They may merely hope to learn what the decision holds, its "bottom line," and add this information to a descriptive map, one that all but the specialists and experts may soon enough forget. The good case is merely coherent enough to permit description. Others may subject the results and justification to some test of the public good or of their own moral beliefs and political ideologies. A good case reinforces one's moral and political sentiments; a bad case opposes them.

College prelaw majors read cases one way, neo-Marxist law professors another way, Straussian political theorists yet another way, ad infinitum. But is the answer that "it all depends on your point of view," satisfactory? If the question is, "How should we experience sighting the fingernail moon in a clear western sky at dusk?," or "What does the first piercing birdsong that breaks the silence of dawn mean?," the answer surely "all depends." The moon may excite A with thoughts of a romantic night ahead but remind B of a lover just lost. The birdsong may fill me with joy as I suddenly hear its resemblance to a motif from a Beethoven symphony at the same time it awakens my wife prematurely from a restless and too brief sleep.

Here the constitutional plot thickens. The United States Constitution is the "supreme law of the land." Laws, unlike moons and birdsongs in mainstream American culture, claim to command and proscribe behaviors. Laws do not routinely make allowances and exceptions for "your point of view." Judicial decisions say what the law means. For the very reasons that an antilittering law ceases to be law if each potential litterer remains free to define litter in his own way, so the supreme law of the land as declared by the Supreme Court cannot remain law if its meaning "all depends" on each citizen's independent point of view. In addition, I have left out of my list of case evaluators the losing litigant. Tocqueville wrote that "men are not corrupted by the exercise of power or debased by the habit of obedience, but by the exercise of a power which they believe to be illegitimate and by obedience to a rule which they consider to be usurped and oppressive." (See also Barrington Moore, 1978.) Losing litigants might justifiably believe that decisions anchored only in the judge's personal "point of view" are "usurped and oppressive." In a community that values the rule of law, where power must justify itself apart from the will of the powerful, the answer that "it all depends" is unacceptable.

Each theory of constitutional meaning and each framework for evaluating the quality of a constitutional opinion therefore claims for itself potential universality. The prelaw undergraduate, the losing litigant, the neo-Marxist, and Straussian professors need not see my moon or hear my bird, but each, it appears, must see my constitution, or I must see theirs. But here the thickening constitutional plot threatens to seize up solid because *the dominant and central position in twentieth century philosophy holds that knowledge and understanding of phenomena do depend on the individual's, the perceiver's, point of view.* Liberty, justice, equality, charity, cooperation, and knowledge do not merely collide in the academic world of ethical theory. We each know them differently. They cannot and will not reduce to an objective system that saints will accept and sinners reject. We yearn for one objective Constitution, one that judges merely interpret, yet it would appear that each decision creates new constitutional meaning; indeed it creates different meanings for different readers.

MODERN PHILOSOPHY
AND JURISPRUDENCE

Readers not yet familiar with the fundamentals of Western social philosophy may not understand how philosophy arrived at its present state. Chapters three and five address the matter at some length, but the unfamiliar reader will benefit from an introductory sketch here.

The central feature of "modernism" in Western societies is the separation and bureaucratization of roles and functions. The differentiation of politics and government from social and religious life does not mark most human societies, nor does the bureaucratization of thinkers—their separation not only from the religious and political life of the community but into departments that separate them from each other. These two kinds of separations have profoundly changed the nature of political thought itself.

For our purposes Locke's "social contract" theory marks the completion of the separation. Once government becomes something other than the citizenry itself, something with which the citizenry metaphorically contracts, and once the *polis* in politics refers not to the life of the community but to the life of the government, the question necessarily arises how citizens can determine whether government keeps to its contract, whether government is performing "correctly." One answer, which we associate with Jeremy Bentham, holds that government keeps its contract to the extent that its policies seek the greatest good for the greatest number. Bentham's "utilitarian" answer, assisted by the growing belief in the power of science to measure both human attitudes and preferences and their consonance or dissonance with actual social conditions, had a powerful effect on social science and on public policy. By the beginning of the twentieth century, the dominant scholarly consensus was that, as in biology, scientists could determine the functions of social conditions and assess the costs and benefits that varying conditions caused in the quality of individual social life.

However, given the increasing differentiation of schools of social thought, it was perhaps inevitable that other theories of good government would arise to compete with utilitarianism. The most natural of these grew out of and extended conventional notions of legal contract itself. Government's side of the social contract bargain required it to observe the "rule of law."

While utilitarian and legal criteria for evaluating the goodness of government differ, note one fundamentally important similarity: Both formulations for good government—the ideal distribution of wealth and compliance with the commands of rules—hold out the promise of attaining single "correct" answers to questions of public policy.

Why, then, does the consensus in contemporary philosophy deny that government can be assessed by these criteria? We must be careful not to see the issue as a debate between hardheaded, realistic scientists and soft, fuzzy-headed philosophers. Modern philosophy takes quite seriously the essence of science, which is careful observation, logical rigor, and ideological skepticism. Modern philosophy "observes" with no less rigor than science that the assumptions on which utilitarian functionalism and the rule of law depend don't work. The point is central to my argument, so let me elaborate further.

Utilitarianism depends on the discoverability of preferences. To know what is good for any number depends on knowing what goods people prefer. But social scientists have great difficulty discovering preferences, partly because preferences changes as conditions change, and partly because the choice of a common standard by which to measure differences in preferences cannot itself be defined by those preferences. Utilitarianism, in other words, assumes an unrealistically high degree of conformity and commonality in both human nature and in social life, and it overestimates the power of scientific observation and measurement.

Scholarly analyses of political decisionmaking, including the works of political jurisprudence I cited previously, observe many political forces that shape policy quite apart from information about utilitarian functions. Furthermore, descriptions of the processes of discovery in the natural sciences themselves, of which Thomas Kuhn's *The Structure of Scientific Revolutions* (1970) is the most well known, reveal how pervasively unconsciously held political values do shape what scientists believe constitutes objective "truth."

Finally, if rules of law are to govern objectively, people must be able to discover some common meaning in the language of legal texts or, if not that, then some fixed sense of their original purposes. But modern linguists, led by Wittgenstein, observe that words and texts gain meaning only in relation to the circumstances and cases to which they relate. Because these contexts are to an extent unique in every instance of application, rules cannot be said to have a fixed political meaning, and they cannot therefore be said to provide a fixed measure of political or governmental "correctness." Thus, modern hermeneutics, the philosophy of interpreting the meaning of past events, has concluded that it is generally impossible to recover a meaning of a rule in the historical setting in which it was enacted that logically determines answers to a range of questions in the present.

OPTIMISTIC MESSAGES

Later chapters will explain in more detail the failure of conventional jurisprudence.[2] I introduce the dilemma here merely to persuade you, if only tentatively at this point, that no simple resolution of the tensions between conventional jurisprudence and modern philosophy exists. Philosophical relativism, historicism, the hermeneutics of Gadamer and Habermas, and

---

[2] For recent stimulating analyses of the state of modern philosophy see Alasdair MacIntyre, *After Virtue*, (1981), and Richard Rorty, *Philosophy and the Mirror of Nature*, (1979).

Richard Rorty's proclamation of the death of moral philosophy all threaten conventional assumptions about the nature of law and judgment.

Having written so pessimistically, however, let me remind you that this book carries several specifically optimistic messages. One of these is that since the mid-1970s legal scholarship has begun to address the constitutional dilemma head-on. The "Critical Legal Studies" movement and the "Conference on Critical Legal Studies," which now numbers over a thousand members, seek actively to redefine the nature of the legal process in light of modern philosophical developments. The movement is the most significant jurisprudential development since the Realism movement of the 1920s and 1930s. The movement's advent, and the need for a political science assessment of it, in fact gave the initial impetus to this book.

"Critical" themes will emerge in each of this book's chapters, but let me try to whet your appetite here. The fundamental question in constitutional jurisprudence is whether it is possible for courts, through their opinions, to generate among readers the sense that they share with other citizens a morally good community. The massive "Critical Legal Studies" symposium issue of the *Stanford Law Review* (January, 1984) begins with an article entitled "Roll Over Beethoven," which addresses that very question. This article, a dialogue between law professors Peter Gabel and Duncan Kennedy, debates whether formal philosophizing, jurisprudential or otherwise, can produce meaningful knowledge. The participants seem to accept the proposition that moments of true communication between and among people—moments of "intersubjective zap," they call them—happen. But Gabel argues that thinking and writing, including legal writing, can extend these moments, while Kennedy argues that "zap" exists only in face-to-face experience and that formal philosophy blocks us from direct experience. Kennedy's position, if true, makes futile all attempts to assess the rightness and wrongness of authoritative communications, including court opinions.

One of this book's optimistic themes reports the possibility of jurisprudential breakthroughs, or rather "break-outs," from the sometimes isolated world of legal education to the larger consensus in science and philosophy. But the more optimistic theme, and this book's principal theoretical lode, holds that even if we concede the truth of the pessimistic philosophical conclusions I have just sketched, constitutional opinions nevertheless have the potential to sustain (and equally to undermine) intersubjective experience of political goodness.

MAIN THEMES

Thomas Reed Powell's 1925 book review that began this chapter continued: "The new book which Mr. Beck has written about the Constitution is a very different kind of book. You can read it without thinking." I hope what follows is a different kind of book. It is neither a book about the law nor about judicial politics, and it does not offer a theory of "what the Constitution means." However, thinking is its essence. To answer the seemingly simple question, "How shall I evaluate the quality of a judicial opinion?" pushes you into the most difficult and controversial questions in modern philosophy. The jurisprudential position in which you find yourself at the end will, in the process of getting there, require you to decide whether and in what sense scholarship, or anything else, matters.

Whatever this book may be, however, it is not a mystery story. Therefore, let me outline my argument's main themes:

First, I do not challenge the conclusions of modern linguistics, hermeneutics, and perceptual psychology. "Truth," defined as it is by personal experience, varies according to each of our separate and unique experiences. Truth is private. We do live in an age where the fundamentalist preacher condemns the same bastards and fornicators that the social welfare journals have transformed into morally neutral "nonmarital children" and "POSSLQs."[3] The language, culture, and experiences of the citizens within a single neighborhood may vary tremendously. To an unprecedented degree, people make and live in different worlds.

Second, granting the premises of modern philosophy, we may still share the experience of goodness in public affairs. Interpersonal understanding—"intersubjective zap"—can and does happen in formal, or if you prefer, philosophical, communication as well as face to face. The psychologist Henry A. Murray reminds us that the phrase "the shock of recognition" comes to us from a typically philosophical Melville novel (Shneidman, ed., 1981, p. 82). Works of art create these zaps or shocks of recognition. John Dewey, who titled his 1931 lectures at Harvard "Art As Experience" (1934), insisted that the "work" of art is not the finished object, but rather what it communicates to us about our experiences. "The task," he wrote, "is to restore continuity between the refined and intensified forms of experience that are works of art and the everyday events, doings, and sufferings that are universally recognized to constitute experience" (1934, p. 3). In the same vein, James Agee reportedly once said of art, "For God's sake, don't think of it as art!"

Third, it is precisely the task of a legal opinion to refine and intensify—to dramatize if you will—the nature of our experiences. Court opinions are artistic works, and we may read them evaluatively, that is, for moral meaning, if we adopt aesthetic standards rather than conventional jurisprudential ones. Aesthetic theory is itself a theory about communication and rhetoric. I argue that in the search for legal meaning, just as in the search for poetic, musical,

---

[3] "Persons of opposite sex sharing living quarters."

or visual meaning, discovery and creation are inseparable. Cardozo himself described the nature of the judicial process over fifty years ago in just such terms. Ultimate or objective truth does not induce the "shock" of recognition; the shock is a reaction to a successful refinement and clarification of the meaning of our everyday experiences.

Fourth, by way of elaboration, I argue that justice done well creates a persuasive vision of a coherent world that in turn makes the case outcome plausible. The psychologist Henry Murray is again helpful. "Next to the seizures and shapings of creative thought—the thing itself—no comparable experience is more thrilling than being witched, illumined, and transfigured by the magic of another's art" (Shneidman, p. 82). The art and magic of persuasive creation sound like ancient and therefore presumptively untrustworthy rubrics, but they should not mystify us. We do experience shocks and zaps from Plato, religious texts, Melville, and other distant sources. Experiencing justice is simply one species in the genus "shock/zap" that includes poetry, visual and plastic arts, dramatic and musical performances, and so on.

Fifth, I believe that if constitutional history contains common patterns or denominators, these patterns are best understood as aesthetic phenomena. When the Court has succeeded, it has succeeded not by persuading legal scholars of the technical acceptability of its result. Rather, it has persuaded a political audience that it has made sense of its members' knowledge and experience. This was just as true in its time for *Dartmouth College v. Woodward* (1819), whose legal conclusions we reject today, as for *McCulloch v. Maryland* (1819), whose conclusions we generally still accept. I also believe that aesthetics explains why communities of jurisprudential scholars have persisted so long in writing about a legal system and a Court that have never existed. The division of labor and the departmentalization of academicians have created separate intellectual communities outside politics. The work of the Court and the work of jurisprudential philosophers both illustrate what Wittgenstein called "language games." Richard Flathman has said of these games, based on what Wittgenstein called "fine shades of behavior," that "they are rarely if ever covered by rules governing the activity. Hence we cannot adequately explain them or the learning of them in terms of rules or rule application and following. Yet regular participants in and observers of such activities will know their place in them" (1976, p. 21). Scholars today play a language game of their own devising, one of whose fine shades of behavior requires scholars to appear to have discovered rules rather than the fine shades of behavior in the games they analyze. The proper task of the social sciences and of philosophy is rather to examine the language games of political action (Winch, 1958). I hope to show that those scholars whose work has received the widest audience—especially John Rawls—have succeeded not because they are "correct" (Rawls is open to numerous criticisms) but because they have performed convincingly. The nature of John Rawls' performance, not his conclusions, should concern us most.

In his *Ways of Worldmaking* (1978, pp. 138–139), Nelson Goodman summarizes a version of the aesthetic framework that I use to evaluate judicial performances:

> Briefly, then, truth of statements and rightness of descriptions, representations, exemplifications, [and] expressions . . . is primarily a matter of fit: fit to what is referred to in one way or another, or to other renderings, or to modes and manners of organization. . . . And knowing or understanding is seen as ranging beyond the acquiring of true beliefs to the discovering and devising of fit of all sorts.
>
> Procedures and tests used in the search for right versions range from deductive and inductive inference through fair sampling and accord among samples . . . . [R]ightness of categorization . . . is . . . a matter of fit with practice; . . . without the organization, the selection of relevant kinds, effected by evolving tradition, there is no rightness or wrongness of categorization, no validity or invalidity of inductive inference, no fair or unfair sampling, and no uniformity or disparity among samples. Thus justifying such tests for rightness may consist primarily in showing not that they are reliable but that they are authoritative.

I hope you sense in this quote, without necessarily getting all the fine points, the potential compatability between aesthetic theory and more conventional legal concepts like "authoritativeness." The aesthetic character of evaluation in art and science (Goodman rightly insists they are identical) incorporates at least some criteria familiar of legal goodness as well.

INTERPRETATION, CREATION, AND JUSTICE

When I first conceived this book, I unthinkingly titled it "Contemporary Constitutional Interpretation." As I worked my way into it, however, I soon concluded that the Supreme Court does not "interpret the Constitution" in the way that most readers presumably understand the term. The Court does not discover constitutional law, it makes it. The problem arises because interpretation implies discovering some pre-existing thing and explaining it without changing it (Dworkin, 1982). This turns out to be tricky business indeed. The anthropologist Clifford Geertz (1973) has insisted that interpretation is "thick description." It thrives on an exhaustive, microscopic analysis of phenomena that the Court rarely if ever attempts. Anything more superficial inevitably substitutes the evaluator's preconceptions about a phenomenon for the phenomenon itself.

More telling, the task of "thick description" never finally closes on its subject. In a charming passage Geertz writes (1973, p. 29):

> Nor have I ever gotten anywhere near to the bottom of anything I have ever written about. . . . Cultural analysis is intrinsically incomplete. And worse than that, the more deeply it goes the less complete it is. It is a strange science . . . in which to get somewhere with the matter at hand is to intensify the suspicion, both your own and that of others, that you are not quite getting it right.

Judges cannot make this confession. His or her opinion must claim to reach closure and finality and rightness for the matter at hand. Thus, to reach closure at all, judges inevitably pay the price of changing what they seek to explain.

At this stage I can only give you hints of the shape this book's redefinition of justice will take, but hints may help. First we must accept that the legal decision itself makes no claim to finality beyond the legal, factual, and normative materials that the case itself gives the justices to work with. We think it proper to react to paintings, plays, and rock concerts on their own terms. We do not think each good only in relation to others of its species, or worse, of the same genus. Cases make no claim to universal rightness or truthfulness, and if we treat them that way they shall always fall short. We must also accept that cases are, as I wrote near the beginning of the chapter, fictional events. That reality should not put us off. Paintings and plays fictionalize raw experience, yet we do not hesitate to judge the goodness of paintings or plays or, for that matter, novels and stories that we routinely categorize as fictional. After all, fictions play a prominent part in legal analysis, witness the common law's famous "reasonable man." All teaching is based on fictions.

I think standard dictionary definitions of partiality and impartiality point in the direction of our redefinition. That which is partial is "incomplete." It lacks some part its whole requires. Thus the impartial decision is not neutral or unbiased; it is complete. The impartial judge convinces us that some materials bear on the case, that others do not, and that he or she has given proper consideration and weight to those which bear. The impartial judge convinces us that he has created a complete fit among these elements.

The just decision therefore transcends formal rules. Commenting on St. Paul's and Solzhenitsyn's condemnation of legalistic relationships (They create "an atmosphere of spiritual mediocrity that paralyzes man's noblest impulses."), Thomas Shaffer comes close to the mark when he writes, "Justice is the gift we give one another as we go about living under the law, and as we go about making the law fit our lives. Our truthfulness in doing this is where justice comes from" (1981, pp. 178–179). Justice is thus a temporary experiential state; it resembles our reaction to paintings, performances, and rock concerts. Justice, like love and works of art, exists in the making. The effect of the making does not last, which is why we must continuously remake it. If this sounds excessively abstract to you, please be assured that by the end of the book I shall defend the proposition that our "great judges," specifically Benjamin Cardozo and Roger Traynor, were great because they performed their roles in just this aesthetic way. You must understand, however, that my argument compels me to avoid the claim that I can "prove" to you that I am "correct." This book necessarily resembles Clifford Geertz's "strange science" more than a persuasive constitutional opinion. How much you accept depends on your own beliefs and experiences.

Finally, as you may by now have suspected, I believe the modern Supreme Court is woefully out of touch with the nature of its constitutional role and authority. It is victimized by a false hope of objective, value-free science that scientific philosophy itself long since abandoned. (See Kordig, 1978, and Elias, 1982.) Scientific constitutional metaphors—Powell titled his essay rightly!—belie the magic of authoritative creativity. The Constitution is a structure that invites and permits the "evolution of political ideals and governmental practices" (Tribe, 1978).

Chapter 2 THE

SUPREME COURT
IN AMERICAN
POLITICS

[T]he natural and proper timidity and delicacy which belongs to the female sex evidently unfits it for many of the occupations of the civil life . . . . [The] paramount destiny and mission of women are to fulfill the noble and benign offices of wife and mother. This is the law of the Creator.
—Justice Bradley, concurring in *Bradwell v. Illinois* (1872)

INTRODUCTION: INTO THE LISTS

This chapter presents short courses in the basics of jurisprudence, constitutional law, and constitutional history. I have condensed some of these materials into little more than lists of Supreme Court decisions and academic theories. This review will bring novices up to the speed at which this book travels. However, experienced jurisprudential readers should not skim these lists too lightly. For nearly two centuries the Supreme Court has performed political acts of constitutional lawmaking. I believe that both this history itself and the various academic attempts to fit political reality and democratic theory together strongly confirm the fundamentally aesthetic character of formal communications in groups of all kinds. This chapter's lists and descriptions hence offer data to support the book's main thesis.

The aesthetic character of constitutional lawmaking has not changed since John Marshall's time, and I hope these lists elevate this overview high enough to reveal this pattern. My dictionary defines *lists* as "an arena for tournaments or other combat." Another entry defines *list* as "an inclination to one side . . . ; a tilt." These lists, then, "contest" much conventional wisdom, and they try to tilt you toward another point of view. The device I have chosen with which to tilt you imagines what a fictional woman from Mars might make of our constitutional experience if she observed it without conventional legal and political preconceptions. I shall introduce her shortly.

JURISPRUDENCE
AND THE ART OF POLITICS

Effective political actors—a father commanding a child, a corporate executive making personnel changes, and a judge ruling in a case—manage to solve a common problem. They take seriously their responsibility to justify their decisions. Whether a justification actually persuades the governed, and particularly those the political action directly affects, depends in part on beliefs and perceptions the actor cannot fully control or shape. Whether a decision actually persuades is always problematic and partial. Nevertheless, the effective political actor presumes his audience is persuadable. He knows what his audience knows and speaks to it within its own framework of normative understanding.

The near identity of the words *community* and *communication* is no accident. Communities *are* those networks of people who believe their past communications had meaning and who have faith that future communications will also have meaning. Community members do *not* necessarily share substantive beliefs. Good friends who disagree strongly about ideologies, scientific propositions, and questions of taste remain good friends as long as they continue to use the same communicative framework. The effective political actor respects his audience because his justification presumes that governor and governed can and do communicate. The justification implicitly asserts that past conversations were "good" and that conversations in the future will remain so.

Thus, the successful exercise of power in community respects the norm that authoritative decisions should flow not from the decider's own "will," but from a communicative framework that governors and governed share. Effective governance creates or maintains community by sustaining confidence in the intelligibility of communications and conversations. In the families I have known, the father who justifies an order to do the dishes with "Because I say so!" (or who spanks the child for his curiosity in asking "Why me?" or "Why now?") maintains the family community less effectively than the father who explains that mom is sick to her stomach and has gone to bed, or who reminds the child that he agreed to do the dishes in negotiating the current level of his allowance.

Politicians—anyone with power deliberately to alter the fortunes and behavior of others—possess many communicative tools and strategies for appearing to be "in" rather than "above" the community. The effective use of these tools distinguishes political authority from brute force. One strategy appeals to rules. "I wish I could help you, but the law of our community requires me to . . . ." Another is to negotiate a community agreement, either bilaterally or multilaterally. A third creates a picture of reality, a mix of norms and factual premises that, if it persuades, leads in turn to a logically inevitable conclusion.

Political persuasion, as distinguished from brute force, succeeds when it creates or evokes in the minds of the governed (the child, the employee, the voter) the belief that his action fits in or helps complete a world in which he lives. Effective political persuasion, which we shall see has much in common with effective "selling," is therefore an artistic process. It creates a vision of a world whose parts seem to fit together and in which the governed themselves belong or "fit." Jurisprudence, which studies the subset of political justifications we label "judicial opinions," must account for the aesthetic character of judicial lawmaking.

Those politicians who bear the title of Justice of the United States Supreme Court seek to escape the appearance of willfulness, to be in rather than above the community. Thus Justice Bradley, in this chapter's epigraph, insists that his "sexist" legal conclusion follows inevitably from something he says the political community shares: God's law. So also do scholars seek to show that their assertions fit with the standards of *their* community of academic specialists. The major failing in modern jurisprudence is that what counts as a good academic fit often turns out to differ considerably from what counts as a good fit in the legal and political communities themselves.

THE WOMAN FROM MARS[1]

What would a woman from Mars, a being of great talent for intuitively articulating the frames of reference of others (and a speed reader and a clairvoyant in the bargain), observe about the constitutional enterprise in the United States? Since she can read minds, she can assess what "constitutional" thoughts citizens think, how frequently they think them, and how commonly they share them. With her Herculean powers, she can digest quickly the words of the document itself, the records of constitutional cases, and the opinions the Supreme Court has rendered, and she can thus judge how well constitutional theories mesh with constitutional events themselves.[2] She would discover that constitutional lawmaking claims to play a key role in creating and maintaining the national community, and she would find that the process resembles the art of politics I just described. In 1872 Justice Bradley invoked divine law. Today's Court frequently employs the metaphor of cost-benefit analysis, but in doing so it seeks to accomplish just what Justice Bradley did: to make the result fit not law but a vision of coherent community norms.

However, the woman from Mars would immediately encounter a contradiction: Most citizens neither understand nor care much about constitutional matters in the way that legal scholars, practitioners, and journalists do. Let me explain.

---

[1] For my choice of a woman from Mars, see Carol Gilligan, *In a Different Voice* (1982), which suggests women are less likely than men to reduce observations to gross or oversimple classifications. I am conflicted by my habitual resort to the male pronoun on the one hand and my thoroughgoing disagreement with Justice Bradley's epigraph on the other, so my choice also tries to compensate for my habitual use of the masculine pronoun.

[2] Please accept this ploy as a device to distill a vast amount of law and scholarship for beginning readers. The device also implicitly tells you what I expect you to believe without extended argument. I realize that the philosophical position I develop in subsequent chapters denies that even a Herculean outsider could see the subject matter in our terms at all.

Assume she begins her inquiry by examining the circumstances in which people think and act with deliberate and conscious reference to law in general. Because she focuses on the political character of law, she asks first what role law plays in the lives of the laity. She would find that most citizens do not spend much time thinking or acting with reference to law. And she would see that when people do become conscious of legal concerns, these concerns do not focus on the precise meaning or mechanistic application of formal rules. Something *has* "gone wrong" or something *will* "go wrong" unless people act to avoid it, but in either case rules do little more than encourage people to have conversations with others that would not, absent the rule, occur.

If I run a red light, I am strongly encouraged to converse with the officer who pulls me over, perhaps later with the judge, and still later with my insurance agent if my insurance rates go up. The law and the threat behind it to punish me provoke these conversations, but the woman from Mars would see that the conversations themselves often involve matters that relate only indirectly to the rule. "I was rushing an injured child to the hospital." "I was unfamiliar with the intersection or with the fact that the city just changed the cycle on the light near my home to which I had become unconsciously accustomed." Do these experiences excuse my behavior? Rules create opportunities and necessities to converse with others about the moral nature of our actions.

She would find constitutional law worked in much the same way. The Fourteenth Amendment does not mandate abortion policies, public school prayer practices, or criminal interrogation procedures. The assertion that they are linked in law instead initiates conversations about the moral nature of abortion, prayer, and law enforcement. These conversations, a few of them in courts but most of them outside, would debate bundles of questions and assumptions that reached beyond the text or history of the rule itself. Rules without conversations do not exist, and the moral conversations that rules stimulate hardly reach certain and predictable conclusions. The studies of constitutional compliance unequivocally show this much. (See, for example, Peltason, 1961; Muir, 1967; Dolbeare and Hammond, 1971.)

Now suppose the Martian examines our constitutional rules more carefully. She would see a paper document, a row of court decisions on library shelves that treat the clauses of the document as "the supreme law of the land," and people who spend some portion of their wealth to keep these decisions flowing. She would also see that news media accessible to the general public report a small fraction of these decisions periodically, and she would see a subsidiary world of teachers, students, and writers spending some small fraction of their time talking and writing about them and the Court that pronounced them.

She might find the number of dollars, hours, words, and people engaged in the constitutional process comparable to those she would observe in association with a process of hitting small, hard, dimpled balls through fields, woods, sand, and water into sequences of immaculately tailored holes in neat lawns. Using unobtrusive measures of intensity of feeling, she would probably find more positive and negative emotional energy associated with golf than with constitutional law, but in some moments she might conceivably find as many students studying law, and as many religious fundamentalists exercised about the Court, as she finds golfers.

In short, she could not conclude that constitutional law, conceived as a body of rules, principles and commands legally defined, carries a significant load in political and social affairs. Law in the abstract does not preoccupy us any more than golf does. Legal concerns, including constitutional ones, seem much less important than do the primary concerns for love, food, accomplishment, and so on. She would conclude that the constitutional phenomenon is instead a collection of specific personal encounters with concrete problems. A litigant believes he has lost his job because he refuses to work on his Sabbath. An undergraduate reads *Lochner v. New York* and fails to see why her professor's lecture condemned the case so strongly, and so forth. The question thus becomes whether any patterns link these discrete experiences together at all.

SOME CURRENT CONSTITUTIONAL ISSUES

Thus the visitor proceeds to identify and categorize the specific conversations constitutional rules stimulate. She surveys first the Supreme Court's most recent constitutional decisions, but she realizes that, with the exception of litigants and legal scholars, newspaper editors and editors of casebooks determine the constitutional impressions citizens receive. Here, for example, is a summary of what *Wall Street Journal* readers would learn about constitutional lawmaking patterns in a recent, three-year period. Nearly all the entries report unnamed Supreme Court decisions. The general press reprints excerpts from published opinions only on the rarest occasions, and the large majority of opinions receive no coverage at all.

1984

- Court rules 5–4 that the Fourth Amendment does not protect against "unreasonable searches and seizures" in prison cells. (Amendment protects "persons, papers, and effects," but prisoners have no expectation of privacy in cells.) (7/5/84, p. 6)
- Court holds 7–0 that states may require the Jaycees to accept women members. (State power to eliminate discrimination by sex in public accommodations overrides First Amendment right of Jaycee male members to freedom of association.) (ibid.)
- Court rules 6–3 that evidence seized by police under an invalid search warrant is not excluded by the exclusionary rule if officer executing warrant

reasonably believed it valid. (Court will weigh the costs of the constitutional rule against the social benefits, which are in these circumstances minimal because the exclusionary rule can have no deterrent effect.). (ibid.)

- Court upholds against due process and Eighth Amendment challenges New York law permitting detention of arrested juveniles up to 17 days before fact-finding hearing if there is a "serious risk" the juvenile will commit a crime in the interim. (ibid.)
- U.S. Justice Department intervenes to block as racially discriminatory settlement of suit in which the state of New York agreed to increase the quota of black residents in New York City's public housing projects. (7/2/84, p. 8)
- Court unanimously reaffirms its 1976 ruling overturning nineteenth century precedent and allows states power consistent with Article I to tax imports in their original packages. (4/19/84, p. 3)
- Court 5–4 holds First Amendment establishment clause does not prohibit local governments from erecting Nativity scenes at Christmas. (Nativity scene in Pawtucket depicts the historical origins of Christmas. Its secular purpose neither advances religion nor entangles government in religion.) (3/6/84, p. 7)
- Senate defeats amendment to permit nondenominational prayers in public schools. (4/20/84, p. 1)

1983

- Court strikes down without opinion or argument a Connecticut law requiring out-of-state breweries to pledge that Connecticut prices would be no higher than those in bordering states. (10/18/83, p. 5)
- Court refuses to hear Second Amendment appeal challenging ban on private possession of handguns by ordinance in town of Morton Grove, Illinois. (10/4/83, p. 4)
- Court 5–4 issues guidelines restricting procedures available to death-row inmates of state prisons to appeal death sentences in federal courts. (7/7/83, p. 2)
- Justices uphold 5–4 Minnesota law giving parents state tax deduction for educational expenses of children. (Disproportionate benefit to those whose children attend parochial schools held not violative of First Amendment establishment clause.) (6/30/83, p. 4)
- Justices rule 5–4 that persons found not guilty of crimes by reason of insanity may be kept in mental institutions longer than the jail sentence they would have received if convicted. (Report notes future potential effect of decision on confinement of John Hinckley, who attempted to assassinate President Reagan in 1981) (ibid.)

- Court 7–2 voids as inconsistent with legislative lawmaking procedures of Article I statutory clauses preserving congressional power by either or both houses to veto actions taken by executive or administrative officers. (6/24/83, p. 2)
- Court 5–4 struck down a New Jersey plan for apportioning members of congressional election districts despite the fact that the maximum variance in the plan was less than 1%. A companion case upheld a state legislative districting plan with more than 10% variation among districts. (Equal protection clause governing states permits greater variation than does "apportionment clause" governing congressional elections.) (6/23/83, p. 10)
- Justices unanimously uphold power of states to prohibit construction of nuclear power plants in state despite previous exercise of federal commerce power in field. (3/23/83, p. 4)
- Court holds 5–4 that public employee (a prison guard) may be held personally liable for punitive damages for recklessly disregarding the civil rights of an inmate. (ibid.)
- Court unanimously holds unconstitutional under First Amendment a federal law banning picketing of Supreme Court. (Law void for including within its prohibition public sidewalks adjacent to Supreme Court building.) (ibid.)

1982

- Court held 5–4 that Mississippi University for Women violated equal protection clause by excluding men from its nursing school. (7/2/82, p. 14)
- Court ordered trial in 1976 lawsuit filed by students against public school board charging First Amendment violations in banning books by Bernard Malamud, Kurt Vonnegut, Eldridge Cleaver, and Desmond Morris from school library. (Seven justices issued separate opinions; no majority position defining the legal basis on which the trial on the merits should proceed emerged.) (6/28/82, p. 9)
- U.S. presidents held immune from suits for damages while in office, but White House aides can be sued. (6/25/82, p. 6)
- Court holds 8–1 Alaska distribution of oil royalties to Alaska residents based on years of residency void under equal protection clause. (6/15/82, p. 4)
- Court 5–4 strikes down under equal protection clause Texas law permitting children of illegal aliens to attend public schools only if they pay tuition. (6/14/82, p. 4)

The observer might notice, as she absorbed these media reports, in addition to these specific constitutional actions, a large number of cases decided under antitrust and civil rights statutes. These include decisions prohibiting the National Collegiate Athletic Association from monopolizing the award of rights to televise athletic contests, the Bob Jones University tax exemption case (1983), and extension of Title VII to prohibit law firms from discriminating against women in the decision to promote to partner. (The epigraphic *Bradwell* case from 1872 had upheld a state law prohibiting women from engaging in the practice of law!) She might be unable to distinguish normatively the interests these statutory cases protect from those protected "constitutionally."

She would also observe media speculation about other issues which the Court might or might not hear in the future. These include equal protection and First Amendment claims of homosexuals, the extension of legal rights to unborn fetuses, the challenges by religious fundamentalists to the teaching of evolution in public schools as a "fact," and the creation of the equivalent of an establishment clause setting limitations on government publication of politically significant information in its exclusive possession. She might also note with some interest that in 1983 a federal judge dismissed a suit filed by the Attorney General of the United States against the U.S. House of Representatives on behalf of a presidentially appointed executive officer, Anne Gorsuch, who had refused to comply with a subpoena requesting documents. The House had cited her for contempt.

CONVENTIONAL LEGAL THEORY AND CONSTITUTIONAL HISTORY

The Martian's review, either of the small fraction of cases summarily reported to the public, or of all the constitutional issues that litigants raise and that courts of all sorts resolve, would confirm her preliminary conclusion that the constitutional process is a collection of discrete events. Nothing in the raw material suggests obvious ways of categorizing the issues. No political theory of human rights, no theory of the meaning of the American polity, no theory of the constitutional role of courts ties them together. On a more mundane level she might expect at least some patterned links between the words of the Constitution and the outcomes, but she wouldn't find them. Indeed she could not even conclude that "common sense" ties the cases together. The recent taxation cases make good common sense, but the legislative veto cases (and most of the recent criminal procedure cases) throw common sense to the wind.

At this point the Martian seeks help from traditional legal scholarship. What patterns in subject matter and methods of justification do conventional legal theories teach students to look for? In the hope that history's longer view might regularize what appears close up as a jumble, she applies each potential pattern against the evidence of constitutional history. She would again be disappointed. She would find evidence in early and late constitutional history alike that both supported and refuted virtually every pattern she tried to apply. Since many of these patterns contradict each other, her historical foray would only reinforce her tentative conclusion that constitutional lawmaking is discrete and unpatterned. Judicial choices would seem to resemble those we make when we choose a midnight snack from whatever looks good in the refrigerator at the moment. Since this "pattern of no pattern" is central to my thesis, I develop the evidence for it at some length next.

Doctrinal consistency in the short run

Ancient: Through *Ogden v. Saunders* (1827) the court consistently applied the contract clause to strike down laws that retroactively altered contractual arrangements. *Modern*: Since *Near v. Minnesota* (1931), the Court has maintained a strong presumption against prior restraints on publication. *New York Times v. U.S.* (1971), the "Pentagon Papers" case.

Doctrinal inconsistency in the short run

Ancient: In 1829, in *Willson v. Blackbird Creek Marsh Co.*, Chief Justice Marshall upheld a Delaware law authorizing the damming of a creek that a boat licensed under an act of Congress used. Yet the grant of a federal license had been central to Marshall's holding in *Gibbons v. Ogden* (1824) setting aside a steamboat monopoly granted by New York State. Also, *Leisy v. Hardin* (1889) held the commerce clause foreclosed state prohibitions on importation of liquor, but *Plumley v. Massachusetts* (1894) held the clause no bar to state prohibition on the importation of colored margarine. (Contrast also *Myers v. U.S.*, 1926, with *Humphrey's Executor v. U.S.*, 1935.) *Modern*: The conditions in which a citizen deserves a due process hearing before an administrative agency that deprives him of some right or entitlement (and indeed the conceptualizations of protectable rights and entitlements) since *Goldberg v. Kelly* (1970) have changed constantly. Contrast *Bell v. Burson* (1971) with *Dixon v. Love* (1977), *Goss v. Lopez* (1975) with *Ingraham v. Wright* (1977), and *Wisconsin v. Constantineau* (1971) with *Paul v. Davis* (1976). See also the justiciability cases (*Warth v. Seldin*, 1975, but *Singleton v. Wulff*, 1976) and the death penalty decisions since *Furman v. Georgia* (1972), which, Robert Weisberg writes, "reveal the art of legal doctrine-making in a state of nervous breakdown." (1984, p. 306)

Doctrinal consistency in the long run

Consistent limiting of Fourteenth Amendment's "privileges and immunities" clause to a very narrow class of cases since initial *Slaughter-house cases* (1873).

Doctrinal inconsistency in the long run

Legal protections afforded property rights under the Fifth and Fourteenth Amendments "due process" clauses and the "contract" clause. (See also the obscenity cases since *United States v. Alpers*, 1950, including Justice Stewart's criterion, "I know it when I see it," in *Jacobellis v. Ohio*, 1964.)

Reasoned elaboration of the historical purpose of a constitutional clause

Ancient: *Gibbons v. Ogden* and general development of federal commerce power. *Modern*: Grants to states under Twenty-first Amendment of power to regulate commerce in alcoholic beverages that conventional commerce clause doctrine would deny.

Express disregard for historical purpose of a constitutional clause

Ancient: *Slaughter-house cases*. (See also implicit disregard of presumed constitutional structure of federalism in *Swift v. Tyson*, 1842, creating a federal common law independent of state law in federal courts with diversity jurisdiction, overturned in 1938.) *Modern*: Indigent's right to assistance of counsel in criminal cases; many establishment clause cases.

Elaborate assessment of policy consequences as justification for case outcome independent of constitutional words and purposes

Ancient: *McCulloch v. Marland* (1819), insofar as it justifies liberal reading of Congressional power under "necessary and proper" clause. Also *Gibbons v. Ogden*. *Modern*: Resolution of competing state jurisdictional claims over divorce proceedings under "full faith and credit clause." Also *Wickard v. Filburn* (1942) upholding congressional power to regulate farmers' consumption of their own crops.

Refusal to consider policy implications of decision

Ancient: *Dred Scott v. Sandford* (1857). *Modern*: *United States v. O'Brien* (1968), upholding statute prohibiting destruction of draft card and eschewing analysis of policy objectives of the statute. *Immigration and Naturalization Service v. Chadha* (1983), the "legislative veto" case, disregarding major functional differences among different legislative uses of the veto device.

Involvement in heated political controversies of the time

Ancient: *Marbury v. Madison* and *Dred Scott*. *Modern*: Desegregation and reapportionment cases. *United States v. Nixon* (1974).

Refusal to become involved in political questions

Ancient: *Luther v. Borden* (1849). *Modern*: *O'Brien v. Brown* (1972), a challenge to the seating of the California delegation to the 1972 Democratic Party convention under the California "winner take all" primary, and *Massachusetts v. Laird* (1970) avoiding constitutionality of Vietnam War.

Declarations of abstract legal principles
(for example, "natural law") as basis for decision

Ancient: *Bradwell*, the epigraph above, upholding state prohibition against admission of females to legal practice. *Fletcher v. Peck*, (1810) and many economic "substantive due process" cases from 1880s to the 1930s. *Modern*: Concept of ordered liberty cases by which some but not all Bill of Rights doctrines are applied to the states through the Fourteenth Amendment, including second *Flag Salute* case and *Roe v. Wade* (1973) respecting the right of a mother to an abortion in the first trimester of pregnancy.

Pragmatism and compromise as declared bases for decision

Ancient: *Blackbird Creek, Plessy v. Ferguson* (1896) upholding separate but equal segregation by race in public accommodations. *Modern*: *Roe v. Wade* (1973) respecting the increasing power of the state over abortion policy as the term of pregnancy progresses. *Mathews v. Eldridge* (1976) and other due process "balancing" cases, plus First Amendment "balancing" cases, and cf. *Regents v. Bakke* (1978) affirmative action case.

Express reliance on dispositive precedent

Ancient: *Marshall v. Baltimore and Ohio Railroad Co.* (1853) following 1844 precedent granting corporations capacity to sue in federal court under Article III diversity jurisdiction. *Modern*: *Flood v. Kuhn* (1972) holding professional baseball not covered by antitrust laws created over congressional commerce clause power.

Express overruling of dispositive precedent

Ancient: *Collector v. Day* (1871) striking down dictum of *McCulloch v. Maryland* to the effect that state employees not necessarily immune to federal taxation, since overturned. *Modern*: Second *Flag Salute* (1943) case. *Gideon v. Wainwright* (1963) (indigent right to counsel).

Confessed or blatant disregard
of plain constitutional language

Ancient: *Marbury v. Madison*; *Hammer v. Dagenhart* (1918), reading word "expressly" into the Tenth Amendment. *Modern*: *Home Building and Loan v. Blaisdell* (1934) upholding state law altering terms of previously existing mortgage contracts despite contract clause.

Confessed or blatant distortion
of or disregard for prior case law

Ancient: *Pollack v. Farmers' Loan and Trust Co.* (1895), the federal income tax case, distorting previous constitutional definitions of direct and indirect taxes; *Gitlow v. New York* (1925) disregarding statement in *Prudential v. Cheek* (1921) that the Fourteenth Amendment imposes no obligations on states to protect First Amendment freedom of speech or press. *Modern*: *Feiner v. New York* (1951) upholding conviction of political speaker despite lack of evidence of major political hostility, in contrast to *Terminiello v. Chicago* (1949) overturning conviction of political speaker speaking in extremely tense and hostile environment. The shopping center cases, *Lloyd v. Tanner* (1972) and *Hudgens v. NLRB* (1976) overruling *Amalgamated Food Employees Union, Local 590 v. Logan Valley Plaza* (1968). All cases ignoring the maxims of judicial self-restraint announced in *Ashwander v. TVA* which would, if applied, be dispositive, e.g., *NAACP v. Alabama* (1958).

Disregard for incontrovertible facts
presented in case and/or transparently flawed or
incomprehensible legal reasoning throughout opinion

Ancient: *Marbury v. Madison*; *Dred Scott*; *Lochner v. New York* (1905), disregarding incontroverted evidence of association between disease in bakers and employment conditions in bakeries. *Modern*: *Shelley v. Kraemer* (1948), holding racially discriminatory contract judicially unenforceable, and *Katzenbach v. McClung* (1964), holding that congressional commerce power extends to those who consume goods shipped in interstate commerce. Both opinions not logically limited to facts, yet plausible extensions of the principle would revolutionize constitutional law in these fields. She also *Kunz v. New York* (1951), in which the majority opinion by Chief Justice Vinson states two mutually contradictory justifications for the result. (Administrative regulation of religious speech is automatically invalid as a prior restraint, on the one hand, but the city, New York, must draft standards for administrative regulation of religious speech on the other.)

CONSTANTS IN
CONSTITUTIONAL LAWMAKING

Thus far, our observer has tried to detect constitutional patterns by employing conventional jurisprudential standards. The startlingly consistent lack of fit between these standards and what the Court does alerts us to the possibility that constitutional practice and conventional scholarship are fundamentally different enterprises, different "language games," in Wittgenstein's terms. We shall be better positioned to assess this possibility after we canvass jurisprudential scholarship more thoroughly. For the moment, assume that the observer now shifts from the legal to the political science perspective. At last some patterns would begin to form. By switching gears this way, she might well conclude that, in reaching a collective decision, the justices routinely negotiate the form the justification will take, and that this explains the "pattern of no pattern" she noted previously. The political viewpoint would reveal at least six other historically consistent patterns as well.

1. Since Chief Justice Marshall's time, the Court has stated explicitly its refusal to bind itself to any mechanistic theory of legal reasoning. Marshall wrote in *McCulloch*, "This provision is made in a constitution, intended to endure for ages to come, and consequently, to be adapted to the various *crises* of human affairs." (Marshall emphasized the word "crises.") Chief Justice Marshall justified the result in *McCulloch* by invoking five different sources of constitutional authority: the text, the theory and structure of sound government, the policy consequences of the choices open to him, the history of the adoption of the Constitution, and precedent (Brest and Levinson, 1983, p. 35). Justice Holmes reemphasized the validity of a nonmechanistic jurisprudence in *Missouri v. Holland* (1920): "The case before us must be considered in light of our whole experience and not merely in that of what was said a hundred years ago." So did Chief Justice Hughes in *Home Building and Loan* (1934): "It is no answer to say that this public need was not apprehended a century ago, or to insist that what the provision of the Constitution meant to the vision of that day it must mean to the vision of our time." *Weems v. United States*, a "cruel and unusual punishment" case, held that clause "is not fastened to the obsolete but may acquire meaning as public opinion becomes enlightened by a humane justice." (See Freund, 1961, chapter one; and for more recent examples see Carter, 1984, chapter six.) The justices have not deemed it politically necessary to practice conventional legal reasoning.

2. In true "crises"—military extremity and political turmoil involving threatened or actual violence directed against the national regime—the Court has consistently *not* advanced constitutional liberties claims. Since the Civil War, the Court has upheld suspension of habeas corpus, permitted the summary deprivation of the property and liberty of American citizens of Japanese ancestry during World War II, buckled during the height of the "Red Scare" after that war, and, in the case of the Vietnamese conflict, refused to examine the executive's authority to conduct the war in the absence of a congressional declaration of war.

3. With respect to its review of the legislative decisions of the Congress of the United States, the Court has never acted as a bulwark defending civil liberties against the power of government (See Railton, 1983).

4. Constitutional decisionmaking resembles what logicians call "practical reasoning" (Golding, 1983, and MacCormick, 1978). Practical reasoning is moral or normative reasoning of the form: "X is a desired state of affairs. I

believe action Y will increase the attainability of X. Therefore, it is morally correct to enact Y." Since practical reasoning does not easily square with some widely held theories about the place of courts in a democracy, judges do not usually state their practical reasons directly. In collegial courts, an opinion may serve to hide differences among those who reach the same result. Thus we can only speculatively reconstruct the reasons, but if we did, the results might look like this:

> *Marbury v. Madison.* It is desirable that the federal government operate with three relatively coequal branches of government, and/or it is desirable to perpetuate the power of the Federalist judiciary after the election of Thomas Jefferson in 1800. Judicial authority to nullify legislation under Article III will increase the attainability of these goals. Therefore, it is appropriate to read Article III in that manner and to ignore the many logical obstacles to such a reading on the facts of the case.

> *Brown v. Board of Education* (1954). Discrimination by race is morally wrong, and/or racial discrimination will eventually lead to violent opposition to the regime. Prohibiting racial segregation in public schools will reduce racial discrimination and hostility. Therefore, it is constitutionally proper, regardless of the intent of the framers of the equal protection clause, to read the clause to prohibit racial segregation. (The same pattern describes *Shelley v. Kraemer* and *Katzenbach v. McClung*, noted above.)

> *Flood v. Kuhn.* It is desirable to promote the efficient operation of the business system and/or to keep baseball sacrosanct as "the national pastime." Strictly adhering to precedents about baseball will promote fair reliance on the law. Therefore, the commerce clause as applied in the antitrust laws does not include baseball, despite the fact that baseball is a big business and despite the fact that the Court has required every other major professional sport to comply with the antitrust laws.

Thus our outside observer seeking political patterns in constitutional lawmaking would readily see the practical reasoning behind legal form of decisions from 1803 to the present. She would spot many cases in which the Court let the end justify the means.[3] Viewed politically, the justices seem not so much to do "law" as to combine their hunches about social conditions and their normative values to reach practically reasoned results. After all, Jefferson

---

[3] Consider *McClung* more closely. If Congress may regulate whom a restaurant serves based on its purchase of supplies in interstate commerce, the formal principle necessarily permits Congress to limit the shrubbery I grow in my yard because I purchase food in interstate commerce. My choice of shrubs does not relate to my food purchases, but the quantity of food shipped in interstate commerce is not affected by a private restaurant owner's decision whom he will serve. People have to eat. Indeed, people denied restaurant service will save the cost of restaurant overhead and will therefore have additional money to spend on food and other goods. The Court could, of course, have found that racial discrimination itself has cumulatively negative effects on national commercial life, which Congress may constitutionally control. The practical reasoning we suspect underlies *McClung* has merit, but the Court saw no political necessity to express it.

himself wrote a friend in 1810 that "to lose our country by scrupulous adherence to written law, would be to lose the law itself, with life, liberty, property and all those who are enjoying them with us; thus absurdly sacrificing the end to the means" (quoted in Murphy and Pritchett, 1979, p. 580).

5. At virtually every point in constitutional history some inchoate theory, some enveloping vision of national need, does seem to drive constitutional decisions. These visions do not rise to the level of legal theories or doctrines. They are assumptions about social order that popular and intellectual discourse of the time make plausible. In John Marshall's time, the failure of the Articles of Confederation to provide for smooth commercial expansion created a felt need for uniform—hence national—rules for the conduct of commerce. This vision determined the bulk of Marshall's constitutional decisions. Taney's time emphasized the importance of permitting the states to police social processes. The Spencerian doctrine of the social "survival of the fittest" influenced the Court for the better half of a century after the nation recovered from the Civil War. Inchoate theories of politically neutral bureaucratic national government coupled with populist theories of individual dignity combined to drive the post–World War II Court. The visions change, but some political vision orients the Court's work.

6. Attempts to refine or convert these visions and inchoate theories into philosophically satisfactory constitutional statements fail. The failure is not merely academic. Rather, the Court itself is not structured to convert visions into academically satisfying philosophies. Justices who have tried to do so have failed, witness the failure of Justice Black's literalistic jurisprudence to win a substantial following. The contemporary paradigm of individual dignity and its correlate of equality before the law have not generated any "law of equality" under the equal protection clause. The Court, in the name of the equal protection clause, has created not a theory of equality but a feeble rhetoric of relative political power. Some forms of unequal treatment are worse than others; therefore, the courts may scrutinize their "rationality," more carefully than the less suspect classifications (Karst, 1977). So too, the First Amendment's declaration of individual liberties has generated no coherent jurisprudential theory. The concepts of self-fulfillment, advancement of truth and knowledge, participation, and the maintenance of loyalty, the elements of simple textbook theories, are not part of declared constitutional law (Emerson, 1980). The confused state of the law of privacy underscores the conclusion.

To summarize, constitutional doctrine, observed case by case, has never closely approximated conventional prescriptions for legal reasoning. The directions in the law, the extension from a past case to a future case, are usually uncertain. At times lawyers can predict for their clients the risks and potential benefits of litigating a constitutional issue, but it is more likely the recent patterns of winners and losers, not what the Court says, that facilitate these predictions.[4] Some have called the Supreme Court a "teacher in a vital national seminar." The woman from Mars, examining the work of the Court itself, might well suspect the Court's teaching evaluations would prove embarrassingly low.

VARIETIES OF JURISPRUDENTIAL THOUGHT

Each of the political patterns the visitor has found reinforce her initial observations. Constitutional decisions are discrete events. They arise from the always somewhat unique configuration of events: the facts and values embodied in the case at hand and the preferences and political agendas of the justices who must decide it. Decisions from our earliest history often manipulate legal terminology to justify results reached on other undisclosed grounds. Having reached this conclusion, the Martian turns finally to examine the ways in which current jurisprudential scholarship has reacted to this state of affairs.

If the Martian had investigated medical research rather than the Supreme Court's constitutional lawmaking, and if she had examined what scholars had concluded on the matter, she would discover that agreements on some points dominated the "scientific community" at the same time the community hotly debated other issues. Academic communities normally treat certain consensus truths as the core of their knowledge and the unknown as frontiers. Medical researchers share common beliefs about the etiologies of thousands of diseases and the preferred treatments for them at the same time they contest which theories might better explain what appears anomalous. Natural scientists find interesting that which they cannot explain.

If the observer examined law in primitive communities, she might well find close connections between social behaviors and religious beliefs stated as rules and enforced by institutions that roll religious and political functions into one. These would "constitute" the political community. She might conclude that consensus about norms associates with common backgrounds and beliefs and with stable and predictable daily behaviors. Reasoning from the converse, she would expect that pluralistic cultures, whose citizens' individual beliefs, social backgrounds, political and religious preferences, and so forth vary, would possess "minimalist" legal systems, ones marked by normative controversies, considerable confusion at the level of doctrine, and much informal scrambling behind legal and religious formalities to prop up short-term compromises and understandings.

---

[4] For an analysis of the historical development of state constitutional law in California that reaches the same conclusions, see Harry Schreiber (1984).

This is, of course, a fair description of contemporary American constitutional (and theological) practice, and our outside observer would expect that scholarly theories about law and religion would move outward from that core description. But philosophy and the social sciences are not as neat. If the outside observer turned to scholars in law and politics for explanations, she would find no consensus distinguishing core from frontier in the first place. Jurisprudential scholarship is itself a fight to define the core. Scholars cannot agree whether the emperor is clothed or naked, and each scholar who asserts nakedness wants to be the new tailor (Tushnet, 1979). The next list therefore introduces seven loci of scholarly disagreement, which later chapters will describe and assess in more detail.

A. *Normative starting points.* The U.S. political community is and should be evaluated as: A republic (Berns, 1976); a constitutional democracy (Murphy, 1980); a liberal democracy (Walzer, 1983); a decaying and increasingly repressive postindustrialist state (Kairys, 1982); a pluralist system defying ideologically derived labels (Dahl, 1956).

B. *Definition and application of concepts.* For some a "constitutional democracy" is one in which a constitution limits political power only insofar as judges apply it as they would a conventional legal document, i.e., only to the extent the fair reading of its words and the historical weight of the evidence about the farmers' purposes permit. For others the same term denotes a judicial system with considerable authority to substitute its choices for those of electorally more responsive units of government. For others, it is a statement of specific substantive principles, particularly political protection of individual liberty through the protection of the concept of private property. The definition of "liberal democracy" is equally uncertain and hotly contended. The authors who tackled the question in Pennock and Chapman, *Liberal Democracy* (1983), either conflict with each other or confess simply that no coherent definition of "liberal democracy" is, under the circumstances, possible.

C. *Theoretical prescriptions for constitutional lawmaking.* Competing theories may predict or explain the same outcomes. They have done so in the natural sciences, where wave and particle theories of light once explained the same phenomenon. But jurisprudence does not predict or explain, it prescribes, which is why, as in theology, scholars debate different positions so energetically. For example:

• John Rawls (1971) believes that consensus on the distribution of wealth is theoretically attainable. Hochschild (1981), however, arrays the competing principles of justice for the distribution of social wealth and finds no overarching logic or principle for choosing among them. She also reports considerable ideological disagreement among citizens on the point. Kenneth

Arrow's (1977) attempt to express Rawl's logic in formal (mathematical) terms failed. Michael Walzer (1983) believes criteria for distribution depend upon the social conventions found in a society.

- Archibald Cox (Harvard) believes the Court's principles should be "sufficiently absolute to give them roots throughout the community over significant periods of time, and to lift them above the level of pragmatic political judgments" (1976, p. 114). The late Alexander Bickel (Yale) agreed in theory but felt such principles often either inaccessible or excessively costly to invoke (1962 and 1975). Martin Shapiro (1965) casts doubt on the attainability of such principles, and he doubts their indispensability to the daily functioning of legal institutions. He believes the judicial process inevitably develops policy incrementally. David O'Brien (1981) favors incrementalism but believes the Court often creates law holistically without the factual basis that incremental approaches permit.
- Jesse Choper (1980) believes the Court should drastically curtail its refereeing of interbranch (powers) and interlevel (federalism) questions and preserve its political capital for the protection of civil rights and liberties. McDowell (1981) argues that the Constitution primarily defines and separates intragovernmental powers.
- Walter Murphy (1980) asserts that the normative values in the Constitution are orderable in such a fashion that it is possible to conceive of an "unconstitutional" amendment to the constitution. Paul Brest (1980) disagrees.

D. *Interpretation or creation.* The debate here concerns both the definition and desirability of the concept of legal interpretation. Raoul Berger (1977) and Michael Perry (1982) agree that careful examination of the political history of the adoption of constitutional clauses yields clear answers to many constitutional disputes, but they disagree on the necessity or the desirability that the courts actually follow these interpretations. (Both, for example, agree that the Fourteenth Amendment does not by interpretation yield the conclusion that its equal protection clause prohibits racial segregation in public schools.) Bruce Ackerman's *Reconstructing American Law* (1984), on the other hand, describes modern jurisprudence as "legal constructivism," a process that builds upon concepts of modern policy analysis ("externalities," "Pareto efficiency," and "Rawlsian maximin," for example) that bear no relation to the act of interpreting the document. Owen Fiss of Yale begins his 1982 essay, "Objectivity and Interpretation," with the line, "Adjudication is interpretation: Adjudication is the process by which a judge comes to understand and express the meaning of an authoritative legal text and the values embodied in that text." Paul Brest of Stanford (1982) replies that Fiss's position can amount to no more than wishful thinking.

E. *The character of interpretive acts.* Geertz (1973) asserts that interpretations are "thick-textured" events, always open-ended and never authoritative or final. They are antithetical to the authoritative pronouncements of a legal system. Geertz believes that only "local knowledge" can answer questions of justice. Gadamer is slightly less pessimistic (1975). He believes that legal texts, interpreted within their political and historical contexts, can reveal fundamental principles, but his description of this interpretive process does not resemble the constitutional work of the Supreme Court. Tushnet, in any event, insists that Gadamer's hermeneutic theory cannot provide legal closure in specific cases (1983). All modern hermeneutic theory is sharply at odds, however, with the jurisprudence of Judge Robert Bork, formerly of Yale, who argues that the "underlying premise" of each exercise of judicial review must be "fairly discoverable in the constitution itself," and that judges must follow where logic leads (1979).

F. *Appropriate level of analysis.* Robert Cover (1983) endorses the careful analysis of specific cases as examples of the normative moods of their time. Donald Horowitz insists that another level—the Court's institutional characteristics and its capacity to gather and process the information on which intelligent policy choices depend—determines the quality of outcomes (1977 and 1983).

G. *The role of the scholar.* Some scholars feel they must be committed to advocacy and prescription. Others believe scholarly objectivity depends on "detached observation" and empiricism. The contributors to the 1984 *Stanford Law Review*'s "Critical Legal Studies Symposium," introduced in chapter one, debate the issue at length.

Felice Lewis (1976) concluded in her analysis of obscenity law that Justice Stewart was forced to adopt the "I know it when I see it" approach not by his own inadequacies as a legal analyst but because his political culture failed to provide philosophically coherent definitions of obscenity and politically acceptable criteria for identifying it. Our Martian might conclude that such intellectual pluralism made inevitable and inescapable this babble of constitutional scholarship.

The Martian might well conclude that constitutional lawmaking is a thoroughly paradoxical process, one that reduces to moral antinomies—Paul Freund's triumph but fraternity, knowledge but privacy, personal security but moral responsibility (1962), and Duncan Kennedy's individualism but altruism (1976). Or as *Esquire Magazine* (Rothenberg, 1983, p. 201) summarized the philosophical debate between Robert Nozick and John Rawls (both of Harvard): "Give me liberty or give me equality." Having concluded that the citizenry is largely ignorant of constitutional matters and that those who take constitutional matters seriously cannot agree on much of anything, our visitor goes home.

WHY BOTHER TO STUDY
SUPREME COURT DECISIONS?

Even after discounting heavily for the artificiality of the woman from Mars exercise, which is primarily an excuse for delivering large quantities of scene-setting information in a short space, and whose leave we now take, the exercise does make a strong prima facie case that conventional analysis of constitutional opinions has very limited payoff potential. The Court has never conformed to conventional legal reasoning principles. Golding and MacCormick rightly described constitutional reasoning as stylized practical reasoning, but that description is hardly an evaluative theory. With the exception of its development of Fourteenth Amendment rights of blacks, the Court has not served as a teacher in a vital national seminar or consistently protected individuals against the tyranny of the majority when it counted.

It is sometimes argued that, while the individual opinion usually muddies more water than it clarifies, the "line of cases" provides legal coherence. The observation is both obviously true and obviously false. Lawyers and judges faced with choices in the case before them can usually "construct" a coherent theory of the line of cases that will favor their desired choice, but the construction is meaningless except within the frame of reference of the problem on the table at the moment. But the student, lacking the case on the table, finds the line of cases even less coherent than an individual case. This was, after all, the point Thomas Reed Powell made at the beginning of chapter one.

There are many more reasons why we might well not bother assessing the quality of decisions. Lord Mansfield once said that "our judgments are better than our reasons." Juries need not give reasons for decisions. Therefore, students should perhaps analyze outcomes and treat opinions as rituals and, for analytical purposes, irrelevant. The Court is a political body responding to a constituency. It reads the election returns, and its opinions are post hoc rationalizations that would earn mediocre if not outright failing grades in introductory college courses in logic. The opinions at best provide heuristic springboards for academic discussions of applied political philosophy, and this only because the court speaks authoritatively. "Truth comes more easily out of error than of confusion," Bacon is reported to have said, and the meat in most opinions lies in the pedagogical fun we can have with their failings.

Furthermore, to the extent constitutional law may predict or measure political change, its capacity to do so is surely no greater than that of network television programming or the latest trends in popular music. To the suggestion that one should study collections of cases, "jurisprudential moods," in order to predict the future, C. H. S. Fifoot, in his *Judge and Jurist in the Reign of Victoria* (1959, p. 56), commented:

Faced with the fragments of life, the current law of any place and time can but approximate to a principle or indicate a tendency. Looking back upon the individual torts as they had emerged at the end of the nineteenth century, it requires an act of faith to postulate that principle or to indicate the goal to which they were tending.

Perhaps political action itself so differs from philosophizing about action that philosophers can never narrow the gulf between themselves and political practices.

Granting for the sake of argument the conclusions thus far, analysis can proceed in one of three directions. The first demotes constitutional justifications to a technical role, of no more intrinsic interest to political and social philosophy than accountants' many schemes for presenting numbers in ways that achieve their goals. The extensive evidence that very few Americans know anything significant about either the Court or its justifications, coupled with the fact that constitutional decisions have in the course of history altered a minuscule fraction of public policies, cautions strongly against taking constitutional opinions very seriously.

Or, scholars may take pluralism seriously and play academic politics with jurisprudence. Scholars can always find a market for virtually any conventional approach. The "back to the constitution" advocates discussed in the next chapter find a variety of markets: universities and colleges with conservatively defined missions, the growing number of private "funds" and "institutes" that sponsor conservative causes, and, perhaps paradoxically, liberal institutions that practice the laudatory principle of academic freedom, and therefore bend over backward to accommodate those who seem out of step with conventional wisdom.

The third direction, which this book takes, grants that pluralist conclusions are inevitable within that frame of reference, but argues that another frame of reference plausibly fits our constitutional experience better than the theories reviewed thus far. This model builds from the Martian's first observation. Law is an invitation to conversation, and differences in constitutional decisions do stimulate different kinds of conversations on a level quite apart from doctrinal coherence, fidelity to the Constitution, overarching and hence acceptably neutral principles, or rigorously disciplined legal reasoning. The next and penultimate list restates the case for bothering with constitutional opinions.

1. Games must have umpires. Umpires do not merely make calls and solve disputes so the game can continue; they operate within *some* frame of reference or the game cannot continue. Some frame of reference presumably guides the constitutional process. Opinions, the formal "calls" in the constitutional game, therefore presumably conform to something. If jurisprudential theory can't find it, the problem is presumptively in the theory. Those who criticize the Court for failing to do today what it has never consistently done in the past rather resemble a physicist or chemist who, when his experiments

regularly confirm the null hypothesis, insists that Mother Nature has sinned and should mend her ways. Both judicial opinions and the academic babble about the Court, in other words, are data that disconfirm conventional theory and prompt the search for other theories.

2. Lower court judges and lawyers do treat the Supreme Court as if it were sending messages. Former Justice Arthur Goldberg (1982, p. 14) reported that lower court judges read into recent death penalty opinions the message "get faster executions." Quite apart from the substance of the message, it is worth assessing how effectively the Court communicates. If the message is purely political, if legal rhetoric cloaks policy preferences, the Court's working audience is not so naïve as to miss the messages. If, as I suggest later, modern constitutional messages seem incoherent with disturbing frequency, whatever the combination of causes (work load pressures or the attitudes of the justices themselves toward clarity in legal communications, for example), these decisions will invite or stimulate confused and disheartened conversations.

3. I think substantial evidence supports the propositions that people live in a normative world and that constitutional opinions play an important part in that world. Each decision *is* a discrete legal event. Usually only a small audience learns of it. Opinions are only loosely linked to other opinions, to formal rules and to legal theories. Most have a short half-life. Yet none of these conditions prevents them from generating or sustaining normative conversations. I doubt that the many refreshingly sincere and searching constitutional conversations about the potential impeachment of Richard Nixon would have happened without the stimulus of a tradition of constitutional law that accepts the moral foundations of law. Indeed, if you spend a day attending to the public media, you will almost certainly encounter citizen discussions of political matters framed in what citizens believe are constitutional terms. My casual attention to the news in the past 48 hours encountered discussions of women's rights to "control their bodies" and the right of townspeople to choose, contrary to a state statute, not to fluoridate their drinking water. Constitutional law matters because these conversations matter.

Richard Saphire, in an article titled "The Search for Legitimacy in Constitutional Theory: What Price Purity" (1981), bemoaned the effect on his students of the scholarly preoccupation with interpretive theory and methods. His students longed to wrestle with the moral problems raised by the abortion cases. They had no enthusiasm for the question whether *Roe* was or was not the modern equivalent of *Lochner*. He cited William Bennett (1979, p. 213):

> I believe we misallocate our resources and energies if in teaching about constitutionalism we neglect to talk about the "ordinary" values citizens—our students—must have in daily commerce with each other . . . . It seems to me that the spirit of constitutionalism requires, perhaps primarily, a commitment to the possibility of citizens' reaching sound conclusions about right and wrong through

the deliverances of judgment and sound principle, and the commitment to sound action on that basis. A skeptical, cynical citizenry that likes to say "it's all subjective" or "you'd do it too if you could" is a diminished citizenry insufficient to the task of the maintenance of civility . . . .

Perhaps the failure of constitutional jurisprudence boils down to a misconception of the nature of authority. If authority is an abstraction of policemen and soldiers, guns and bombs, if we are rightly suspicious of those with guns and bombs, and if the Justices have authority, then we approach them distrustfully. If, on the other hand, authority, in family, religion, or politics, defines the questions people must answer to know themselves and their communities, we may properly approach authority with cautious hope for instruction toward furthering our moral conversations.

ALTERNATIVES

This chapter's lists attempt little more than a descriptive summary of the current state of constitutional theory and practice. The analysis, such as it is, by design raises many more questions than it answers. A wide chasm separates what the Court appears to do, on the one side, and virtually all current jurisprudential theories (diverse as they clearly are), on the other. Some major rethinking of the nature of the constitutional enterprise is therefore in order.

My rethinking has led me to the conclusion that we can better understand the Court if we see its history as a series of performances that attempt to sustain conversations about the normative nature of our national community. By the end of the book I hope you will appreciate three points: first, that this model better describes both what the Court does and how we yearn to evaluate it than do legalistic models; second, that the Court's political position effectively prevents it from operating in any other fashion; and third, that aesthetic theory provides a more constructive framework for evaluating the goodness of specific opinions than do more familiar jurisprudential models.

I think that the Court is worth bothering with because sustained moral conversations are an essential ingredient in the health of any group. I do not mean that the Supreme Court's decisions are the only force sustaining national dialogues. Good political speeches do so; good movies, plays, and television programs do so. I would like to believe that the television series "Hill Street Blues" will a century from now rank with Dickens' novels as great morally instructive literature. But the Court has often contributed something to these ongoing conversations which is reason enough to bother with it.

However, readers may grant the adequacy of this chapter's descriptions and the necessity for significantly reorienting the field yet remain skeptical of, or even baffled by, the aesthetic direction chapter one promised. Here then is one final list, a list of four other plausible ways of bothering we might adopt if we accept that the Court does not and will not conform to legal models. I put you through one more list in the hope that it will prepare you to read critically what I propose. The more these alternatives appeal to you, the less comfortable you will be with the chapters that follow.

1. The demise of the authoritativeness of the Constitution is real and serious. The court, for the reasons stated, is reacting to its culture, but culture and Court, seduced together by false promises of scientific objectivity, head toward moral disaster. Academicians, therefore, have no choice but to play a political role. Detached empiricism has as many consequences as active advocacy. Indeed, the myth of detachable empiricism is a major contributor to the increasingly vague and insipid pronouncements from the modern Court. Therefore, the scholar concerned about the nature of constitutional reasoning has no moral choice but to criticize head-on the substantive constitutional results he dislikes and to reinforce those he approves. The scholar's task is to rebuild attractively authoritative substantive theories about liberty, equality, and fairness. We have no guarantee that the effort will rescue the nation, but without such theories the ideal of the rule of law is doomed.

2. All, or nearly all, of the angst scholars express about the apparent confusions in constitutional law and about the apparent distance between scholarly theories and the decisions themselves are false alarms. The Court has indeed followed the patterns described in this chapter, yet it has remained a politically viable, functioning part of American government. Its legitimacy and its ability to function day to day simply do not depend on the criteria that scholars keep insisting should govern the process. The principles of everyday pluralist theory not only explain the reality, they also create a large zone of indifference around the Court. As long as its decisions do not consistently appear to "take sides" on partisan causes (or worse, become captured by some scholar's utopian theories that the mass of politically active Americans reject), the Court is not worth much worrying. The very willingness of Justice Bradley in the name of the Constitution to speak so shockingly of sexual inequality under God in 1872 shows us we have no fear of legalistic inflexibility from the Court. Indeed, a recent constitutional law casebook (Schmidhauser, 1984), arrays the entire history of constitutional law according to the changing moods of U.S. political history. Lawyers will continue to argue cases, presidents will continue to appoint politically sensitive justices, and the egregious errors will wash out no slower than new ones are committed. The scholar must accept the fact that he plays the role of technician. He must identify the occasionally egregious error the Court commits and help fine-tune doctrine as it develops case by case because scholars are an important part of the continuous mechanism of democratic political adjustment. Scholars should learn a little modesty and get on with earning their livings like other folks.

3. Of course doctrinal elegance and consistency over time are pipe dreams, and the political position of the Court does depend far less on the content of

opinions that only a handful of people read than on broad and not very mysterious political forces. Nevertheless, the substance of specific decisions does matter. Some specific choices, made by a divided Court, affect individual lives profoundly. Imagine yourself on death row if you doubt the fact. Furthermore, form shapes substance. Even under the assumption that law and the Constitution serve primarily symbolic roles in society, we nevertheless must maintain a system of incentives for trusting the legal process. The hierarchical structure of legal authority binds judges throughout the country to its decisions. A collapse in legal trust would mark the social equivalent of nuclear war. Such dangers require the Court to hold consistently to the artificial but symbolically important devices of legal form. The Court's failings, and particularly those since World War II, are not substantive failings. Virtually any substance will do as long as its form generates trust, and scholars must defend and preserve those forms.

4. The preceding three alternative approaches to constitutional lawmaking reveal once again the tendency of academicians to aggrandize the social relevance of academic thought. Maybe the dangers are real, maybe not. If academicians have any sense, they will realize that social forces dwarf them, that the unanticipated consequences of their speculations (in the unlikely circumstance that political actors take them seriously) are likely to be just as great and every bit as negative as the anticipated and desirable products of their speculations. Scholars should keep their eyes on the obvious. There is an obvious disjunction between their theories and political practice. Such disjunctions call for explanations, but they will only matter to the audience of others scholars. Bothering with the Court matters, but not for the sake of law, politics, or anything "national." Large groups are not groups at all. Only small communities have moral value. Scholars should bother about maintaining their own scholarly communities, which means they must honor the language of their scholarly discourse, no matter how removed it may be from the languages of law and politics.

Each of these alternative reasons for bothering possesses some intellectual attractions. This chapter concludes with the suggestion that each of the four responses neglects an aspect of appellate law that lawyers are taught to take very seriously: legal "craft." The invocation of craftsmanship undoubtedly has a commencement-address ring to it that I do not intend, at least not directly. My point here is descriptive. Much is made in law school of craft, just as the medical professional takes seriously the Hippocratic Oath. Law schools indoctrinate the craft of coping with uncertainty, not the principles of legal reasoning or fidelity to texts or respect for democratic theory. At the very least, academic theories of legal process must take the nature of that craft into account. More to the point, if the authority of law depends on the exercise of craft for its own sake, it is worth asking whether from this viewpoint some of the incoherences, paradoxes, and inconsistencies noted above might disappear. American constitutional law has heroes: Chief Justices Marshall and Hughes, Justices Holmes, Brandeis, Cardozo, Frankfurter, certainty the first and perhaps both Harlans, perhaps Chief Justice Warren. They hardly followed the same jurisprudential star or reached identical answers to common questions. How then can we account for their reputations? Near the end of this book I shall examine the possibility that each of the heroes was an exceptional "performer." In the interim, readers may want to reflect on why the electorate elected a former movie actor of modest talents to the governorship of California in 1966 and the presidency of the United States in 1980 and 1984. I suspect the answer is obvious. Ronald Reagan, the performer, managed to create for his audience visions of a virtuous national community.

Chapter 3　THE FAILURE
OF INTERPRETIVE
THEORY

[T]he specialized roles assigned the individual, or adopted by him, are not a full substitute for citizenship because citizenship provides what the other roles cannot, namely an integrative experience which brings together the multiple role-activities of the contemporary person and demands that the separate roles be surveyed from a more general point of view. It means further that efforts be made to restore the political art as that art which strives for an integrative form of direction, one that is broader than that supplied by any group or organization. It means, finally, that political theory must once again be viewed as that form of knowledge which deals with what is general and integrative to men, a life of common involvements.

—Sheldon Wolin

Heaven is no more than a fantasm generated by the excess energies of the pooled imaginations of the blessed.

—Thomas Disch

BACK TO THE CONSTITUTION?

Thus far constitutional law seems to present us with a paradox. We presume that the Constitution helps "constitute" our national political identity. It is a primary source "of what is general and integrative to men, a life of common involvements." To promote this common life, we assume the constitutional lawmaking process must embody some fixed or objective truths. Perhaps constitutional lawmaking must obey the rules of "correct" legal reasoning— observing the best reading of the text in the context created by the intentions of those who framed it, for example. Or perhaps the process must continuously reeducate us in the fundamental values that unite us as a people. Somehow we must find a "there" in the constitutional scheme. The paradox is that this is exactly what the disinterested observer does *not* find.

There are at least four prominent jurisprudential responses to the paradox. The first, the subject of this chapter, holds that the Constitution, if only we would treat it as a legal document, does yield demonstrably correct legal conclusions to litigated cases. Scholars committed to this approach insist that the Supreme Court, seduced by temptations to satisfy expediently the political demands of the moment, has sinned mightily against the discoverable objective law of the Constitution. These scholars seem to believe that if they preach convincingly enough, the Court will confess its sins and go back to the Constitution. The second and third alternatives, which we take up subsequently, propose political and normative alternatives to legal interpretivism. The fourth, the main theme of this book, holds that the paradox does not exist. Professor Wolin correctly identifies the critical importance of the art of politics, but effective performance of the political art does not depend on either the legal or the normative objectivity and constancy that scholars seek. These scholarly arguments are language games that play to small academic communities which are largely isolated from the political life of common involvements. Across our history the Court has performed far better, on average, than most scholarly theories would indicate.

PRESERVATIVISM

The "back to the Constitution" school insists that the only proper constitutional decision is one that "accords binding authority to the text of the Constitution or the intentions of the adopters and is significantly guided by one or more of these sources" (Brest and Levinson, 1983, p. 395). The case for constitutional interpretation bound strictly to text and history is only slightly stronger than the case for the proposition that we inhabit a flat earth. Yet the persistence of this or any discredited point of view generates some fascinating insights. These scholars have created for themselves an academic polity. As in all polities, even "The Flat Earth Society," core normative agreements give that community its "integrative experience." These scholars protect their community by defending their core at all costs. For them these costs include widespread academic criticism. The same dynamics sustain the radically different "Critical" community as well.

This school of jurisprudence includes political scientists, many of them disciples of the University of Chicago's Leo Strauss and/or Herbert Storing, and law professors, many of whom also have a "Chicago connection." Philip Kurland has led the law professor contingent vocally and, as chairman of the editorial board of the University of Chicago Press and editor of *The Supreme Court Review*, powerfully. Some call this community the "Chicago school" of jurisprudence, although academia harbors many "Chicago schools," not all philosophically reconcilable with one another. Also, a "Chicago connection" hypothesis does not fully account for the strictest interpretivist of all, Raoul Berger, though he did earn his law degree at nearby Northwestern University in 1935.

Modern jurisprudence labels this approach "strict interpretivism" or "originalism." Both of these terms mislead. "Interpretivism" takes for granted the proposition that the justices could interpret if they wished. It criticizes them for failing to choose this option, which misleads because the justices do not have this option in the first place. "Originalism" also misleads, both because it implies that constitutional clauses had original meanings with reference to contemporary constitutional issues and because I, at least, associate originality with "creativity," something originalists condemn.

So, with apologies for adding another label to academic discourse, I shall call this the "preservative" school. It seeks to preserve a past that it imagines. It insists that preserving an imagined past is the only objective the Court can properly pursue. No branch of contemporary scholarship seem more obviously, sometimes ludicrously, out of touch with the mainstream of modern political and social philosophy. It asks the Court in its constitutional role to switch off centuries of common-law habits. It ignores the history of constitutional lawmaking described in chapter two. Its methods often paradoxically combine exhaustively detailed historical descriptions with crudely generalized empirical speculations about modern politics and with normative conclusions rhetorically asserted but not documented. Its methods sometimes resemble the very practices it deplores in the Court's constitutional reasoning.

We study this discredited constitutional approach for three reasons. First, the rhetoric of the Reagan presidency suggests that preservative ideology may serve as the "cover" behind which politicians seek to conservatize the federal bench. Second, and more important for my purposes, the preservatives are, unwittingly, on to something. Those who advocate reasoning bound to the constitutional text and its political history have heard Sheldon Wolin's call for a broader and more integrative politics. Wolin has identified the underlying Grecian yearn of the preservatives. Their constitutional heaven may be no more than a fantasm created and maintained by their energetic imaginations, but if communities need some heaven to survive, then upward may be the right way to point. Third, the more widely accepted scholarship described later has developed in part in reaction to preservatism. The reasons the preservatives fail will explain why most of the reactions to it also fail. We must try to understand the political world the Court lives in, not a fantasy heaven created by academicians.

MEMBERS OF THE PRESERVATIVE SCHOOL

I have attempted no comprehensive content analysis of the views of law professors and political scientists, but my reasonably attentive scan of the mainstream professional literature in recent years uncovers the following law professor preservatives: Philip Kurland, Raoul Berger, Frank Easterbrook, Henry Monaghan, Joseph Grano, Bernard Siegan, and Robert Bork, who is now a judge rumored to have Supreme Court potential under a Reagan regime. Gary McDowell, Jeremy Rabkin, John Agresto, Christopher Wolfe, Walter Berns, and Ralph Rossum typify preservative political scientists. Some illustrations will set the stage for an analysis of difficulties with preservativism.

Gary McDowell

McDowell (1982) takes his credo from a passage in "The Letters of Junius":

[L]et me exhort and conjure you never to suffer an invasion of your political constitution, however minute the instance may appear, to pass by, without a determined, persevering resistance. One precedent creates another—they soon accumulate and constitute law. What yesterday was fact, today is doctrine. Examples are supposed to justify the most dangerous measures; and where they do not suit exactly, the defect is supplied by analogy. Be assured that the laws which protect us in our civil rights, grow out of the constitution, and that they must fall or flourish with it.

In a short editorial page essay in the *Wall Street Journal* (January 26, 1983, p. 30), McDowell proposed to erase the bulk of twentieth-century constitutional law, which he believes is an invasion of our political constitution. He advocates enacting a constitutional amendment holding that nothing in the Fourteenth Amendment incorporates any of the principles of the Bill of Rights. This "federalism amendment" is necessary, he argues, because we must remain faithful to the constitutional text. The Court's application of the Bill of Rights to the states resulted from the "creative and unrestrained judicial imagination, not constitutional provision." Federalism, the framers' fundamental goal, has thus deteriorated. After all, John Marshall himself held in 1833 that the Bill of Rights applied only to the national government. The framers adopted the Bill of Rights at the behest of antifederalist interests as a way to check the tendency of the national government to devour the states. "It is striking that what was intended to *limit* the power of the national government over the domestic affairs of the states, the Bill of Rights, has been so turned on its head as to be one of the major avenues whereby national power runs roughshod over the states."

McDowell insists that his proposed amendment is politically neutral. A conservative Court appointed by conservative presidents might strike down state policies allowing abortions or prohibiting school prayer. His amendment would prohibit the worst consequences of judicial whimsy in either direction.

In a *Wall Street Journal* review (8/26/82, p. 20) of G. Edward White's biography of Earl Warren (1982), McDowell called Warren's jurisprudence "only a string of cases wherein his 'individual beliefs' led to judgments."

Earl Warren's judging and jurisprudence were utterly at odds with the idea of limited constitutional government. For the republican idea of justice that the Constitution was intended to secure does not depend upon the noble intentions of a judge any more than any other public official. It depends, as Herbert Storing has said, on a "government with powers to act and a structure arranged to make it act wisely and responsibly."

McDowell does not trust judges. In his book *Equity and The Constitution* (1982), he cites (p. 18) as his authority Aristotle's preference for statutes that define "the issue of all cases as far as possible, and leave as little as possible to the discretion of judges." There is a wisdom in legislative numbers and the leisure which a legislature has to consider proposals. A legislature need not act at all. "But," Aristotle continues, "what is most important of all is that the judgment of the legislator . . . is universal and applied to the future, whereas the [judges] have to decide present and definite issues, and in their case, love, hate, or personal interest is often involved so that they are no longer capable of discerning the truth adequately, their judgment being obscured by their own pleasure or pain."

Aristotle supposes that politics do not significantly constrain the judges, and McDowell says (p. 134) that this remains true today because the Court has a powerful but one-way impact on public opinion.

> There is an intimate connection between judicial power and public opinion. . . . Judicial opinions tend to be woven into the fabric of the American political consciousness to such a degree that they are taken for granted. . . . On the whole, the people believe the Court to be apolitical and beyond reproach, and that belief is a massive, if not insurmountable, obstacle to Congress exercising any meaningful control over the judicial power.

Of course if McDowell's *Wall Street Journal* specter of a politically appointed conservative Court gunning down liberal state policies is correct, such a Court will not be quite so politically untouchable. His asserted connection between Court opinions and popular beliefs is either untestable or, if converted to testable form, inconsistent with public opinion evidence. McDowell contradicts both himself and incontroverted evidence, but I am getting ahead of my story. I shall lay out the serious flaws in preservative thinking after I describe a larger sample.

John Agresto

In "The Limits of Judicial Supremacy: A Proposal for 'Checked' Activism" (1980), Agresto also asserts that the political process does not check the Court. He argues this is so because we have come to believe, as Stephen Douglas held in the Lincoln–Douglas debates, that constitutional decisions are legally final and authoritatively binding throughout public and private life. This presumption of finality contradicts the framers', and especially Jefferson's, commitment to the checks and balances system. Judicial self-restraint is no answer, partly because the framers did not intend self-restraint and because the historical data show it does not work in practice. Worse, "the Court can, and often has, made serious errors regarding the meaning and demands of the constitutional text" (p. 485). Impeachment, jurisdictional modifications by the elected Congress, and political appointments (both routine and extraordinary, like the Court-packing threat of 1937) have not effectively deterred or corrected these errors. "The cry of 'judicial imperialism' is abroad, and not without reason" (p. 493).

Therefore, Agresto urges restoration of effective checks and balances through a constitutional doctrine in which judicial decisions bind only the parties to that decision and the judiciary itself. Political actors in other branches of government should retain the recognized authority to resist judicial errors by making separate and independent constitutional interpretations.

Christopher Wolfe

In an exchange in the *Journal of Politics* between Professor Wolfe and me, Wolfe (1981) echoes the call for a rigorously interpretive approach to the Constitution. Wolfe agrees that to hold his position requires rejecting the core of contemporary social philosophy. He concludes (p. 325):

> But in the final analysis, I would rather reject the broad relativism itself, believing that the founders embodied sound political principles in the Constitution, which can be "interpreted," and that what the Constitution does not provide rules for should be left to the workings of a democratic process soundly designed by those founders (trusting to amendment to rectify any serious infirmities). Adherence to these principles requires neither scholasticism . . . nor linguistic naïveté, but merely, in my view, fidelity to the political wisdom of the founders.

Professor Wolfe believes that, contrary to the consistent pattern of no pattern we saw in chapter two, a "golden age" of sound interpretive lawmaking existed prior to the Civil War, and that we have lost it.

Walter Berns

McDowell, Agresto, and Wolfe are legalists. They believe the Court must obey the Constitution to preserve the legitimacy of the legal system, and ultimately the political system as well. Walter Berns, by contrast, is a philosopher. In *The First Amendment and the Future of American Democracy* (1976), he specifically endorses "the political wisdom of the founders." Berns, like most Straussians, takes us back to the Constitution not because the legal words and history require the return or because democratic theory "illegitimates" noninterpretive judicial lawmaking. Berns believes that the founders formulated a correct substantive vision of republican government, one which it is suicidal to abandon.

His final chapter deserves a hard look. Berns' closing argument begins by citing Justice Black's dissent in *Adamson v. California* (1947). The *Adamson* majority declined to require the states, under the Fourteenth Amendment, to follow the federal courts' Fifth Amendment proscription of prosecutorial comment on defendant's refusal in a criminal trial to take the stand in his defense. Black dissented on the ground that, although the framers did not anticipate the modern problem, it was of the same kind as those the framers intended to cover. Black's approach, says Berns, "casts the Court in the role of defender of democracy, of the people. And the Bill of Rights does indeed speak of the people" (p. 229). But Black's appeal hides from us the nondemocratic character of judicial review. Worse, it turns the purpose of republican government on its head. It pretends that the Court's task is to promote democracy when it in fact should protect the few from the many. Recent applications of the First Amendment, whose justifications often fit Justice Black's pseudodemocratic theory, is "calculated adversely to affect—if not destroy—those institutions on which American democracy depends" (p. 232). The Court's decisions shape character, and

> that character depends on the condition of religion, the family, the schools, and on the strength of the people's attachment to republican principles. The Court in its First Amendment decisions has proceeded in blissful ignorance of this, promoting pornography in the name of freedom of expression; casting aside, as so many irrational encumbrances, the conventions of decency that used to govern public discourse; refusing to permit financial support to religious education; and subtly undermining the venerable character of the Constitution itself. (pp. 232–233)

The law should look to the past for precedents, but we look "almost in vain for references in the Court's opinions to what the great commentators—Story, Kent, and Cooley, for example—have written on freedom of speech and religion, or what the Founders intended with the First Amendment" (p. 233). "Justice Brennan cited Jefferson and others in his opinion in *New York Times v. Sullivan* [1964], and, having misunderstood them, came up with a 'central meaning of the First Amendment' that Jefferson and the others would not have recognized" (pp. 233–234). "Among [the people,] the family is still a respected institution, and they continue to ·be suspicious of the fashionable idea that sexual fulfillment is the measure of a truly human life. Hence, they find it difficult to accept the related proposition that all the laws that somehow inhibit sexual fulfillment, or that channel it in the direction of marriage, are unconstitutional. They suspect this is not the Constitution they and their forbears have lived under, and of course they are right. What is disquieting, however, is that public opinion is, inevitably, beginning to follow the Court and the 'elites' the Court follows" (p. 235).

Berns closes (p. 237) with a jurisprudential bang warning against impending and quietly whimpering social decay:

> Why is free speech good? The Court doesn't know. Was free speech intended to serve republican government and only republican government? The Court doesn't care what the original intention was. Is there a connection between decent public discourse and decent government? The Court doesn't even bother to wonder. Is there a connection between the privacy of sexual behavior and the family and, therefore, with republican government? For a period that may prove to be decisive, the Court did not even acknowledge the relevance of the question. Is there a connection between morality and republican government—or, in Tocqueville's formulation, can liberty govern without religious faith? Whatever the answer, the Constitution is now said to have built an impregnable wall between church and state.

Philosophic men of the past addressed themselves to these questions and provided answers. But the Supreme Court no longer remembers those answers. The
Founders, in their different ways, also provided answers, but the Court no longer
remembers their answers either. Instead, it has allowed itself to be carried about
on the wind of modern doctrine.

What is preservativism's appeal? Walter Berns' final passage gives a clue.
He is threatened less by what the Court claims to know than by the possibility
the Court knows nothing. This moral vacuum threatens us with the possibility
that our moral visions, and therefore our national political identity, have died.
Preservativism appeals because it takes seriously our need for a life of common involvements. The same yearning underlies the work of a law professor
whom Ronald Reagan recently appointed to the federal bench, Robert Bork.

Robert Bork

Michael Perry, whose defense of noninterpretivism appears in chapter
four, selects Robert Bork's as the best justification of interpretivism. Here, in
part to help set the stage for Perry, are some of his selections from Bork (1971,
in Perry, 1982, pp. 29–30). Note that Bork, a lawyer, argues more by syllogism
than do the political scientists cited earlier.

Society consents to be ruled undemocratically within defined areas by certain
enduring principles believed to be stated in, and placed beyond the reach of
majorities by, the Constitution.
. . . [I]t follows that the Court's power is legitimate only if it has, and can
demonstrate in reasoned opinions that it has, a valid theory, derived from the
Constitution, of the respective spheres of majority and minority freedom. If it
does not have such a theory but merely imposes its own value choices, or worse if
it pretends to have a theory but actually follows its own predilections, the Court
. . . abets the tyranny either of the majority or of the minority.
. . . [N]o argument that is both coherent and respectable can be made supporting a Supreme Court that "chooses fundamental values" because a Court that
makes rather than implements value choices cannot be squared with the presup-
positions of a democratic society.
. . . Where constitutional materials do not clearly specify the value to be
preferred, there is no principled way to prefer any claimed human value to any
other. The judge must stick close to the text and the history, and their fair
implications, and not construct new rights.
. . . Where the Constitution does not embody the moral or ethical choice, the
judge has no basis other than his own values upon which to set aside the community judgment embodied in the statute. That, by definition, is an inadequate basis
for judicial supremacy.
. . . Courts must accept any value choice the legislature makes unless it clearly
runs contrary to a choice made in the framing of the Constitution.
. . . There is no principled way in which anyone can define the spheres in which
liberty is required and the spheres in which equality is required. These are matters
of morality, of judgment, of prudence. They belong, therefore, to the political
community. In the fullest sense, these are political questions.

For Bork, whatever is not demonstrably "in" the Constitution must fall exclusively in the realm of personal value choices. As such only the democratic political process can choose among them. They are therefore no business of an impartial, apolitical, court. Bork concludes:

> The Supreme Court regularly insists that its results, and most particularly its controversial results, do not spring from the mere will of the Justices in the majority but are supported, indeed compelled by a proper understanding of the Constitution of the United States. Value choices are attributed to the Founding Fathers, not to the Court. The way an institution advertises tells you what it thinks its customers demand.

Preservatives thus believe that the framers designed, in something like a timeless or natural law fashion, an ideal state, one in which the courts play a limited role. If we can today imagine a system preferable to the framers' system, we are no less constitutionally bound to the framers' system. The Constitution is a legal document which judges must follow according to its terms. These terms command that constitutional changes come by democratic means, not through government by judiciary.

THE PRESERVATIVE STYLE

If the way a seller advertises reveals what it thinks its customers demand, then our analysis of preservative thought should attend first to its advertising style.[1]

Preservative analysis is "legalistic." It resembles Judith Shklar's definition of legalism (1964, p. 1), "the ethical attitude that holds moral conduct to be a matter of rule following, and moral relations to consist of duties and rights determined by rules." This style of unabashed advocacy contrasts with scientific styles of persuasion. The advocative argument starts with a conclusion, normatively laden, and then supports it with a mix of passion and selective evidence. It is not, by contrast, skeptical.[2] Skeptical reasoning is no righter in any absolute sense than any other form of reasoning. Indeed, that truth is central to the argument of this book. But scientific, skeptical argument purports

---

[1] I agree with Bork on this point. Indeed, by the end of the book we shall learn that, in Nelson Goodman's aesthetic theory (1978), performance resembles selling in several important respects. The difficulty with Bork's position in this passage is that the Court often explicitly *denies* that it attributes values to the Founding Fathers. Bork thus practices the sin which he preaches the Court should eschew. My point is not simply that the logic of Bork's position evaporates (though it indeed does) but rather that Bork and the Court engage in a practice necessary to good performance: they simplify and fictionalize raw experience in order to communicate their vision of its meaning effectively. In performance the external values, those suggested by a script, for example, and the values of the performer inevitably interact and merge. Thus Bork's dichotomy between constitutional values and personal predilections has merit only if the Court does *not* attempt to sell us its ideas.

[2] It is the same practical reasoning that characterizes all appellate adjudication. For example: "It is desirable to limit the political power of the judiciary, or honor our forefathers, or shape moral character, etc. Holding strictly to the intent of the framers will do so. Therefore the Courts should adhere to the intent of the framers."

to appeal to the open mind. It defines the conditions for replication and falsification of the experimental findings. Advocacy, on the other hand, does not assume responsibility for dealing comprehensively with counterevidence or for acknowledging the existence of plausible alternative starting premises which, if adopted, could produce different and inconsistent conclusions.

Attorneys seek to persuade judges through advocacy, and there is nothing demonstrably inferior about the method as a mode of persuasion. We must, however, approach it warily. Preservatives surely know that the argument, "because the law says so," is not an acceptable argument in most appellate litigation. The question is *why* the law ought to say one thing or another. David Riesman, the legally trained sociologist, came to the conclusion that lawyers do not take law seriously precisely because their training enables them to generate from law multiple right answers to legal conflicts. The legal style is a consequence of the multiplicity of potential right answers, which is just what the preservatives seek to refute.

If preservatives seek to persuade academicians, they can do no more than preach to the converted. The bulk of contemporary academicians think of themselves as scientists, or as skeptics, and legalistic advocacy is not likely to convert them. If the Court has never consistently practiced preservative jurisprudence, nothing less than a revolution will suffice.

The preservative style usually makes it unnecessary systematically to defend its central premise: the premise of the authoritative past. Gary McDowell titles the final chapter of his 1981 book, "Toward a Recovery of the Past," a title consistent with his view that Junius and Aristotle serve as authorities for his position. This basic premise rejects the familiar argument that social conditions change and law must adapt. Chief Justice Marshall himself seems to have endorsed the position the preservatives reject. Jefferson certainly did. But on what basis does one reject Marshall's familiar argument, particularly when it seems accurately to describe all of our constitutional history?

Wolfe rejects relativism, but he explicitly chooses not to defend that courageous position. And why the choice of republican versus democratic starting models? The answer that the Constitution says so or that the framers intended it yields only the vicious circle of a presumed conclusion. While the preservatives might well reply that all argument must begin somewhere, that no one ever defends his or her starting premise (for the defense of a starting point only pushes back to a prior undefended assumption), they also tend to assume their conclusions, which is a different matter.

The legalistic style generates a host of critical but unanswered questions:

- How are we to distinguish Junius' evil precedents that "accumulate" from those good ones that "grow out of the constitution?" McDowell cannot posit a linguistically unambiguous constitution. The age one must attain to become president is specific, and the Third Amendment's peacetime applications seem pretty clear, but the clauses that the preservatives wish to preserve, the First, Fifth, and Fourteenth Amendments, for example, gain meaning only in context. Junius, if he is apt at all, must refer to encroachments on the meanings and usages the framers intended their words to carry. Well, how certain must we be of framer intent to know we are in the "growth" rather than "accumulation" category?

- How does the Court's "national power run roughshod over the states" in McDowell's sense? He does not mean by upholding congressional power under the commerce clause, for those decisions come from elected bodies, and bodies elected through state political organizations and electoral machinery at that. We possess a properly restrained Court in such instances, so McDowell must mean civil liberties decisions. But the very decisions he cites by definition limit national and state power equally. Incorporating portions of the Bill of Rights into the Fourteenth Amendment only limits state power according to principles that previously limit national power. If the Court runs roughshod over the states, it seems to do so in defense of individual liberty, not of raw national power. It is a curious position. Why not say, as Berns believes, that the Court allows individual interests to run roughshod over community interests expressed through the exercise of political power?

- If we are to credit McDowell's quote of Herbert Storing, on what basis should we deny that, say, the reapportionment decisions help make government "act wisely and responsibly"?

- Since we have a Constitution whose words, rightly or wrongly, do leave much to the discretion of judges, of what use is the rest of McDowell's quote from Aristotle? On what basis should we assume identity between the practices of judges in Greek city-states of 2,500 years ago and Supreme Court judges? The recent journalistic efforts to uncover something like corruption in the Court—Woodward and Armstrong's *The Bretheren* (1979) and Bruce Murphy's *The Brandeis/Frankfurter Connection* (1982)—turn up trivial and contextually distorted gossip (see especially Cover, 1982). These diggings do *not* turn up evidence that love, hate, and the interest in gaining personal pleasure or avoiding pain from the outcome determine judicial decisions. These vices may well have occurred in the tight communities of free men in Greek city-states prior to the professionalization of the legal system, but they are hardly major factors today. If the defeat of the Fortas, Haynesworth, and Carswell nominations is any indication, the Court is squeaky clean. Again, the style somehow makes it unnecessary to demonstrate a connection between Aristotle's premise and McDowell's conclusion.

- If in Agresto's diagnosis the growing power of the Court attaches inevitably to its political position and responsibilities, do not those conditions doom a checks and balances theory no less than the other failed restraints?

- Given Walter Berns' concern for the countermajoritarian character of judicial review, on what basis is it "disquieting" if public opinion follows the Court?

Robert Bork's work is especially laden with non sequiturs:

- Granted that the Court must have a theory, why must that theory be "from" rather than "about" the Constitution in order to avoid abetting tyranny? Why is the preposition so important?
- Where the Constitution does not clearly specify (Why "clearly?" How "clearly?") preferred values, how does sticking "close to the text and history" solve the problem? If the Constitution offers two competing but equal values, the text is the problem, not the solution.
- If the objection to the modern Court is that it is too political, on what basis is the Court not part of that political community which Bork believes should address questions of morality, judgment, and prudence?

The preservatives could clarify these confusions without destroying their case. The point here is that their style of persuasion makes it unnecessary, from their perspective, to do so.

The preservatives often employ passionate and sometimes angry rhetoric. To the extent it suits their message, it is effective rhetoric, and by and large it suits the message quite well. The preservatives are angered by the fearful prospect of legal decay. Professor Kurland speaks often of judicial whim. The inclusion within the Fourteenth Amendment of the protection of religious liberty happened "solely at the whim of the Court," said Kurland in an article splenetically titled "The Irrelevance of the Constitution" (1978, p. 10). Walter Berns seems to posit that the Court has contributed to rising divorce rates, and he is angered by that "fact." The evident anger in this rhetoric will not raise the confidence of the persuadable skeptic that the factual descriptions are comprehensive and the logic well crafted. Preservative rhetoric serves to avoid the question: why must the intent of the framers matter? If the framers did not intend the Fourteenth Amendment to include the protection of religious liberties, the fact does not prove that the framers' intent ought to settle the larger argument. Kurland himself (in the *New York Times*, June 23, 1971, p. 43) put the point well: "[C]ertitude is only an anagram and not a synonym for rectitude."

But perhaps style and substance do not interact. Perhaps despite the non sequiturs and overgeneralizations, the preservative approach triangulates with other bodies of knowledge. If so, then it is petty to carp on the lack of fit between the preservative style of argument and standard accepted methods of argument in modern science and philosophy. The next section searches for some triangulation of the preservatives with other schools of thought. We will eventually find some very modest triangulations, but they will confirm, ironically, style more than substance. Some "critical" legal scholars are angry too, if for very different reasons. Certitude *is* more than an anagram for rectitude. The preservative lust for certainty is a drive widely shared. In chaotic times people may grasp and hold even to an Adolf Hitler. Even in normal times the conversations that build communities need authoritative and hence undisputed starting points. The great theologian Karl Barth once wrote, "We must learn again to speak to each other with authority and not as the scribes. For the present we are all much too clever and unchildlike to be of real mutual help."[3] Judges and scholars alike must speak with authority in order to sustain political conversations effectively. I again remind you that the preservatives are on to something.

THE PRESERVATIVE SUBSTANCE: YOU CAN'T GO HOME AGAIN

The preservatives contradict, or more precisely, neglect, a large body of evidence and theory about modern political life. Above all, they neglect modern theories of the nature of interpretation itself—hermeneutics. To master the complexities of hermeneutic theory, we must first canvass some of the more familiar objections to the preservative position. It lays foundations for both the hermeneutic and political discussions to come.

Contemporary Theories of Legal Reasoning

To commit to the preservative position requires a rejection of a widely accepted understanding of common law reasoning. What makes legal reasoning particularly difficult for the preservatives to overcome, and why they ignore it, is that practicing judges, reporting the lessons taught by legal history and learned from self-examination on the bench, have contributed as much as have scholars to modern reasoning theory. Holmes over a century ago wrote of the common law:

> The life of the law has not been logic; it has been experience. The felt necessities of the time, the prevalent moral and political theories, intuitions of public policy, avowed or unconscious, even the prejudices which judges share with their fellow-men, have had a good deal more to do than the syllogism in determining the rules by which men should be governed. (1881, p. 1)

The more reflectively elegant Cardozo confessed that the judicial process "in its highest reaches is not discovery, but creation" (1921, p. 166).

Much modern theory denies that mechanistic reasoning techniques determine case outcomes. Consider the technique of reasoning from precedents. A judge only perceives that case X serves as a precedent for the case before him

---

[3] Quoted in Shaffer (1981, p. 21). A few hours after I first drafted this section, Governor Mario Cuomo of New York addressed the 1984 Democratic National Convention in Chicago. He spoke authoritatively about the nation as a family and a city. The press used such metaphorical adjectives as "electrifying" in its write-ups of the speech, and began immediately speculating on Cuomo's chances for the presidential nomination in 1988. (See, e.g., the *Wall Street Journal*, July 19, 1984, p. 1.) Cuomo's address illustrated Barth's point nicely. We are, of course, far too pluralistic to become a national family. How childish to assert the possibility!

after choosing to call the two cases factually similar despite their many factual differences. Furthermore, the elliptical nature of opinion-writing usually provides multiple alternative conclusions from just one case, in the uncommon instance in which only one potential precedent case applies.

The preservatives call for fidelity to the Constitution, not precedents. Since these arguments and their supporting literature receive full treatment in Levi (1949), Rumble (1968), Bennett (1984), and Carter (1984), it suffices to note that many of the same difficulties with getting right results from precedents apply to the interpretations of historical evidence of the framers' intent. Chief among these is the inescapable factual uniqueness of the case at hand. Judge Jerome Frank wrote that "in a profound sense the unique circumstances of almost any case make it an 'unprovided case' where no well-established rule 'authoritatively' compels a given result." Felix Frankfurter wrote to Hugo Black in 1939, when both were relative newcomers to the Court:

> I, too, am opposed to judicial legislation in its invidious sense; but I deem equally mischievous—because founded on an untruth and an impossible aim—the notion that judges merely announce the law which they find and do not themselves inevitably have a share in the lawmaking. Here, as elsewhere, the difficulty comes from arguing in terms of absolutes when the matter at hand is conditioned by circumstances, is contingent upon the everlasting problem of how far is too far, and how much is too much.

Justice Frankfurter's emphasis on the "impossible aim" of speaking in terms of absolutes might have been written to a modern preservative. It virtually was, since Justice Black claimed to read the Constitution literally. But of course Black's "preservativism" contributed to many of the decisions the preservatives condemn. And, over time, Black appeared to contradict himself.[4]

Even those who profess strict fidelity to the past often arrive at contradictory conclusions. Raoul Berger, Charles Fairman, and William Crosskey all sought truths from the details of historical records, but they came to very different legal conclusions (Berger, 1984; McAffee, 1984; Krash, 1984). Similarly, Thomas Grey's analysis (1975) of the records of the founding convinced him that the framers knowingly created a legal document whose vague words would, over time, come to mean what the framers themselves did not intend or envision. No lawmaker, after all, intends that the law mean only what he personally hopes it means. He knows others in different contexts will derive other meanings from the words. Gary Jacobsohn (1984, pp. 40–41), examining much of the same evidence, believes otherwise:

> When, then, in the next several paragraphs, Paterson invalidates the Pennsylvania statute, declaring it to be "inconsistent with the principles of reason, justice, and

---

[4] So, for that matter does the preeminent preservative and enemy of "philosophizing," Raoul Berger. See McAffee (1984).

moral rectitude," as well as "contrary to both the letter and spirit of the Constitution," there is no question that these two sources of adjudication are inextricably linked in his mind, that the written constitution contains the principles of justice for which Professor Grey seeks external justification.

Once again we see that the principles the preservatives take as legally certain are actually the object of intense disagreement.

Since the preservatives call for a jurisprudence that discovers the intent of the framers, they must as least resolve the "level of analysis" problem. Does intent include speculation about what the framers would think if confronted with a modern problem? Many constitutional clauses—the cruel and unusual punishment clause, for example—would not mean much if limited only to the conditions of the times, but to admit speculation about what the framers might have thought in modern times, e.g., of the mortgage moratorium laws of the Great Depression, which contradict a literal reading of the contract clause and the political purposes its framers may have intended it to serve, gives Junius' noninterpretive camel permission to thrust his nose under the edge of the tent. In other words, the preservatives do not provide a reason to reject the extension of constitutional doctrine by analogy. The combination of textual ambiguity and intervening technological and sociological innovations supports such extensions. The second Justice Harlan, no wild-eyed judicial legislator, after all found such a basis in the Fourteenth Amendment when he voted for the majority's conclusion in the birth control case, *Griswold v. Connecticut* (1965).

The biggest hurdle for the preservativist in modern legal reasoning doctrine is that all legal interpretations of intent are speculative and inconclusive. William Anderson wrote in 1955:

> Every man, being a different individual, unavoidably has intentions that are somewhat different from those of someone else. Such a thing as a solid, unified intention of all the members in any group would be hard if not impossible to find . . . (p. 345). I simply am unable to imagine what types and quantities of records would be needed to clinch any important point in the several major problems that arise. Neither can I imagine how any known method of psychoanalysis, content analysis, or plain crystal-ball gazing applied to such records or to the people who left them could give thoroughly reliable and irrefutable answers concerning the intentions of these later framers. The transition that needs to be made from the enduring and objective facts of the written words used to the fleeting, largely unexpected, and subjective facts of the intentions of framers who passed away many years ago is beyond human capacity to make. (p. 350)

Murphy and Pritchett (1979), noting Anderson's analysis, point out that the records of the founding are far less complete than modern congressional legislative history. Madison's notes, the most complete source, are not complete, and he admitted to editing them more than 20 years after the founding. Not surprisingly, the preservatives frequently cite as authority the familiar sections of the *Federalist Papers*, but these clauses do not claim to speak for the lawmaking body. They are advocate's arguments, not reports of what a group, empowered to make law, intended. If intent has legal force, its force comes only by convincing us of the legal position of the lawmaking majority. Opinion-polling provides the only measure of group intent. But the poll put to legislators and framers asks only one question: Do you wish a given proposal to become law? That measure of intent gets the preservatives to their starting line, but no further. That much intent we have already safely presumed.

In sum, American jurisprudence in the twentieth century has debated many points, but not the proposition that constitutional decisions inevitably weigh competing social interests. Such diverse thinkers as Benjamin Cardozo, Karl Llewellyn, Jerome Frank, Roscoe Pound, Edward S. Corwin, H.L.A. Hart, and Ronald Dworkin all concur in rejecting preservatism. If the preservatives seek a world in which the justices reason like expert historians and thus restore us to our past, they buy a product that does not exist. The position depends upon a philosophical system that would demonstrate that the *Holy Bible* could have only one meaning binding for all time those who profess commitment to it. A tall order!

The Insignificance of Public Opinion

Many of the preservatives speak in terms of a reified mass of public opinion, which presumes that the citizenry pays careful attention to the constitutional work of the Court. McDowell posited "an intimate connection between judicial power and public opinion." Philip Kurland (1978, p. 26) wrote: "Surely, in a would-be democracy, the people are entitled to know who their masters are." Yet most citizens, when asked openendedly to describe what the Court has done, cannot do so with anything like the accuracy and understanding the reified version presupposes. (The evidence is summarized in Sarat, 1977.) Survey items that formulate the issue for the respondent provoke higher rates of coherent responses, but they depend on the wording of the question. "Do you favor the Supreme Court's position on abortion?" will receive a lower favorable response than "Do you agree or disagree that 'A woman's decisions about her pregnancy should be left between her and her doctor'?" In any event, such public opinion as is measurable shows every evidence of relating not to the nature of the constitutional justification but to the respondent's perception of whether a good or evil ox has been gored, and the severity of the damage. In such cases, people do know who their masters are.

Two final obstacles to the reified public opinion position. First, if as Berns fears the Court shapes opinion, it does so by indirect means, and sociological research has not succeeded in finding them. The mechanisms may exist. The mediating mechanism would probably be television, but of course television, subject as it is to national regulation, hardly resembles the Fourteenth Amendment "usurpations" that so worry the preservatives.

Second, the preservatives express concern for the "legitimacy" of the Court as an institution and of the practice of judicial review. But "legitimacy" as an institutional characteristic has no operational definition in social science. It is political science's modern equivalent of "phlogiston," a symbol without content that plugs a hole in an argument. Given the tenuous or nonexistent linkages between public opinion and the justifications of the Court, it is difficult to conceptualize how the Court's political survival rides on the style or structure of its opinions.

The Lessons of Comparative Government

The preservatives are fond of claiming that judicial review in the United States has so few analogs in other democratic political systems that it thereby becomes presumptively deviant. Walter Murphy (1980) has shown that comparable democracies are tending toward rather than away from the practice. (See also Kommers, 1976.) The new Canadian constitution resembles the United States Constitution as the Court has constructed it far more than the preservatives' vision of the original.

The Jurisprudence of Unique Cases

The analysis thus far suggests that judges cannot go back to the Constitution no matter how much they might desire to do so. But assume for a moment that they could and did. To commit to the preservative position, a judge or scholar would have to reject as insignificant or erroneous what I call the jurisprudence of unique cases. By this phrase I mean that each litigant confronted with a "constitutional problem" sees not an abstracted legal issue but a rich and, in most instances, personal moral claim.

The litigant will sense, sometimes quite erroneously, that some of the elements of his case involve "his rights." The desire to have one's rights vindicated is less a legal claim than a claim to reassert dignity and self-respect. In a common-law system the courts, not the legislatures, hear such claims. If a person seeks vindication of his dignity in a court, then the preservative position, even assuming its doability, poses a major obstacle, for it presents the citizen with an automatic result. Where the claim of dignity takes the form of a constitutional claim, the preservatives's static and fixed constitution forecloses vindication. The citizen will not seek vindication in court at all. The law will be clear in advance, and courts will play bill collector. If an individual's claim of right is in part dignitarian, however, then participation in a process may matter apart from winning or losing the legal issue.

From this point of view, rights are always personal. By definition, the political or collective definition and structure of individual rights must incorporate the promise of transcending political calculus. The legal process must not operate in a way that makes irrelevant or meaningless the citizen's desire for dialogue because the event of the dialogue, not the legal outcome, may provide the dignitarian vindication. Vindicative conversations, with one's lawyer in private as well as in court, must in this view be truly two-sided, caring, and open-ended. Uncertainty and the capacity for the legal system to change its rules over time are therefore essential characteristics of a system that cares to preserve the integrity of moral claims. Without uncertainty and the potential for legal change, citizens would have no incentive to participate.

This theory presents a testable hypothesis. If individual vindication comes from winning on the legal issue, then experiment and opinion research comparing winners and losers should find winners substantially more satisfied with the legal process than losers, quite independent of the procedure employed. If participation contributes in substantial part to vindication of dignity, however, satisfaction differences should vary with the degree to which processes are in fact participatory, not merely with the outcome. The bulk of recent research leans consistently toward the second conclusion (Tyler, 1984; Cohen, 1984; Thibaut and Walker, 1975).

We need not take this theory to the mat here. The theory merely asks preservatives to demonstrate either that their approach leaves questions of law and vindication sufficiently open to motivate adequate participation or to supply a normative basis for rejecting a jurisprudence that preserves the uniqueness of each citizen's case. Their failure in this respect might even strike us as ironic. Those who demand a "recovery of the past" actually mirror the formal, impersonal, and legalistic relationships we associate with contemporary bureaucratic culture.

But recall that the preceding argument assumes the feasibility of preservativism in the first place. If contemporary legal reasoning theories are correct, however, the argument for individualistic jurisprudence merely suggests an inevitable dynamic in American law that the legal profession can, if it chooses, incorporate in its efforts to improve the quality of the legal system.

Political Practice

Preservative theory insists that the Supreme Court is institutionally poorly equipped and situated to make policy effectively. Consider, largely by way of anticipation of chapter four, Alexander Bickel's (1962) statement of the difficulty:

> The judicial process is too principle-prone and principle-bound—it has to be, there is no other justification or explanation for the role it plays. It is also too remote from conditions, and deals, case by case, with too narrow a slice of reality. It is not accessible to all the varied interests that are in play in any decision of great consequence. It is, very properly, independent. It is passive. It has difficulty

controlling the stages by which it approaches a problem. It rushes forward too fast, or it lags; its pace hardly ever seems just right. For all these reasons, it is, in a vast, complex, changeable society, a most unsuitable instrument for the formation of policy.

Each of Bickel's reservations about the Court—remoteness, narrowness of vision, inaccessibility, weak control and timing of policy changes—characterizes American politics in general. They are the planned inefficiencies of democracy itself, not just judicial weaknesses. Chapter four will, among other things, suggest that the Court's suitability or unsuitability as a policymaker depends on the characteristics of the case and the Court in combination. Furthermore, suitability depends in practical affairs on a comparative test. Is the Court less suited than the White House to decide questions of military and other foreign affairs? Probably so. The Court does not have access to the information on which such policies often hinge. Is the Court less suited than a police department to decide the specific meaning of the rights of a suspect? Probably not. The police agenda understandably wants to maximize returns on dollars of law enforcement money invested. The Constitution inhibits organizational "effectiveness," in this regard. In addition, unlike foreign policy, criminal justice dynamics fall squarely within the professional training and experience of those lawyers who become judges. Finally, the immediate self-interest of legislators directly hampers some kinds of policy changes. Is the Court better suited to correcting legislative malapportionment than are the legislators who benefit from sustained malapportionment? Almost surely so.

The Court does not, of course, always understand these distinctions or act on them wisely, much to the preservatives's dismay. The preservatives seem at bottom to demand judicial perfection. The Court must convince nearly all of us in nearly every case that it has decided correctly. Anything less will destroy the Court politically. Political experience should lay the fear to rest. It is one thing to converse, like children, with authority, and another to claim perfection. We may delight in the thrust and parry of a discussion where each side seeks to persuade the other of the authority of his or her position because both sides may be right. Conversations with perfectionists are, on the other hand, tiresome.

"WHAT IS REAL?
HOW IS ONE TO KNOW?"[5]

Preservative jurisprudence boils down to the assertion that the text of the Constitution and the intentions of those who framed it prescribe a way of knowing the reality of, or the "truth of," certain quite specific legal principles. Moreover, perservatives presume that all lawyers and judges—indeed all citizens—can and ought to arrive at the same truths by virtue of this method. For

[5] Peter Berger and Thomas Luckmann, *The Social Construction of Reality* (New York: Doubleday, 1966), p. 1.

preservatism to persuade us of its validity, it must first persuade us that people are capable of reaching a common knowledge of reality in this fashion.

We do, of course, suppose that people know things to be real in the living of their lives. We know that tangible things like tables, chairs, hamburgers, and cassette tapes are real, and we also know the reality of love, melody, fear, and other less tangible things. People must know reality in order to survive both individually and collectively. When an individual's answers shatter, we say he is insane. When collective answers fail, the collective community no longer exists.

But how do people know such things? In the late twentieth century a consensus in social philosophy and social science contradicts the preservative model of knowing. People believe in objective realities that are created and strongly conditioned by their social environments. "Primitive" beliefs in gods and demons are just as "true" for people whose families, friends, and leaders believe in gods and demons as the "scientific" statement that smoking causes lung cancer is true for people whose social environment accepts the truth of scientific method (Alexander, 1981).

We need not reify individual beliefs, which are the only acceptable unit of analysis in the study of ideas, into the abstractions of "societies and cultures." These abstractions can only consist of collections of beliefs that individuals hold to be true. Beliefs develop through an interactive process in which shared knowledge shapes what people in daily affairs think they see as common sense reality.

In pluralistic political communities, where people from different cultural, religious, economic, and educational experiences seek to operate together through many highly differentiated and tightly structured organizations (schools, families, churches, gangs, businesses, labor unions, and so on), we should expect to find that people frequently disagree on the nature of reality. The United States is just such a pluralistic political community. Agreements tend to be fragile and short-lived.

The theory of understanding I have just described, the construction of which owes much to Hegel, Marx, Nietzsche, and more recent members of the German school (Mannheim, Wittgenstein, Gadamer, and Habermas, for example), has important consequences for constitutional jurisprudence that scholars are just now beginning to recognize. Pluralist communities have no single way of knowing that all members can and should adopt. Since lawmaking is a community act, there can be no single method for knowing a "correct" set of legal truths. Thus what you or I believe is real depends not on realities or truths "out there" but on the nature of the social communications, the conversations about reality, that we experience.

When I say something to a listener, I usually try to communicate a belief in some reality. As the song, "How Could You Believe Me When I Told You That I Loved You When You Know I've Been A Liar All My Life," reports, words alone do not necessarily express my beliefs. But we do communicate through verbal and bodily language. Speakers presumably hope listeners will get the message the speaker thinks he sends. Communications theory, a direct extrapolation from the core consensus I outlined above, predicts that in face-to-face communications among people with common languages, cultures, experiences, and so on, listeners' interpretations of messages can come relatively close to the messages senders hoped to send, or at least the parties will act as if that were true.

Lawmakers send messages to a political community. How are we to interpret the messages they send across time? "Hermeneutics" is that branch of communication theory that asks how we may know the meaning of messages sent in or from the past. But as William Anderson pointed out above, this is no easy task, for it makes almost certain, particularly when one looks back several hundred years (across what C. S. Lewis calls "the great divide" in Western thought separating pneumanistic from scientific ways of knowing), that we as listeners cannot replicate the world of the message sender and therefore cannot interpret the message accurately. We may think we do, but our reconstruction of the messages the Constitution's framers sent, of the messages the authors of the *Holy Bible* sent, of Plato's and Thucydides' messages, will not replicate the original message; it will reconstruct it consistent with our own understanding (See also MacIntyre, 1981).

The questions for hermeneutics, therefore, are: How close can we come to an accurate interpretation of the past? By what standards can we judge that reading X is close but Y is closer? In the early part of this century the common answer held that one can do so through "historicism." Only a painstaking recreation of the world in which the message was sent can provide close approximations. The method is painful because the researcher must consciously lay aside what his common sense, derived from his personal experience, tells him to be true and right and put himself in an unfamiliar world. And to do that conscientiously requires the examination and consumption of huge quantities of information about the past.

Gadamer and Habermas, the current leaders of modern hermeneutic thought, point out the flaw in historicism. The interpreter cannot by definition shake off the contexts and traditions of his own time. What we know from our own experience is all we can ever know. Our own experiences inevitably shape our definition of the interpretive problem in the first place, and they shape what we think the makers of the text in the past thought they were doing. The interpreter cannot transcend the present, cannot bring past and present together into a higher fusion.

Hermeneutic philosophy, therefore, holds unattainable the very objectivity on which the preservative position rests. As Bleicher (1980, p. 3) puts it: "The aim of understanding . . . can consequently no longer be the objective recognition of the author's intended meaning, but the emergence of practically relevant knowledge in which the [interpreter] himself is changed by being aware of new possibilities of existence and his responsibility for his own future." This is one reason why I wrote in chapter one that the Supreme Court does not interpret the Constitution.

Gadamer and Habermas emphasize that extralinguistic factors will inevitably shape both the behavior of lawmakers and the motives and goals of interpreters. Sender and receiver operate under political and personal agendas and constraints hidden not only from each other but from themselves as well.

At this point Gadamer and Habermas part company. Gadamer believes that through an intensive interactive process between the interpreter and the textual materials it is possible to believe that one has come closer to a shared understanding of the past. He would presumably hold that Raoul Berger's painstaking review of the history of the passage of the Fourteenth Amendment (1977) makes it meaningful and proper for him to assert that the amendment's framers did not intend the amendment to incorporate sections of the Bill of Rights or to prohibit public schools segregated by law. Gadamer would hasten to add that Berger cannot claim to have identified "the correct interpretation of the message in the Fourteenth Amendment," a claim Berger seems in fact to make. Rather, Berger's close encounter with the text and its political surroundings permits him to claim that his interpretation is presumptively closer to the legal message sent than would be the conclusion of someone who did not engage the material so closely.

Habermas, on the other hand, would deny Berger even that claim. Habermas holds that the interpreter must start by recognizing that the most that can come from interpretive attempts is to sensitize the self to the possibilities for betterment in the political here and now. Interpretation is not a means of objective verification of timeless truths. It is a way of enriching, articulating, justifying, and applying what we already believe and know. It is a political act, part of a larger process that seeks to build consensus, or paradigmatic agreement, in the present.

Bleicher (1980, pp. 161–163) stresses Habermas' conviction that power limits, conditions, and controls communicative acts. Hermeneutic acts, for Habermas, serve not to verify a truth but to affect the quality of communication, to emancipate communication from power and thereby to contribute to the individual dignity of the interpreter. Thus Habermas would permit Berger to claim that he, Berger, has expanded and opened political communication and that we should respect the individualism and self-determination that characterize Berger's behavior as a scholar.

In other words, Habermas holds that truths are those beliefs that people come to understand through collective discourse. "True consciousness" is not the correct discovery of the past; it is the state of knowledge attained when the conditions insure for every citizen full and equal potential to participate in conversation. We can distinguish the conditions that encourage from those that oppress the communicative acts on which consensus depends. These are sincerity, honesty about one's interests, equality of position (truth claims should not be judged according to the ascribed status of the speaker), and official indifference to the substance of communications. In this respect Habermas comes close to Lon Fuller's statement (1964, p. 186), "If I were asked . . . to discern one central indisputable principle of what may be called substantive natural law . . . I would find it in the injunction: Open up, maintain, and preserve the integrity of the channels of communication." For that matter, Holmes' 1881 description of the common law, which I quoted on page 52, is in the modern hermeneutic ball park.

Two cautions here: First, the hermeneutic theories of Habermas and Gadamer are not identical to the academic consensus that I mentioned at the beginning of this section. They extend the consensus, to which we return in chapter six. Gadamer and Habermas operate on philosophical frontiers. The preservatives do not so much fail because they ignore modern hermeneutics; they fail because they do not accommodate more conventional and widely shared academic beliefs about social knowledge in pluralist communities. Second, do not leap from method to substance, at least not yet. Gadamer and Habermas do indeed endorse a constitutional jurisprudence that tilts toward the protection of individual dignity and equality of opportunity, but hermeneutic theory makes here a methodological point: The materials of history do not and cannot in themselves produce right answers.

Here are three illustrations of hermeneutic indeterminacy in constitutional theory.

1. Raoul Berger concludes that the framers of the Fourteenth Amendment did not intend it to require integrated public schools (1977). Tushnet (1983) concedes they did not consciously intend so, but he urges that:

> . . . freedom of contract was extremely important because it was the foundation of individual achievement, and they certainly wanted to outlaw racial discrimination with respect to this freedom. . . . Our hermeneutic enterprise has shown us that public education as its exists today—a central institution for the achievement of individual goals—is in fact the functional equivalent not of public education in 1868, but of freedom of contract in 1868. Thus *Brown* was correctly decided in light of a hermeneutic interpretivism (pp. 800–801).

Tushnet does not in fact endorse this form of interpretivism. Rather, he shows that within its framework interpretivism may yield inconsistent but equally defensible answers.

2. The preservatives often appeal to John Marshall as a quintessentially correct interpreter, but Marshall, according to William van Alstyne, pursued his own very special constitutional theory: "[A]cts of Congress (other than those affecting the judiciary!) would not be subjected to the same judicial predisposition as acts of the several states. Rather, acts of Congress would be treated as presumptively constitutional . . ." (1983, p. 213).

3. Assuming the justices should emulate the framers, what should they emulate? G. Edward White (1984) indicates that the framers understood law and political theory synonymously. On one level they wrote a legal document, but at another they struggled to attain political knowledge. Could not the Court claim that its authority is to continue that struggle, that what was vital in the founding was the belief that law depended upon an inquiry into knowledge, so that the Court recreates the search, not its result? If not, why not?

These illustrations remind us that hermeneutic methods do not determine for us which of the many inconsistent levels of historical analysis is the most "truth-filled" level, the level most relevant for solving a legal dispute in the present.

I said previously that in thinking through this book, I came early to the conclusion that the Court does not interpret the Constitution. If the justices engaged in the "best" possible hermeneutic analysis as Gadamer and Habermas describe it, they would not interpret in the way legal scholars of nearly every stripe define interpretation and interpretivism. But the more significant reason that the justices do not interpret is that they do not seriously attempt to do hermeneutic inquiry in the first place. The justices are political actors, not scholars. Hermeneutics implies that one does not interpret legal texts at all unless one engages in an intensive dialogue among the self, the text, and the evidence surrounding it. Judges in theory could interpret the Constitution in this fashion if they choose to become scholars. But judges do not seriously engage historical materials in the first place. It is highly unlikely that the legal profession will produce in the near future a body of judges and clerks committed to the methodology of hermeneutic inquiry, and even less likely that a president would desire to appoint judges who did so. The judicial audience does not expect it. The resources we can afford to invest in cases do not permit this luxury. In any event, recall that modern hermeneutic theory gives no guarantee that nine justices would reach the same conclusion even if they all struggled faithfully to practice the best form of interpretive research.

THE THEORY OF SOCIAL KNOWLEDGE

Peter Berger and Thomas Luckmann (1966) offered what has become a classic theory of "the social construction of reality." The metaphor of construction—"making something"—relaces interpretation—"discovering something"—in this theory. We inhabit in everyday life a world we believe is real, but we construct that reality using as tools the symbols, the languages, that our social institutions teach us to use. Each individual may construct for himself a unique reality, one that no other person can fully know. There are multiple, if not infinite, realities. But each person must believe his reality is objective, that his world is coherent, discoverable, and by definition sharable.

Each makes his reality from the social world, which is to say the symbolic world, around him. But languages (symbols) are the only medium for sharing and objectifying reality. They automatically simplify and distort reality (p. 25). Symbols necessarily distort because each individual's experiences are to some degree unique to him, yet he can only share them through a common language. He must translate one to the other. The common denominator of language necessarily "leaves something out."

Language, being symbolic and abstracted from raw experience, transcends pure experience. Berger and Luckmann write (p. 38):

> Any significative theme that thus spans spheres of reality may be defined as a symbol, and the linguistic mode by which such transcendence is achieved may be called symbolic language. On the level of symbolism, then, linguistic signification attains the maximum detachment from the "here and now" of everyday life, and language soars into regions that are not only *de facto* but *a priori* unavailable to everyday experience. Language now constructs immense edifices of symbolic representations that appear to tower over the reality of everyday life like gigantic presences from another world. Religion, philosophy, art, and science are the historically most important symbol systems of this kind. . . . Language is capable not only of constructing symbols that are highly abstracted from everyday experience, but also of "bringing back" these symbols and appresenting them as objectively real elements in everyday life. In this manner, symbolism and symbolic language become essential constituents of the reality of everyday life and of the commonsense apprehension of this reality.

We must of course add law to the list of abstract symbolic systems. Institutions—churches, universities, research laboratories, courts, and law offices—are the mechanisms in society that make and sustain the languages that bring order from chaos. Institutions prescribe and enforce simplified categories for worldmaking. The astonishing survival, despite their frequently deflected goals and/or corrupted actions, of formal institutions like the Roman Catholic church or the common law presumably measure how much people need these stabilizing forces to survive.

Institutions in turn employ rules, taboos, and the like to justify and give dignity to the power they necessarily exercise. In this process of "legitimation," Berger and Luckmann (pp. 85–118) point out that all institutions, across societies, cultures, and times, do not simply make rules that differentiate right from wrong and command the right. These rules appear to work only to the extent that the people they govern see them as derived from "knowledge"—not "academic" or "scientific" knowledge as college students are told to conceive it, but stories, myths, narratives, dramas, the things, in short, that religions are made of. These stories give those within the institution's domain a "self-identity," but providing self-identities serves the deeper purpose of *explaining* why "things are what they are" so that one should obey the institution's rules (p. 87).

Above all, the bundles of rules, offices, traditions, and stories called institutions allow people to function in the face of the inevitability of their own deaths:

> All legitimations of death must carry out the same essential task—they must enable the individual to go on living in society after the death of significant others and to anticipate his own death with, at the very least, terror sufficiently mitigated so as not to paralyze the continued performance of the routines of everyday life. . . .
>
> It is in the legitimation of death that the transcending potency of symbolic universes manifests itself most clearly, and the fundamental terror-assuaging character of the ultimate legitimations of the paramount reality of everyday life is revealed. . . . The symbolic universe shelters the individual from ultimate terror by bestowing ultimate legitimation upon the protective structures of the institutional order. . . .
>
> The symbolic universe also orders history. It locates all collective events in a cohesive unity that includes past, present and future. With regard to the past, it establishes a "memory" that is shared by all the individuals socialized within the collectivity. With regard to the future, it establishes a common frame of reference for the projection of individual actions. Thus the symbolic universe links men with their predecessors and their successors in a meaningful totality, serving to transcend the finitude of individual existence and bestowing meaning upon the individual's death. All the members of a society can now conceive of themselves as *belonging* to a meaningful universe, which was there before they were born and will be there after they die. . . . (pp. 94–95)[6]

Sociological and anthropological descriptions, like those of the hermeneutic philosophers, see law as inevitably political. A legal scholar who said he *discovered* the intent of the framers would more honestly have to say that he *created* a version of their intent from the symbolic material that has meaning for him. Moreover, institutions *make* realities within the relativistic boundaries of time and place. Contrary to preservative prescriptions, courts inevitably function to maintain collective political consciousness. Courts are therefore necessarily influenced by the political ideologies around them.

WHAT THE PRESERVATIVES ARE ON TO

The "back to the Constitution" scholars presuppose political conditions that contradict the heavy weight of empirical descriptions and analyses of public opinion, of legislative, executive, and administrative politics, and of judicial behavior. Worse still, their insistence that the past dictates fixed truths to the

---

[6]Mark Twain put the truth against which institutions fight this way: "There is no God, no universe, no human race, no earthly life, no heaven, no hell. It is all a dream—a grotesque, foolish dream. Nothing exists but you. And you are but a *thought*—a vagrant thought, a useless thought, a homeless thought, wandering forlorn among the empty eternities." ("The Mysterious Stranger," 1916, p. 151.) Ingmar Bergman's film *The Seventh Seal* powerfully describes both the horror of a world without meaning and the triumph over that horror by creating through religious faith a transcendent world in just the fashion Berger and Luckmann describe.

present contradicts both modern hermeneutic theory and the consensus belief that people construct realities from institutional mediation between personal experience and shared language. To fix truth in the past denies the meaning of present experience. For example, it denies that accumulated experiences of racial discrimination and hatred matter in the shaping of constitutional policy. Preservatives claim that the Court should adopt a jurisprudence of discovered rather than created decisions, but the broad sweep of modern philosophy says such a jurisprudence cannot succeed, either methodologically or politically.

In this light it is easy to understand why throughout our constitutional history the Court has never successfully practiced what the preservatives preach. But if they preach the impossible (and if the Court will not in any case listen even if preservation were possible), what can the preservatives nevertheless be on to?

All the criticisms of the preservative perspective presented thus far presume that the preservatives are scholars and should be judged by the consensus of academic knowledge and by the tests of impartiality in method and perspective that scholars use. But whichever side in an academic argument prevails at a moment is not likely to matter much in political life. As Berger and Luckmann put it (p. 116):

> The intellectual is thus, by definition, a marginal type. Whether he was first marginal and then became an intellectual (as, for example, in the case of many Jewish intellectuals in the modern West), or whether his marginality was the direct result of his intellectual aberrations (the case of the ostracized heretic), need not concern us here. In either case, his social marginality expresses his lack of theoretical integration within the universe of his society. He appears as the counter-expert in the business of defining reality. Like the "official" expert, he has a design for society at large. But while the former's design is in tune with the institutional programs, serving as their theoretical legitimation, the intellectual exists in an institutional vacuum, socially objectivated at best in a subsociety of fellow-intellectuals.

Perhaps therefore the preservatives really accept the truths of modern philosophy but seek to escape the irrelevant state Berger and Luckmann assign the scholar. Or, to be even more generous to the preservatives, they may so respect and fear the horror of a meaningless world as to sacrifice their safe and secure position in academia. They may assume, like Dostoyevski's Grand Inquisitor, the burden of preserving by authoritative means traditional beliefs about the rule of law and judicial impartiality that they know possess no intrinsic truth or merit whatsoever. Thus we might justify the preservative position in terms of the modern academic consensus itself. This sophisticated defense of preservativism might take the following more specific forms:

Law and the Constitution are core institutions that help shape our national identity. They objectify our national reality. The modern Court is losing, if it hasn't already lost, touch with what Berger and Luckmann rightly say institutions must do. By abandoning the framers and precedents, the Court throws away our stories, our narratives. Without them we have as members of one nation no common buffer against the reality of life's corporate meaningless-ness. Without them we have no protection against the ultimate terror of our death. Without them we have no hope of achieving the communal and inte-grative experience Sheldon Wolin calls for. As Henry Fairlie (1981) pointed out, conservative Republicans won the presidency and the Senate in 1980 because "they believed in something."

Alasdair MacIntyre (1981, p. 67) recently stated:

> The best reason for asserting so bluntly that there are no such [natural] rights is indeed of precisely the same type as the best reason . . . for asserting that there are no witches and . . . no unicorns: every attempt to give good reasons for believing that there are such rights has failed.

Perhaps the preservatives seek to buffer society from this truth, for if it is true, our institutionalized understandings collapse.

I will show why preservative theory, framed this way, fails on its own "anti-intellectual" terms just as much as it fails the academic tests. However, this sophisticated argument contains a disturbing truth. By and large scholars *are* marginal. Socrates advised his followers that true wisdom lay in recogniz-ing how little one knows, but judges cannot officially follow that line. Institu-tions must speak with authority, as children, and not so cleverly and self-effacingly as did Socrates.[7] No matter how effectively modern hermeneu-tics persuades the academic community, the position that nothing is know-able, that everything is relative and recreated moment by moment hardly yields an institutional foundation for building, for constituting, a complex nation.

The methods of the common law, from which those of constitutional law derive, operate under rules of impartiality and rationality. Owen Fiss (1982, p. 1012) wrote, "It is a belief in the rationality of the law . . . that transforms a statement about what the law ought to be from an exhortation into an argu-ment, and that intellectually sustains those who engage in that activity." Berger and Luckmann would presumably applaud Fiss' appreciation of the importance of transforming a raw command into a moral choice. An institu-tion that seeks to maintain acceptance of its authority to rule by appealing to the symbols of logic and reason may have no more intrinsic merit than primi-tive religious rituals, but if that practice maintains self-identities, if it fits the social construction of reality around it, it is worth maintaining.

Conceived this way, Gary McDowell's Junius exhorts citizens to a vigorous defense of constitutional order because society must protect the integrity of its institutions, of which the Constitution is one. John Agresto rightly urges us to pay attention to the contribution of the Lincoln–Douglas debates, and Raoul

---

[7] Thus Richard Flathman (1976) finds the practice of rights operationally distinct from aca-demic philosophizing about rights. And Jane Mansbridge, a social philosopher, has recently argued that social philosophers should make not the classic texts but participant observation the primary source of philosophical insights (1982).

Berger may insist on honoring the historical evidence surrounding the framing of the Fourteenth Amendment because they are part of our national narrative. If modern philosophy's insistence that "frame of reference" shapes and conditions truth, then that is all the more reason for institutions to respect the work of those we call framers. Robert Bork rightly concerns himself with the perceived illogic and unreason of modern judicial review dogma because reason and logic happen to be this particular institution's claim to authority. Indeed, one of its institutional rules may require that it appear to discover when it creates, no matter how persuasively academicians show that judges always in fact create.

Three more points in the preservatives's defense: First, most of the scholarly writing about the Supreme Court and the Constitution comes from law professors and the political scientists who would emulate them. Constitutional jurisprudence has always carried hidden political agendas. Many, perhaps most, of the leading writers in the field have clerked for Supreme Court justices. They do not write about marginal experiences for an impractical audience. The next two chapters show that much of the "best" legal writing will not survive rigorous philosophical and methodological scrutiny in much better shape than does preservative scholarship. The preservative political scientist qua "little law professor" is not nearly so out of step with the legal community as he is with social science and philosophical scholarly communities. Preservatives may have simply chosen to write for law professors, not social philosophers.

Second, constitutional law decisions inevitably rest on dramatic falsifications. They are falsifications for precisely the reasons Berger and Luckmann give. Only linguistic simplifications can create meaning, and these simplifications transcend raw experience. Scholars must accept that truth and focus attention on the competing criteria for distinguishing the better dramatic falsifications from the worse. The preservatives engage in much falsification, but if they play to an audience of students, practitioners, and other citizens rather than marginal academicians, we must judge them, as we must judge the Court, by the quality of their falsifications, not on whether they falsify at all. All communication falsifies.

Third, the preservative position has much in common with natural law. Natural law has played a much more powerful role in shaping political events (within church and state politics alike) than in modern philosophy. A previous section of this chapter speculated that the preservative approach threatened, if practiced, to so foreclose legal conversations as to stifle a jurisprudence of individualism. But perhaps natural law actually helps keep legal systems open. Sophocles' Antigone says to Creon, when he forbids her for political reasons from burying her brother in accordance with "natural law":

> I never thought your edicts had such force they nullified the laws of heaven,
> which, unwritten, not proclaimed, can boast a currency that everlastingly is valid;
> an origin beyond the birth of man.

It is Antigone's assertion of a natural law right that entitles, or at least emboldens, her to resist Creon's power, and it is worth recalling that such liberation from political power is part of Habermas' prescription for meaningful discourse. Perhaps the appeal to the framers, or at least to something beyond the policy inclinations of the justices sitting at the moment, is essential to a jurisprudence of individualism.

FINAL DIFFICULTIES WITH PRESERVATIVISM

The scholars I have lumped together as preservatives do not claim to be postmodernist philosophers. Perhaps they do not admit their true position because that position depends on the dramatic pretense of traditionalism. But if that is their position (and I see no real evidence that it is), then they must not expect a favorable reception from an academic audience. The academic audience demands an intellectually coherent defense of the position, marginal or not.

The real difficulties, it seems to me, with this benevolent assessment of the preservatives run deeper than the simple suspicion that they are what they seem, i.e., politically conservative scholars defending a conservative political agenda.[8] Granting as I do that the Court must recover a sense of its institutional responsibilities for the reasons Berger and Luckmann give, preservativism does not prescribe a program of recovery. It fails to answer these questions:

1. If institutionalizing the Constitution requires preserving stories and maintaining the integrity of the nation's narrative, does not limiting the source of law to the intent of the framers contradict the notion of narrative by blocking out all subsequent legal and political contributions to it? Similarly, if the virtue of natural law is to permit constant retesting of fundamental principles, does not any theory proposing a static (and earthly) source of law do just the reverse? Does it not tend to close rather than keep open the lines of communication?

2. What might be the political consequences of McDowell's proposed amendment obliterating federal court oversight of state protection of civil liberties through Fourteenth Amendment incorporation? Do we not, at least for political purposes, unthinkingly identify what Wolin calls our "life of common involvements," with national elections, national policy, and national triumphs and tragedies? If so, must we not maintain national definitions of fundamental rights?

---

[8] *Nixon v. Fitzgerald*'s reasoning is every bit as noninterpretive and "penumbral" as are *Griswold*'s and *Roe*'s, but I have encountered no criticism of the case from the preservative quarter.

3. Assuming that historical research can improve our reconstruction of the past, it still will not provide undisputed right answers. Historicist scholars will dispute their findings about the framers' intent. How will the Court resolve disagreements among scholarly readings of the past?

4. If the real role of the Court as Constitution-maker is to construct myths that makes the identity of "self as American" meaningful, must not that process interact constantly with the normative environment of its times? Must it not, in other words, interact with political life around it in order to maintain its authority? Does this not explain the Martian's observation that constitutional law has always lacked much doctrinal consistency? Are we not better constituted as a result?

Chapter 4 POLITICAL ALTERNATIVES TO INTERPRETIVISM

The question is not how the phenomenon must be turned, twisted, narrowed, crippled so as to be explicable, at all costs, upon principles that we have once and for all resolved not to go beyond. The question is: "To what point must we enlarge our thought so that it shall be in proportion to the phenomenon. . . ."
—Friedrich W. J. von Schelling

[T]he university professor is the only free man who can develop legal doctrine in his own way and travel the road he chooses in accounting for his conclusions.
—Harlan Fiske Stone

INTRODUCTION

When the woman from Mars reviewed constitutional lawmaking across the sweep of American history, she concluded that no legal theory consistently explained what the Supreme Court has done. The patterns she did observe seemed suspiciously like patterns of political expediency. At the same time, however, she observed that the members of a relatively small judicial audience—students, scholars, and legal professionals—shared a strong desire to treat the Court's work as a source of political and communal goodness. Despite the evidence that constitutional decisions are relatively discrete events, tied closely, just as the modern philosophical consensus would predict, to the powerful influence of immediate and changing political and social forces, those who study it seek desperately to find some way of assessing the normative goodness of the lawmaking process itself. The dogged determination of preservative scholars to defend such an unpromising model of constitutional goodness illustrates the great strength of this desire.

Constitutional lawmaking is thus a quintessentially political process, and this chapter reviews a variety of proposals for assessing the goodness of constitutional decisions based not on their legal correctness but on their degree of consistency with some norms about politics itself. Near the beginning of this century the historian Charles Beard wrote that the Constitution "is always becoming something else, and those who criticize it and the acts done under it, as well as those who praise, help to make it what it will be tomorrow." (Quoted in Frankfurter, 1939, p. 18.) Given that venerable

71

perspective, we might well expect political scholarship to debate legal substance: Is segregation by race or the official sponsorship of collective prayer in
public schools politically desirable? Answers to such questions would help
shape the Constitution itself.

Yet political alternatives to interpretivism have taken a different tack. They
debate the political justifications for the Court's use of power, not the uses of
that power themselves. The question is whether it is "legitimate" for the
Court to make racial and religious policies about public schools, not what
those policies ought to be.

We shall see that the preoccupation with the "legitimacy of judicial review"
is just as fruitless as the preoccupation with preservativism, and ultimately for
the same reasons. No static academic theory, either political or legal, can hope
to correspond to Beard's constantly changing phenomenon. Nevertheless, the
preoccupation with the legitimacy of judicial review has come about for very
understandable reasons. Judges since at least John Marshall have had political agendas (Haskins and Johnson, 1981). These agendas of whatever sort—
Dred Scott or the social Darwinism cases or the more recent school
desegregation cases—offend opposing political interests, and these interests
respond by attacking the premises on which the Court wielded power against
them. For example, Justice Brewer's speech to the New York Bar Association
in 1893 called the Court "the only breakwater against the haste and the
passions of the people—against the tumultuous ocean of democracy." (And
Justice Field stated that the income tax marked the beginning of the war of
the poor against the rich.) James Bradley Thayer (1893) therefore responded
that the courts may only set aside the acts of politically more responsive
branches when the branches have made a very clear legal mistake.

This chapter reviews the answers legal scholars have given to the question of
the Court's political legitimacy. But readers should know at the outset that the
legitimacy problem is the most overrated problem in social philosophy. The
Court isn't bothered by it. Voters aren't bothered by it. A minority of politicians try to exploit it. Only scholars are bothered by it. Constitutional jurisprudence for a century has struggled to narrow the phenomenon so as to
explain it in terms of fixed categories just when it should be seeking to enlarge
the categories to explain the obvious features of the phenomenon. The problem is overrated not because it is trivial but because the solution is quite
straightforward. "Legitimacy," if it is anything more than a synonym for
"legal," means "widely accepted." We accept judicial review because judicial
lawmaking has always been the essence of our common-law system.

But why should a question with a straightforward answer remain on so
many academic agendas? William James said that habit is the great flywheel
of society, and Morris Cohen added that, unlike pliable facts, which people
can always ignore or rationalize away, stubborn theories "are mental habits
which cannot be changed at will." So perhaps the question feeds itself out of

academic habit. This explanation will not do, however, because most academic questions are removed from the academic table once consensuses on answers emerge. The real reason why no consensus answer clears legitimacy from the table is that the political debate does not really deal with the evidence of what is acceptable or legitimate in the first place. The legitimacy debate is a surrogate for debating fundamental and scientifically unanswerable normative questions of political philosophy.

CATEGORIES OF POLITICAL OBSERVATIONS ABOUT THE COURT

By way of a road map of the varying terrain ahead, this section briefly describes the major political arguments that recur in constitutional jurisprudence.

A. It is legitimate for the Court to override the decisions of other branches of government only if the decision can be justified in terms of a "neutral principle." A neutral principle is one general enough to assure us that courts will apply it across partisan lines, yet specific enough to distinguish the classes of disputes its logic does not reach. Thus economic "substantive due process" failed the neutrality test, at least as the Court applied it over time, because the Court refused to strike down the politically indistinguishable statutes limiting commerce in yellow oleomargarine and lottery tickets.

B. It is legitimate for the Court to refuse to decide cases altogether, or to decide them on technical and procedural grounds, even when a neutral principle would dispose on the merits if a decision on the merits would impose unacceptable political costs on the Court's ability to govern.

C. Since the Constitution allocates power both horizontally and vertically in a federal system, it is inevitably necessary, and therefore legitimate, for the Court to declare boundaries between the power claims of units of government. Claims of rights and liberties, however, are fundamentally political problems and must be left to the democratic political process.

D. The units of government are sufficiently well organized and otherwise politically competitive to negotiate the boundaries of their powers. The Constitution should check the power of government to limit individual rights and liberties. Therefore, judicial review is legitimate when it supports rights and liberties, but it should leave institutional boundary problems to the institutions to resolve.

E. The history of economic substantive due process shows that in the name of individual liberties the Court may side politically with those who have full access to the electoral political process and who have lost fair and square. The Court legitimately protects only the political process itself, through free speech, free press, and related provisions, and legitimately gives a voice in a pluralistic system to those minorities (racial, religious, or for that matter criminally deviant) who, by virtue of discrimination or otherwise, have no effective voice in the normal political process. (A corollary is that the Court properly gives closer scrutiny to the decisions of electorally less responsive units of government, like police departments, than to those of responsive bodies, e.g., legislatures themselves.)

F. The Court legitimately exercises the power of review only when it possesses the institutional structures and resources to analyze policy information with at least as much accuracy as do the units whose decisions it overturns. The tools of public policy analysis thus allow us to evaluate the goodness of Court decisions.

G. Society needs a collective moral voice. The more politically responsive a unit of government is, the more likely it will avoid speaking in a moral voice in order to accommodate and compromise among competing interests. The Court therefore legitimately articulates and guards the core moral values that give the polity its self-identity.

H. Legitimacy and judicial review are trivial problems. The Court is no more or less responsive to political pressures than are other units of government. Furthermore, as with other units of government, it decides incrementally over time (in response to political forces) in such a way as to shape policy about as effectively as any other branch. If and when it gets out of step with the dominant coalition, its decisions will be evaded in the short run and overturned by direct political intervention in the long run. (This is what I called "political jurisprudence" in chapter one.)

I. The legitimacy problem is trivial because all solutions to it ignore the fundamental constitutional mission of protecting individual dignity. The Court, whether active or restrained, merely supports the hegemonic dominance of politics by materialistic, postindustrial, capitalism. Or, as Hilaire Belloc put it regarding change in British politics of an earlier era:

> The accursed power that stands on privilege
> And goes with women and champagne and bridge
> Broke, and democracy resumed her reign
> Which goes with bridge and women and champagne.

I trust this list reveals the degree of disagreement among those who offer political solutions to the "problem" of judicial lawmaking. I hope also you sense that these theories tend toward a simplistic kind of dualism. The Court follows either pattern X or pattern Y (and one of them is usually "wrong"). This is not a useful way of evaluating anything, yet even the preeminent jurisprudent H.L.A. Hart (1983, p. 144) wrote:

> I have portrayed American jurisprudence as beset by two extremes, the Nightmare and the Noble Dream: the view that judges always make and never find the law they impose on litigants, and the opposed view that they never make it. Like

any other nightmare and any other dream, these two are, in my view, illusions, though they have much of value to teach the jurist in his waking hours. The truth, perhaps unexciting, is that sometimes judges do one and sometimes the other.

If jurisprudence boils down to Hart's conclusion, then it and the "legitimacy" debate within it are indeed unexciting. But if judges inevitably do both, jurisprudence may have a few tingles of excitement left in it.[1]

NEUTRAL PRINCIPLES

Most law professors since the advent of the legal realism movement in the early twentieth century have accepted that constitutional text and history do not answer constitutional questions. They insist, however, that legal answers must nevertheless come somehow from "the law." Any legal answer that does not come from the law, in this view, must be a purely political judgment, and political judgments equate with the greatest of legal evils, judicial "whim."

Herbert Wechsler's 1959 attempt to define the legally permissible in fundamentally political terms is as noble an attempt as we are likely to find. He holds that "the main constituent of the judicial process is precisely that it must be genuinely principled, resting with respect to every step that is involved in reaching judgment on analysis and reasons quite transcending the immediate result that is achieved" (1959, p. 15). A neutral principle is one that transcends the case at hand. That is, the court decides according to a principle stated in a way that assures us that future courts can apply the same rule in cases with very different partisan or political implications. According to Wechsler, *Plessy*'s "separate but equal" doctrine is entirely neutral as stated. The opinion in *Brown*, rooted as it is in superficial and incomplete analysis of the empirical consequences of school segregation, is not.

---

[1] My review does not discuss further an important body of political science scholarship that is "scientific." C. Herman Pritchett's paradigm-breaking analysis (1948) of the votes of the justices in the 1930s and the decades of increasingly sophisticated judicial behavior research (at trial and appellate court levels alike) that followed asked, in effect, "If the law does not adequately predict legal outcomes, how helpful is it to say judicial attitudes do so?" Attitudes are, of course, difficult to measure directly. The research generally uses surrogate measures—political party affiliation, cosmopolitan/local background, and cluster or factor analyses of past voting patterns, for example—and correlations definitely exist. Three caveats about this important social science research, however: if justice X's attitude favors the rights of the accused while Y's does not, both justices may nevertheless derive their positions from "the law." If law yields multiple and inconsistent meanings, then both may reason "from the law." The dichotomy between law and attitude as "causes" of legal results is a false one. Second, much of the research depends on analysis of non-unanimous opinions. Unanimity, while it varies with the leadership skills of different chief justices, presumably measures a consensus on a legal outcome that overrides attitudinal differences. Third, criteria that evaluate attitudes and votes make opinions irrelevant. Journalists describe the Court's "solid blocks" and "swing votes" and the changes a prospective presidential appointee might make in the balance precisely because the judicial behavioralists are right, but rightness does not guarantee relevance. The goodness of opinions concerns us.

Wechsler's approach is, I think, far more important than many scholars have assumed. He addresses our fundamental question—How may judges persuade us they have reached good results?—and he tells us to look nowhere but in the opinion itself for answers. "The virtue or demerit of a judgment turns, therefore, entirely on the reasons that support it . . ." (pp. 19–20). I shall return to Wechsler's virtues, but for the moment, ask how much help this formula gives in evaluating the following case.

In *Logan v. Zimmerman Brush Co.* (102 S.Ct. 1149, 1982), Zimmerman fired a shipping clerk, Logan, claiming that Logan's short left leg prevented him from performing his duties effectively. Illinois law protected handicapped workers from losing their job for physical handicaps "unrelated to ability." Logan claimed Zimmerman fired him in violation of this law and filed a complaint with the Illinois Fair Employment Practices Commission in timely fashion. Illinois law required a hearing on the matter within 120 days of the filing of the complaint, for the understandable reason that excessive delays might reduce the reliability of the assessment of the circumstances of the firing.

An employee in the commission's office inadvertently scheduled Logan's hearing 125 days after Logan filed. When the commission attempted to proceed with the hearing, Zimmerman sued in state court to enjoin the commission. Zimmerman won. Logan could not argue that the commission denied him due process of law and equal protection of the laws, but he argued that the interpretation by the Illinois courts did so.

The due process clause protects life, liberty, and property from deprivation by government without due process. It does not govern private citizens, whose obligations derive from statutory and common-law commands. Without the Illinois statute, Logan would have no claim against Zimmerman. The Illinois court reading of an Illinois statute violated the Constitution if anything did. Logan lost something, but did he lose anything the Constitution protected?

Illinois has no constitutional obligation to protect the handicapped. The Illinois legislature could repeal the law without violating the Constitution. If the legislature could deliberately repeal Logan's right to a hearing, why could not the commission do so inadvertently?

For many decades due-process decisions seemed to hold that the clause protected no privileges created by government, only things possessed apart from government action. This rights/privileges distinction implied that the government could terminate welfare recipients, or its own employees, summarily, at least if it didn't fire in violation of an employee's First Amendment freedoms.

The rights/privileges distinction was never merely an abstract philosophical doctrine. In law it simultaneously served to draw practical limits on the judicial power to intervene in government. Government officials promise all sorts of things to citizens that they don't deliver. Suppose I love Fourth of July fireworks and my city council votes to appropriate funds for a spectacular show. I may look forward to the show for months, but if the head of the recreation department embezzles the money and the boxes labeled "FIRE-WORKS!" turn out to be stuffed with bricks, I have no due process action against the city. To maintain the benefits of "drawing the line somewhere," the Court has recently recreated a version of the rights/privileges distinction disguised in the word "entitlements." Presumably this distinction distinguishes the fireworks case from Logan's, but how?

The U.S. Supreme Court overturned the Illinois Supreme Court and ordered the commission to hold a hearing. Justice Blackmun for the Court held that Logan's right of action was an entitlement comparable to a property interest and therefore protected under due process. The Court did not analyze in depth the significance of the fact that it overturned the act of a state court interpreting a state statute. It noted that it had recently held that: (a) a prisoner who claimed his property had been wrongfully taken by a prison guard and (b) a school child who claimed to have been wrongfully spanked by a teacher had no protectable due-process entitlements. It distinguished the cases by claiming that the prisoner and the student could bring private tort actions against the individuals responsible for their harm. It did not demonstrate how Logan would be less likely to process a tort action effectively than would a prisoner or a child.

Assuming that *Logan* is a typical case, it hardly seems convincing or unconvincing on neutral principle grounds. It rather implies that courts cannot articulate truly neutral, general principles for the same reasons they cannot find clear commands in the Constitution itself: The case—Logan's problem—exists on multiple inconsistent levels. To be more blunt, does not each of the following arguments seem principled? "Logan lost something arbitrarily. He should recover because the rule of law protects at the very least against governmental arbitrariness." Or "Logan should win because any unit of government should have discretion to waive its rules when it admits an arbitrary error." But "Logan loses because his case is not distinguishable from other recent definitions of entitlements." Or "Logan loses because the Court cannot afford to review every state interpretation of its own procedures."

When we choose to go east, D. H. Lawrence once said, we forfeit the chance to go north, west, or south. By opting to enrich the legal scope of entitlements, the Court foregoes the chance to speak in principled terms about other directions the analysis might take.

Judge Charles E. Clark (1963, p. 665) confessed that he found it difficult to apply Wechsler in practice because he felt neutrality necessarily tied the decision to follow past doctrines. "We need the unprincipled decision, i.e., the unprecedented and novel decision . . . to mark judicial progress, of the kind in fact which has been a glorious heritage of the Court's history. . . . Of course, I do not suggest a wild orgy of unexpected and unwise judicial excursions. But elderly judges are so conditioned by training and tradition that the danger of this is minuscule."

How can a judge articulate a neutral principle when the law's fundamental commands conflict, as do the two religion clauses, or the free press/fair trial problem? Wolfgang Friedmann pointed out in 1961 that the contending sides in hotly disputed positions in modern constitutional law are equally expressable in neutral terms. Worse, halfhearted stabs at neutrality à la *Logan* hide the real decisional process from the audience. The judge's policy preferences will go undisclosed. Pretending to proceed in that manner undercuts the orderly flow of incremental policy adjustment that is the heart of the common law process.

Yet Wechsler's position is subtler than these criticisms suggest. Wechsler is no advocate of mechanical law-finding. He merely specifies a minimalist kind of requirement for opinion writing: Opinions must state intelligible lines separating the kinds of cases the principle covers from those it does not. The principle may be a bad one substantively. A decision may be principled and bad; it just can't be unprincipled and good. Indeed, two opposing opinions in the same case might both be principled.

Kent Greenawalt (1978) points out that judges who assume the responsibility to articulate minimally neutral principles may maneuver themselves into more rigorous examination of the possible consequences of a decision. Their decisions may better conform to standards of pragmatic rationality. They may also more effectively convince their audience of their freedom from political pressure and personal self-interest in the result. Above all, they send messages to future courts, other political branches, and the public that are not pure nonsense. That is, by seeking neutral principles, judges permit the incremental debate about the nature of public policy to move forward. The aesthetic model of jurisprudence assesses opinions in terms of their capacity to generate conversations. If this is what Wechsler means, he is certainly correct.

But this is not quite what Wechsler means, for recall that his is a theory of legitimacy. Like some of the preservatives, Wechsler posits a linkage between the impartiality of the principle and popular political support for the Court, yet there is no evidence that the public responds to the Court on such terms. Instead, Wechsler points us in a useful direction because he requires us to ask the more fundamental question whether the Court has stated, quite apart from its neutrality, anything coherent at all.

He prompts us to ask, for example, whether *Logan* states a coherent principle. Perhaps it holds that citizens are protected against purely arbitrary government action. Nothing in the opinion limits the principle to Illinois' handicapped population. *Logan*'s failure is that it doesn't state this or any other coherent principle, neutral or otherwise. It implicitly contradicts the emerging body of entitlement law. It gives us no basis for distinguishing my fireworks case. Jobs may be more important than fireworks, but that is not the sort of principle we have in mind. (For a detailed analysis of *Logan*, see Smolla, 1982.)

Logan fails not a neutrality test but a basic intelligibility test. *Logan* itself contains an easily neglected footnote that brings the point home (and which explains my attention to this rather insignificant case). Justices Powell and Rehnquist, concurring in the *Logan* result (on the grounds that the case is so unusual that it should have been decided with no attempt at principle at all!), imply in a footnote that the justices have enough on their hands trying to say anything intelligibly.

> It is necessary for this Court to decide cases during almost every Term on due process and equal protection grounds. Our opinions in these areas often are criticized, with justice, as lacking consistency and clarity. Because these issues arise in varied settings, and opinions are written by each of nine Justices, consistency of language is an ideal unlikely to be achieved. Yet I suppose we would all agree—at least in theory—that unnecessarily broad statements of doctrine frequently do more to confuse than to clarify our jurisprudence. I have not always adhered to this counsel of restraint in my own opinion writing, and therefore imply no criticism of others. But it does seem to me that this is a case that requires a minimum of exposition.

This footnote (p. 1162) is both heartening and threatening. It acknowledges the importance of coherent communication but doubts, and on very practical grounds, its attainability. If our legal history did not provide us with many examples of coherent communications from the Court, we would end the book here. We cannot expect the Court to convince us of the neutrality of its principles, for these depend as much on our beliefs and experiences as on the opinion. But if the Court gives no principle at all, its opinions communicate nothing. *Logan*'s hint that the justices may give up caring to attain intelligibility threatens directly our hope that the Court can create visions of political goodness by performing persuasively for us.

JUDICIAL SELF-RESTRAINT

If the Constitution does not constrain judicial choices the way contracts, wills, and specific statutory languages do, and if we may construct a principle to support virtually any case result, then perhaps the only limit on judicial power lies in wise judicial self-restraint.

The proponents of judicial self-restraint start from the conviction that doctrinal developments over time have profound political consequences. The Court's record of frequent intervention to upset policies affecting the daily lives of citizens, in both economic and social relations, obligates the justices to recognize their limited capacity to make doctrine wisely and consistently, and therefore obligates them to proceed cautiously. Self-restraint doctrines recognize that the debate about judicial review seeks to prescribe to practical political people called justices of the Supreme Court operational dos and don'ts. Self-restraint theories, like moral theologies, rightly locate authority and responsibility in the same place, which is in the minds of those who choose.[2]

Three books by the late Alexander Bickel (1962, 1970, and 1975) develop as elegant a theory of judicial restraint as one could ask for. Bickel, who campaigned extensively on university campuses for Robert F. Kennedy in 1968, was no conservative masquerader. The theory comes in two parts, pragmatic and heroic.

The pragmatic part holds that, like all political bodies, the Court has limited resources that it must neither hoard nor squander but spend wisely. Whether principled or not, some decisions will cost more than they are worth in the short run. Thus, assuming that principles of individual liberty and racial equality make a conclusive case for the unconstitutionality of state laws that prohibit interracial marriages, Bickel believed that the Court wisely ducked the issue in 1956 in order to reserve its resources for the more significant battle over school desegregation (1962, p. 174). Bickel elaborated at some length the many procedural devices the Court may use in pragmatic fashion to avoid deciding constitutional issues. These "passive virtues"—the denial of certiorari petitions, the dismissal of appeals, and the elements of the law of justiciability under Article III's cases and controversies language, for example—allow the Court to accommodate principle to political realities by refusing to decide.

The heroic part of Bickel's prescription insisted, with Burke, that the object of political life is not to purify theory or ideology but to accommodate competing interests (1975, p. 19). Accommodation based on principle must walk the fine line between meaningless patriotic generalities and detailed scholarly abstractions. Principles must be so fundamental as to appeal across the tremendously diverse range of individual beliefs and group agendas. Judges must restrain their enthusiasm for principles because principles are often inadequate to the delicate task of adjusting among competing political interests. Pluralist politics sets priorities among economic goods and noneconomic values. Judicial activism upsets the social and political compromises at its peril. Judicial review's countermajoritarian character usually costs more,

---

[2] Much political propaganda masks itself in the language of self-restraint, however, and readers must stay on alert to spot it. For example, when Robert Nisbet (1982, p. 209) condemns the activism of Griswold and Roe: "[B]y no constitutional or moral standard is the Court authorized to enter such delicate, fragile, deeply personal areas as abortion and the artificial sustainment of a dying life," he either engages in political propaganda or he is confused. If these two decisions protect the deeply personal character of these areas from interference by a tyrannical majority, then Nisbet should aim his accusation of unconstitutional activism at the legislatures whose policies entered such areas, not at a judicial effort to protect the "privacy" of these areas.

by destabilizing the political consensus, than the value gained from the rights its doctrines confer. The Court cannot, as Lon Fuller noted, accommodate to the fundamentally polycentric nature of modern public policy.

Bickel's Court acts properly when it explains, more like a teacher than a lawmaker, why certain fundamental moral principles belong in the policy calculus. The Court must be prepared to do so because lawmakers may neglect principle as they seek short-term and often self-interested goals. Yet, even when the Court is tempted by the vision that it has met these requirements, Bickel believed, with his mentor, Frankfurter, that the Court should still hesitate to act. By minimizing access to courts and thus the temptation to litigate an issue, the Court can maximize usage of the healthier democratic processes of decisionmaking. The Court wrongly relieves the electorate of its burden of debating moral issues in democratic fashion (1962, p. 156).

Does this elegant theory match enough political data to persuade? I think not. Here is a short list of the difficulties.

1. The modern Court pragmatically maintains its resources less by the passive virtues than by modifying the substance of its doctrines. It has set limits on school desegregation and on the availability of abortions, and it has virtually reversed itself on the death penalty without incurring the wrath of public majorities. Paul Mishkin (1983) has even adopted the position that the utter failure of the Court to agree on any principle to justify its affirmative action decision in *Bakke* is *Bakke*'s great achievement. Indirectness and ambivalence—Justice Powell's middle ground in *Bakke*—may have defused the affirmative action decision just as, conversely, Justice Blackmun's far-ranging justification for the abortion decision inflamed reactions to *Roe*. Like Wechsler, Bickel does not give us a politically realistic theory of the role of legal principles.

2. Bickel overstates the power of the Court in its most active moments. Bickel recognizes that the art of politics builds communities through normative appeals and pragmatic accommodations simultaneously. However, the devices for avoiding and evading Court decisions are so effective that to keep even a small light of moral value flickering in practical political life, the Court may need to ignite legal phosphorus. To make the threat of reversal on moral grounds credible, the Court must not seem overly reluctant to carry its threat through.

3. Like any good advocate, Bickel states half an argument. Like Frankfurter, he presumes but neither analyzes nor defends the proposition that democratic and representative politics, without judicial help, can protect against and correct for political inertia, corruption, and neglect of the claims of the powerless. He opposed the reapportionment decisions and seriously questioned the Court's role in racial desegregation. His respect for Burkean pluralistic politics prevented him from considering carefully that the iron law

of oligarchy pushes political and business organizations alike toward monopoly and that the Court might therefore need to push aggressively and politically for the values of individual liberty, dignity, and openness on which his model of political community depends.

4. Finally, the self-restraint concept, like the concept of principle in legal doctrine, exists on multiple, mutually inconsistent levels. Brad Canon (1982) showed how competing definitions of self-restraint empower judicial opponents to cloak themselves in the restraint banner. He found six independent categories by which a judge might claim that a fundamental legal or political value restrained his own policy preferences:

> (a) He defers to majoritarian legislative acts, that is, policies made by elected officials by statute. Such a judge would not necessarily defer to informal administrative practices.
> (b) He values doctrinal stability and defers to precedent.
> (c) He defers to the literal linguistic meaning of the legal command and to evidence of the framer's specific intents and purposes.
> (d) He defers to substantive social policy decisions wherever generated but feels empowered to review the procedures specified by formal law at the implementation phase.
> (e) He eschews judicial responsibility for prescribing the details of remedies and for implementing them judicially.
> (f) He avoids judicial action whenever other units of government seem comparably trained and motivated to deal with the problem.

These categories permit a rather long list of judges to claim they have acted with restraint. *Brown* (1954) followed precedent, e.g., the 1950 case of *Sweatt* (b). The *Brown* court postponed any attempt to fashion or enforce specific remedies (e). Congress' southern-dominated committee system seemed to hamstring proposals for national reform of race policy (f). *Mapp*, *Gideon*, *Miranda*, and the bulk of the criminal procedure cases overturned no statutes (a), affected procedure rather than substance (d), and drew directly on the trained competence of judges, i.e., their knowledge about the workings of the judicial system itself (f).

Judge Richard Posner, a Reagan appointee who had previously taught at the University of Chicago's law school, recently wrote that "contemporary judicial activism is unprincipled" (1983, p. 17). In light of Canon's schema, any such generalization about activism can only mask a political ideology. Both neutrality of principle and judicial self-restraint can do no more than facilitate disagreement by organizing and standardizing the concepts about which people disagree.

In *Hawaii Housing Authority v. Midkiff* (1984), we see this phenomenon precisely. Due to Hawaii's feudal past, as recently as 1967 only 72 private landowners held title to over 90% of all privately held land in the state. Most citizens owned their home but not the land on which it rested. The state therefore passed a land reform act by which the government, for compensation, seized these lands and resold them to homeowners. But the Fifth Amendment prohibits the taking of property except for "public use." Does the scheme designed to change private ownership constitute a public use? Justice O'Connor for the Court stated simply that the statute was "not irrational" and that therefore the courts must not debate its wisdom, a decision which the *New York Times* called a "model of judicial self-restraint" but which *Newsweek* (June 11, 1984, p. 69) and Professor Laurence Tribe called "a ruling of potentially breathtaking scope."

SETTING THE BOUNDARIES OF POWER

Recall that the political perspective this chapter describes seeks to legitimize judicial lawmaking by reading into the constitutional system certain democratic theories and some supporting assumptions about political realities in the United States. Thus neutral principles theory assumes that the Court will discredit itself and its power to govern if it acts in partisan fashion, that is, unlike a law professor's image of a court. The trouble with these political approaches is that the assumptions about political realities are very weak. For example, political support for or opposition to desegregation or school prayer seems to have virtually nothing to do with the neutrality in Wechsler's terms of the opinions in *Brown* or *Abington School District v. Schempp* (1963).

These categories do not really offer much hope of broadening either an academic or a community consensus about the nature of "good" constitutional lawmaking. However, until recently an academic consensus has existed on at least one political justification for activism. Preservatives, modern law professors, constitutional activists, and analytical political scientists have agreed that the Supreme Court must umpire the boundaries that define, both vertically and horizontally, the powers of potentially competing units of government.

No more obvious purpose motivated the framers than the desire to reduce state-imposed impediments to commerce. To do so they gave Congress broad commercial powers. The Court has worked toward increasingly sophisticated accommodations of national, state, and local power over commerce for over two centuries. The concepts of separation of powers would seem similarly to require an umpire to resolve disputes over interbranch powers, and it is difficult to imagine how conflicts among the states, e.g., under the full faith and credit clause, could iron themselves out without an umpire. In such areas settling the matter seems more important than settling it correctly, and with the exception of the 50-odd years leading to the Great Depression the Court's performance has provoked more cheers than hisses.

However, in 1980 Dean Choper published an argument for the proposition that the Court should get out of the business, at least with regard to disputes about the boundaries between federal and state power. Choper notes that policing boundary disputes among branches of government is more likely than civil liberties decisions to overturn the act of some directly elected body. More important, the Court should reserve its resources for liberties cases because of the nature of political power itself. State governments have direct electoral and party ties to the Congress. States and federal government have independent and unquestioned tax bases. Executive and legislative branches within national and state governments possess countervailing powers. But individuals and minority interests have no such power to countervail those of government.

Yet once again a plausible political argument on close inspection rests on a shaky empirical foundation. No trend separates contemporary politics from even recent political history more sharply than the demise of political parties. Primary elections, not party structures, nominate candidates. Caucuses, not party loyalty, select convention delegates. The traditional lines of party power that gave states voice and power in national government and thus might generate political compromises on the scope of powers are collapsing, re-placed by political action committees and iron triangle policymaking.

Furthermore, it is hardly clear that the Court *spends* its resources in bound-ary cases. The theory of political resources and its practical applications are difficult to quantify, and we can only speculate, but it seems plausible that the Court may *gain* resources by its decisions in boundary cases. The Nixon–Watergate case, though not a federalism issue, received much more praise than criticism because it appeared to preserve the integrity and boundedness of executive power. Yet if the balance of power between political branches means the Court need not interfere, then the Court should have declined to rule in Watergate. The difficulty with Choper's position is that boundary decisions may raise powerful normative questions about justice just as civil liberties cases do. After all, the constitutionality of the 1964 Civil Rights Act rested on commerce clause, not civil liberties, doctrine. If the Court leaves the field, it cannot provide moral guidance. Clearly, moral judgment of Watergate and the Civil Rights Act depended deeply on the moral assessment of all the political questions these events raised, and neither the executive nor legislative branches are politically positioned or organizationally structured to do so.

Choper's argument is nevertheless interesting on two important counts. First, with respect to tax policy, the Court is moving in Choper's direction. One of the less tractable boundary issues over the years has required the Court to define those taxes which a state may impose without burdening interstate and foreign commerce. The Court recently has abandoned classic distinctions like the original package doctrine precisely because in practical application they produced the opposite of the intended results. (See *Michelin Tire v. Wages*, 1976.) Recently the Court has allowed the state of Montana to impose a 30% extraction tax on the mining of coal for shipment in interstate com-merce, on the theory that if the burdens become too great, Congress may use its undoubted commerce power to correct the damage. (See *Commonwealth Edison v. Montana*, 1981.)

Second, Choper may engage in a covert form of academic lobbying. I am speculating, but assume that a professor seeks a form of government that maximizes progressive liberal values, say civil liberties protections, strict environmental protections, and the like, and suspects that the Congress of the United States is more likely to represent those values than either the Court or other branches of government. The pro-Congress argument would presume that the Congress is better buffered than other institutions from conservative influences and possesses the largest purse in town. The professor therefore seeks a doctrine that will minimize judicial interference with congressional decisions. Since congressional decisions under current doctrine, especially the civil rights acts since 1964, derive from the boundary concept of Congress's commerce clause power, the professor constructs an argument to protect Congress' broad commerce clause lawmaking scope.

When confronted with a new Burger Court of unpredictable proclivities, Choper argued (in 1974) for a drastic reduction in the Court's review powers over Congress. The speculation that the Burger Court might "turn back the clock" became a plausible fear for a liberal when in 1976 the Court struck down, 5–4, an economic regulation of Congress for the first time in four decades.

Justice Rehnquist's opinion for the Court in this case, *National League of Cities v. Usery* (1976), held that Congress could not require state governments as employers to comply with the minimum wage and maximum hours provisions enacted originally in 1938 to govern the majority of private employees in the United States. Congress' commerce clause justification for including the states by a 1974 amendment presumably was identical to its original justification of private coverage, but Rehnquist's majority held that the Tenth Amendment prohibited the federal government from forcing directly upon the states its choice as to how "essential decisions regarding the conduct of integral governmental functions are to be made." To allow the Congress to dictate minimum wage and maximum hours would "allow the national government to devour the essential ingredients of state sovereignty" (p. 855).

Rehnquist's premise, that the Tenth Amendment should be read as protecting against the destruction of federalism itself, hardly raises eyebrows. The trouble is that the conclusion in the case does not remotely follow from the premise. To assert that it does implies a rewriting of *McCulloch v. Maryland* plus more recent cases requiring states to observe federal wage and salary regulations to combat inflation.

If Congress established under the commerce clause a commission to make all hiring and firing decisions regarding all state employees, or if it sought to prescribe all rules of protocol for state legislatures, such actions might challenge state sovereignty. But the wage and hours legislation neither attempted to make substantive policy nor did it threaten state treasuries in such a way as to threaten state existence.

Alfange (1984) describes other gross defects in Rehnquist's opinion, for example, that the Tenth Amendment only reserves powers not delegated to the Congress and Rehnquist concedes Congress' commerce power at the outset. The point is that Choper's approach may really be a form of academic political pressure to nullify the *Usery* trend. Indeed, the Court seems to be doing just that. In 1981 the Court found that federal law regulating state-operated mining operations did not violate the Tenth Amendment. In 1982 the Court held 5–4 that the federal government could impose conditions on state energy policies. And in 1983 the Court required Wyoming to abandon a rule requiring game wardens to retire at age 55 under the federal Age Discrimination in Employment Act. The result for the moment is, for scholars who believe in doctrine, a doctrinal mess even more untenable than that which Rehnquist originally created, but the net results might please Dean Choper. (The Court overruled *Usery* on February 19, 1985. See 53 *Law Week* 4135.)

FAMOUS FOOTNOTE

Bickel and Choper build their theories of permissible judicial lawmaking from their reading of empirical political conditions. Unlike Wechsler, who implies that the Court might justify *any* substantive decision if it used an acceptable form of argument, Bickel and Choper believe political facts require the Court to stay out of some substantive matters—reapportionment and federalism, for example—altogether.

John Hart Ely's *Democracy and Distrust* (1980) proposed a constitutional jurisprudence that combines formal and substantive concerns. The Court's famous *Carolene Products* footnote (1938), the joint effort of Chief Justice Stone and his clerk, Louis Lusky, provided his analytical starting point:

> There may be a narrower scope for the operation of the presumption of constitutionality when legislation appears on its face to be within a specific prohibition of the Constitution, such as those of the first ten amendments, which are deemed equally specific when held to be embraced within the Fourteenth. . . .
>
> It is unnecessary to consider now whether legislation which restricts those political processes which can ordinarily be expected to bring about a repeal of undesirable legislation, is to be subjected to more exacting scrutiny. . . .
>
> Nor need we inquire whether similar considerations enter into the review of statutes directed at particular religious . . . or national . . . or racial minorities . . . whether prejudice against discrete and insular minorities may be a special condition, which tends seriously to curtail the operation of those political processes ordinarily to be relied upon to protect minorities, and which may call for a correspondingly more searching judicial inquiry . . . (pp. 152–153).

This famous footnote has matured as the most commonly cited justification for modern judicial restraint in economic matters and active protection of civil rights and liberties.

Ely urges that this approach can free constitutional interpretation from the dead hand of a preservative past without substituting the social policy preferences of five to nine unelected justices. In Ely's theory, judicial review in support of racial equality and religious and political freedom augments rather than inhibits the democratic system the Constitution created (p. 109):

> In a representative democracy value determinations are to be made by our elected representatives, and if in fact most of us disapprove we can vote them out of office. Malfunction occurs when the process is undeserving of trust when (1) the ins are choking off the channels of political change to insure than they will stay in and the outs will stay out, or (2) though no one is actually denied a voice or a vote, representatives beholden to an effective majority are systematically disadvantaging some minority out of simple hostility or a prejudiced refusal to recognize commonalities of interest, and thereby denying that minority the protection afforded other groups by a representative system.

For Ely the Court properly overrides political choices to insure procedural fairness in resolving individual disputes and to insure full participation in the political processes that distribute the wealth of the nation. He claims that no other reading of the grand scheme the Constitution created is logically possible. In doing so he offers a new definition of interpretivism. We interpret neither text nor history but rather what the document, taken as a whole, would have to mean in order to be true to itself.

The *Carolene Products* basic theory does describe much of the modern Court's work. It actually allows us to fit many cases within in. The Court has, with a few exceptional blips like *Usery*, abandoned the definition of commercial interests à la *Lochner* and focused on the rights of minorities on legal procedures, and on the integrity of the electoral process. Its recent decisions striking down laws limiting commercial advertising, e.g., *Virginia State Board of Pharmacy* (1976) extol not economic liberties as much as the consumer's right to full information. The Court has refused to permit the state to punish someone for displaying in public on the back of his coat the message "———— the draft." It has limited the circumstances in which individuals can recover damages from the press for printing false information about them (*New York Times v. Sullivan* 1964). The bulk of these cases do indeed seem to advance political participation and to protect those—accused criminals, racial minorities, and the like—who seem to lack political clout.

Despite its descriptive appeal, no recent essay on constitutional theory has received more thorough dissection and more unanimous criticism from scholars of every persuasion than Ely's, and, from a scholarly perspective, rightly so.

Ely offends strict interpretivists by claiming, despite the preservative reading of the historical evidence, that the framers must have intended the Court to have power to expand or balloon constitutional language. Yet Ely does insist on sticking to some version of interpretivism. He condemns *Roe* because the Court failed its "obligation to trace its premises to the charter from which it derives its authority" (1973, p. 949). But he cannot have it both ways. Both the text and its history do speak as if they protected property interests, and Ely does not constitutionally justify abandoning those messages (at least the land-owners in Hawaii whose property the state "condemned" might think so).

Ely offends the rights theorists because he cannot answer the arguments that rights accrue to individuals, not groups or interests. The black comedian Godfrey Cambridge often told of a recurring nightmare he had while living in California. The phone would ring in the middle of the night. He would answer to a voice that announced: "We've just had a referendum vote on slavery. You lost. Report to the block in four hours!" Assuming no impedi-ments to black voting or black political lobbying, why would we not accept the result? The Civil War amendments would nullify such a referendum, but only if Courts say so.

Worse, consider the situation in the absence of the protection of specific constitutional or statutory language. Suppose that after a fully debated refer-endum presuming no restrictions other than age and mental competence on the franchise, California passes a referendum limiting jobs to males, on the theory that the woman's place is in the home. Or, suppose a referendum in California permitting women sole discretion over the choice of carrying or aborting a fetus throughout the first six months of pregnancy, and suppose a Massachusetts law passed at the same time forbade all abortions except to save the life of the mother. Or, suppose a referendum requiring mandatory death by hanging for all those convicted of a felony for the third time, or a referendum requiring as a condition from graduation from school that a student demonstrate he or she has memorized five prescribed reasons for doubting the theory of evolution.

It is in practice difficult if not impossible to untangle the motives behind a policy and hence to tell if and when the political process has malfunctioned (Brest, 1981). Which of these actions, none of which denies any female or potential felon or parent the right to vote or to participate in debate, disadvan-tages "a minority"? The "woman's place is in the home" and the abortion decisions do not. Women are an adult majority. On what grounds does requir-ing knowledge of (not belief in) theological arguments, or the desire to deter crime through heavy punishments amount to "simple hostility or a prejudiced refusal to recognize commonalities of interest"? What is the nature of the constitutional rights in these cases if they vary among jurisdictions depending on the subtleties of the politics of their enactment? Ely's theory denies the Court's constitutional authority to rule on the abortion question. Unborn fetuses are particularly incapable of political participation or communicating with those who do participate. But if the Constitution's grand scheme states moral ideals, does not the legal status of a fetus cry out for a normative answer?

The Court's task of deciding how much representation is enough is equally ephemeral. Does everybody have a right to vote on everything? Why not limit the vote for membership on a local school board to residents who pay taxes or have children in the schools or who rent in the district? (The Court struck down such a restriction in *Kramer v. Union Free School District No. 15*, 1969, and see Tushnet, 1980.) Participation is not an ultimate value, prior to all others, in political affairs, but concede that much and the justices must become experts in theories of representation before they can shape sound doctrine. A theory of constitutional law must state criteria for decision sufficiently forceful to constrain practical political actors. The force of the theory necessarily depends on its moral appeal and its practical applicability. But motives are of all political things least objectively knowable. Different judges will speculate on policy motives depending on their own experiences and values unless a theory of rights, which Ely does not offer, provides a surrogate indicator of motives. Even assuming judges could agree on a method of deciding what the motives are, Ely's argument is completely circular. Courts can declare rights based on motives, but the motives must pass or fail some previous definition of constitutional right.

Let us now step back. John Hart Ely, who clerked for Earl Warren and who now serves as dean of Stanford's law school, is no legal amateur. When a major figure in legal scholarship writes a book that for two years dominates the conversation of the nation's teachers of constitutional law, and when that conversation condemns it at virtually every point, we must expect to learn something fundamental about constitutional jurisprudence. I have said previously that communities, in this case the community of constitutional scholars, seek to protect the integrity of their own ways of communicating, no matter how flawed they may appear to outsiders. The Ely debate confirms the suspicion. This particular community lives and dies in the belief that "the law" itself must provide "a theory," a grand scheme from which all subsidiary truths logically flow. This is their solution to the political problem of legitimacy. Like the preservatives, Ely fails because he is not looking at politics, only at some imagined political world such that he can arrange it into the logical unity his theory requires. These scholars believe that to reject the logic of law, to find answers outside law, is "nihilistic," a necessary rejection of all distinctions in moral values. But if legal logic itself will not avail, as it will not, then the distinctions in moral values must come from some other source.

THE INSTITUTIONAL CAPACITY OF COURTS

Political scientists who teach constitutional law occasionally succumb to the temptation to play law professor. The reverse is equally true. Wechsler, Bickel, Choper, and Ely all rightly attend to political realities in their theories, but they only play at political science. Because they can only converse with each other as lawyers, they offer only legal theories. The aesthetics of academic scholarship demand that these theories yield a set of legal commands for "correct" constitutional decisionmaking. For their purposes, political play suffices, for it enables them to create a dramatic, fictional world in which all of the elements of their argument fit together.

One obvious place to start good political science is to develop a sense of how judicial structures and resources actually affect the quality of legal decisions and to describe the political circumstances in which the Court seems to produce workable results. Indeed Justice Rehnquist, among others, seems to take the jurisprudential significance of the relative capacity of institutions to make wise policy very seriously. In *Bell v. Wolfish* (1979), he wrote: "[U]nder the Constitution, the first question to be answered is not whose plan is best, but in what branch of the Government is lodged the authority to initially devise the plan." Thus Rehnquist thought, in *Wolfish*, that prison officials were better able to judge the costs and benefits of total body searches of prisoners, and therefore rejected a constitutional challenge to that practice.

Horowitz (1977), on one side, and Chayes (1976) and Cavanaugh and Sarat (1980), on the other, frame the debate. Horowitz argues for judicial restraint from observable evidence about judicial decisionmaking:

1. Courts do not self-start. The correctness of their decisions depends on the evidence raised in the case they hear, but the resources and motives of those who bring the case limit the information the court hears in generating its decision. Often the cases are atypical, and hard cases make bad law.

2. The rules of admissible legal evidence artificially limit the information judges permit themselves to hear. Policymaking by other political bodies operates under no such artificial restraints.

3. Judges do not specialize sufficiently to master the intricacies of a policy problem. The judge must switch from an antitrust case that hinges on economic projections of the oligopolistic market effects of a vertical merger today to the definition of human life in tomorrow's abortion case. In the age of specialists the conclusions of generalist judges will almost always contain what the specialists will call errors, and the litigants in the next case will no doubt seek to exploit those weaknesses.

4. Trial judges may try in chambers to negotiate compromise settlements short of trial, but appellate courts are not nearly as well positioned to do so. The obligation to justify the result in terms of some principle produces over-simple, binary decisions that cannot consider complexities satisfactorily.

5. Courts lack muscle to enforce compliance adequately.

6. Political information is transmitted largely through informal networks, networks that judges do not tie into. Thus, for example, Judge Arthur Garrity, the "receiver" for Boston public schools after they failed to desegregate, used geographical lines drawn by the police department, not knowing that the

department had tried to encourage racial peace by drawing the lines so as to maximize racial homogeneity in police districts. Had Garrity participated in the richer informal network of Boston politics, he would have learned that fact and used some other guide for designing desegregation plans.

Cavanaugh and Sarat (1980) document quite persuasively that Horowitz's fears, drawn from a small sample of cases, do not consistently characterize a larger sample of judicial interventions.[3] Furthermore, nearly every criticism that Horowitz levels at courts has analogs in legislative and bureaucratic policymaking. (See Carter, 1983, especially chapters 13 and 14.) More significant, Abram Chayes (1976) has argued that in constitutional matters these criticisms attenuate. I shall quote at some length because Chayes (pp. 1307–1316) reminds us that the normative nature of constitutional law necessarily limits how much mileage we can get from empirical inferences about political practice.

[D]espite its well rehearsed inadequacies, the judiciary may have some important institutional advantages. . . .

FIRST, and perhaps most important, is that the process is presided over by a judge. His professional tradition insulates him from narrow political pressures, but, given the operation of the federal appointive power and the demands of contemporary law practice, he is likely to have some experience of the political process and acquaintance with a fairly broad range of public policy problems. Moreover, he is governed by a professional ideal of reflective and dispassionate analysis of the problem before him and is likely to have had some experience putting this ideal into practice.

SECOND, the public law model permits ad hoc applications of broad national policy in situations of limited scope. The solutions can be tailored to the needs of the particular situation. . . .

THIRD, the procedure permits a relatively high degree of participation by representatives of those who will be directly affected by the decision. . . .

FOURTH, the court, although traditionally thought less competent than legislatures or administrative agencies in gathering and assessing information, may have unsuspected advantages in this regard. Even the diffused adversarial structure of public law litigation furnishes strong incentives for the parties to produce information. . . . And, because of the limited scope of the proceeding, the information required can be effectively focused and specified. Information produced will not only be subject to adversary review, but . . . the judge can engage his own experts to assist in evaluating the evidence. . . .

FIFTH, the judicial process is an effective mechanism for registering and responding to grievances generated by the operation of public programs in a regulatory state. Unlike an administrative bureaucracy or a legislature, the judiciary *must* respond to the complaints of the aggrieved . . . . The legislature, perhaps, could balance, but it cannot address specific situations. . . .

---

[3] Cavanaugh and Sarat write, "However cast, arguments about failures in competence or capacity tend to be political statements about the desirability of particular court decisions or aspects of legal doctrine. Such analyses of judicial capacity regularly reveal impatience with the substantive outcomes produced by courts" (p. 386).

SIXTH, the judiciary has the advantage of being non-bureaucratic. It is effective in tapping energies and resources outside itself and outside the government in the exploration of the situation and the assessment of remedies. . . .

[T]he growth of judicial power has been, in large part, a function of the failure of other agencies to respond to groups that have been able to mobilize considerable political resources and energy. And, despite its new role, the judiciary is unlikely to displace its institutional rivals for government power or even to achieve a dominant share of the market. . . .

In my view, judicial action only achieves . . . legitimacy by responding to, indeed by stirring, the deep and durable demand for justice in our society. I confess some difficulty in seeing how this is to be accomplished by erecting the barriers of the traditional conception [of courts] to turn aside, for example, the attacks on exclusionary zoning and police violence, two of the ugliest remaining manifestation of official racism in American life. In practice, if not in words, the American legal tradition has always acknowledged the importance of substantive results for the legitimacy and accountability of judicial action. . . . Perhaps the most important consequence of the inevitably exposed position of the judiciary in our contemporary regulatory state is that it will force us to confront more explicitly the qualities of wisdom, viability, responsiveness to human needs—the justice—of judicial decisions.

I think Chayes rightly encourages us not to underestimate the fact-finding capacity of courts nor to diminish how the role expectation that judges must decide impartially affects actual judicial choices. But his broader point is that institutional capacities analysis simply cannot satisfy the "demand for justice." If I were a property owner in Hawaii, I would not find the Court's statement that the plan was "not irrational" morally satisfying. If I felt abused by prison officials, I would think judicial deference to the judgment of prison officials would violate the fundamental principle that they not judge their own cause.

POLITICAL JUSTIFICATION FOR NONINTERPRETIVE CONSTITUTIONAL RIGHTS

Recall that Ely's "representative reinforcing" role for the Court failed to resolve three difficulties. He asserted that the text and the intent of the framers objectively interpreted logically required greater judicial activism in protection of individual rights and liberties than of commercial interests. But the text makes no such distinctions, and the history of the founding presents plenty of evidence of concern for protection of property interests against excessively representative regimes. Second, his theory does not apply cleanly to the cases he says it covers. Finally, Ely does not answer the charge that rights belong to individual citizens and therefore by definition cannot depend on political calculations.

This and the next two sections of this chapter report three different escape routes from the apparent deadlock of law and politics. The first proposes to embrace noninterpretivism itself. The second abandons any pretense of achieving legality on lawyers' terms and sees the courts in purely political terms. The third tries to combine the two. The Critical Legal Studies movement attempts the third escape, and in the final section, having met it earlier, we begin to get to know it.

Arthur S. Miller (1982) and Michael Perry (1982) endorse unequivocally noninterpretive constitutional lawmaking. Miller is especially loud. His shouting, like all shouting, requires him to simplify the message, but the core of it is significant. Madison in *Federalist 51* held that pluralism, the contending of interests, would yield better principles of justice and the general good than would autocratic means. Madison in effect endorsed the Burkean computing principle that Bickel could not abandon. But, holds Miller, Madison, Burke, and Bickel are wrong. At least in the highly organized iron triangle politics of interest groups, bureaucracies and legislatures, principles of justice and the general good simply don't reliably enter the political calculus. Grant the premise that communities cannot survive without moral value, and grant that the world of electoral politics cannot supply this community need, and we are left with the courts as our last and only moral resort.

Perry's argument seems on first glance similar to Miller's. He defends the legal acceptability of noninterpretivism: "If noninterpretive review serves a crucial governmental function that no other practice can be expected to serve, and if it serves that function in a manner that somehow accommodates the principle of electorally accountable policymaking, then that function constitutes the justification for noninterpretive review" (p. 24).

Perry, however, arrives at his conclusion more subtly. As we saw previously, he quotes Bork at length and holds that within their framework preservatives like Bork are quite correct. If we interpret the Constitution honestly, we will find exactly what Berger and Bork find. Perry accepts the conclusions this framework generates, but he argues the framework is profoundly wrong. All the debaters assume that all legal questions have right answers. The flaw in both the restrained and activist thought is the unquestioned assumption that it must find a method for getting the right legal answer. The adversaries debate where and how to discover or create the right answers, but they all assume the answers must be right. If, on the other hand, constitutional questions, particularly questions of equality, liberty, and fairness, are moral questions, then the grounds of the argument shift, for moral questions do not have right answers. The value lies in continuous moral evolution.

Perry argues that "Our religious understanding has generally involved a commitment to the notion of moral evolution" (p. 99). We are sinners who continuously seek grace. Legislators, driven by the desire to stay in office and to compromise among contending interests, are not institutionally situated to articulate the moral bases of public policy. The Court must therefore serve as prophet or teacher of values in order to stimulate "an ever deepening moral understanding." Judicial review of constitutional rights is simply a different political operation from the normal resolution of disputes. The courts must try to focus and crystallize the visions beyond transient majorities and political compromises that bind us as a nation. Judicial review should not find right answers; it should speculate on mysteries. It must therefore be open-ended and future-oriented. It will never actually settle right answers any more than does the church. Judicial review is simply that part of political life that strives to keep political practice in some "harmony with our evolving, deepening moral understanding" (p. 99). Political practices continually change, and so does moral knowledge. The struggle for harmony will continue for the same reasons that those who profess to belong to a religious community will regularly "go to church."

Stated this way, Perry's position is close to my own. If he had proceeded to define and illustrate the standards by which we might assess how well or badly the Court deepens our moral understanding in specific cases, I might not have bothered to write this book. Instead, Perry reverts to the standard forms of argument of his community of legal scholars: the preoccupation with political legitimacy and the demonstration, despite what he has just written, that *his* position possesses the greatest logical elegance of them all. For example, since the Constitution is law, and since judicial activism does resolve disputes in a countermajoritarian manner, Perry feels he must tell us what constrains the Court, not how to evaluate its decisions.

Perry's legitimacy solution builds on Article III. He would not diminish the formal authority of a constitutional decision. However, since noninterpretive review is less legitimate than interpretive review, Perry would allow Congress under Article III to deny the Court jurisdiction to decide noninterpretive cases. Thus the Congress could remove the Court's jurisdiction to nullify laws limiting the right to an abortion (a noninterpretive result), but could not limit the Court's jurisdiction to protect religious freedom under the First Amendment. Therefore, the liberation of the legitimacy debate from its legalistic preoccupation with right answers evaporates. I count the evaporation as further evidence of the compelling need in this academic community to honor its communicative forms.

Perry does not present a theory of rights that increases judicial confidence about where and how to intervene. What if, following Perry, the Court struck down a state law permitting abortions as a violation of the due process rights of the fetus? Perry seems not to approve such a result, but the disapproval hardly follows from his theory. At least Ely preached a theoretically operational model: Find out from political scientists where and why the system of representation breaks down and work to minimize those representational failings. Perry operates on such a high level of abstraction that he may well leave his audience on the ground.

Perry's main shortcoming arises in his overly simple distinction between interpretive and noninterpretive review. Perry actually doubts the constitutionality of *Home Building and Loan*'s reshaping of the contract clause, firmly ensconced in law though it is. But if the hermeneutic philosophers are right, then people will disagree about what is and isn't interpretive in the first place. Congress will have no way of telling which decisions are and which are not interpretive. If interpretative acts bring interpreter and interpreted together, but each interpreter is to an extent unique, then how shall Congress or anyone else decide that opinion X in interpretive while Y is not? Yet Perry's scheme depends precisely on that distinction. Grant the premise of the "living constitution" and even *Roe* might count as interpretive (Alexander, 1983). Perry might permit Congress to overturn nearly all of the Warren Court's work under Article III as noninterpretive, but the second Justice Harlan, no liberal on interpretive matters, found in the due process clause of the Fourteenth Amendment sufficient grounds for nullifying Connecticut's contraceptive laws.

Sanford Levinson summed up this problem: "There is something distinctly odd about an author whose major theme is the propriety of noninterpretive functionalism adopting an essentially interpretivist limit when conceptualizing the role of Congress. Who cares, frankly, about the text of Article III if one is able to accept the legitimacy of noninterpretivism in the first place?" (1983, p. 576). Or consider this problem: If Congress does withdraw judicial jurisdiction to hear, say, challenges to a statute prohibiting the shipment in interstate commerce of depictions of sexual intercourse, then no citizen would have the power to address whether the ban fell within interpretive or noninterpretive powers in the first place. What of the prosecution of a shipper sending materials for medical education, or the shipper of ancient works of art valued by museums? (Lupu, 1983, p. 610). In short, by regressing to the familiar vocabulary of legitimacy, Perry contradicts the very essence of prophetic vision.

Despite the great differences among Choper, Ely, and Perry, and the immense criticism the works of each have stimulated, the three do have something in common. In spite of the wide array of political ideologies that contend in American politics—religious fundamentalism, socialism, social Darwinism, and so forth, these three scholars reach similar conclusions about the role of the Court. The Court should be about, one way or another, the protection of roughly those liberties that the Warren Court advocated. This triangulation within the profession might mean only that law professors are, for the most part, a liberal bunch. But if this conclusion also triangulates with the conclusions other paths of inquiry reach, the fact may deserve a second look.

MORE POLITICAL REALISM

Robert B. McKay (1983, p. 140) summarized the judicial review debate:

> The Supreme Court of the United States, like other courts, is not perfect. It is not possible, perhaps not even desirable, to define a coherent and altogether defensible theory of judicial review. The Court is not disturbed that consistency is not entirely possible. In the practice of judicial review the Supreme Court has admirably served the cause of justice for nearly two centuries. My advice is not to worry too much about the matter. So long as we are free to tell the Court, the world—and each other—about its failings, things should turn out pretty well.

This chapter has reviewed theories of judicial review that legitimize the noninterpretive judicial creation of constitutional law and policy. These scholars behave very much as Harlan Fiske Stone's epigraphic quote predicted. Each defines legitimacy so that only legal analysis can provide it, and then each proceeds to create his own legal solution. In the larger sweep of things, however, McKay may be closer to the mark. If political arrangements, which lawyers help make but hardly control, determine the acceptability of institutional performance, then we must examine those arrangements as directly as possible. And when we do we will not find a public outraged by the Court's methodology.

Ira Lupu (1983) has written that the misunderstanding of the nature of political consent dooms these law professors's political jurisprudence. They have not shaken off the Lockean presumption that public consent exists to the extent government keeps its contractual bargains with citizens. But citizens do not think in such political terms. Consent is no more than a label we put on some minimal level of post hoc public acceptance. We may say that citizens consent to the Court, and to political regimes in general, only insofar as they do not actively spend their resources seeking political change. Consent to the Court is closely tied to regime consent. Since courts rarely stray from the political agendas of the regime, consent is, absent political crises, presumed to exist. As Shapiro (1981, p. 34) put it in his comparison of the political position of courts in several countries:

> No regime is likely to allow significant political power to be wielded by an isolated judicial corps free of political restraints. To the extent that courts make law, judges will be incorporated into the governing coalition, the ruling elite, the responsible representatives of the people, or however else the political regime may be expressed.

Here are several arguments that political jurisprudence offers to dispel lawyers' preoccupation with a myth of consent. I omit from the list the evidence that the Court itself directly represents in the sense that it listens to complaining citizens and that it possesses resources for competently assessing information about policies that are comparable to the resources of other lawmaking units of government, some branches of the federal bureaucracy excepted. Chayes touched on these, above, and so does Tribe (1980).

1. Social scientists are not much more likely to resolve these questions to everyone's satisfaction than are law professors, but the social science literature leaves little room for doubt on two points. First, public opinion about the Court is too diffuse and uninformed and changeful to provide a useful measure of public acceptance either of the Court as an institution or of the quality of all but a very few highly publicized decisions. Change and relativity in law do not threaten its legitimacy. Second, the Court does respond over time to the pressures of public opinion when they coincide with consensus among elites (Dahl, 1958, and Schmidhauser, 1984). Martin Shapiro, who is dean to political science students of courts as Bickel was dean of the sophisticated judicial restraint advocates, has argued that the Court routinely adopts the dominant paradigms of social knowledge, but with a lag time. Thus the post–World War II Court brought "to its final conclusions a set of values and policy preferences that had achieved an overwhelming consensus produced by one of the few great crises and value reorderings in American political history" (Shapiro, 1983, pp. 237–238). If the New Deal consensus has broken down since the Vietnam war, no coherent political alternative has yet replaced it. Under this standard political analysis, one would predict a confused and drifting Court, which is just what the Burger Court appears to be. Felix Cohen, a law professor, made a comparable point in 1935 (p. 843):

> A judicial decision is a social event. Like the enactment of a Federal statute, or the equipping of police cars with radios, a judicial decision is an intersection of social forces: Behind the decision are social forces that play upon it to give it a resultant momentum and direction. . . . Only by probing behind the decision to the forces which it reflects, or projecting beyond the decision the lines of its force upon the future, do we come to an understanding of the meaning of the decision itself.

2. Part of the breakdown of the New Deal coalition involves the breakdown of the hegemony of the legal profession, the decline of the assumption that, as "professionals," lawyers on legal matters know best. Hence, until now the legal profession has failed to appreciate the obvious conclusions of the social sciences because "professionalism" made it unnecessary. Legal education has begun to take other disciplines seriously only in the last decade, and it is only in this decade that the Critical Legal Studies movement has taken shape.

3. Courts are organizations that depend on environments for support. Much of the research on early compliance and noncompliance with desegregation orders noted how strongly trial judges were influenced by their communities (Peltason, 1961). If the Court, despite the regular appointment of judges politically congenial to the president who appointed them, dotes upon an idea that will not carry the day in the long run, the lower courts will buffer it for the same reasons they resist in the short run ideas that win in the long run. In any event, major Court-made social innovations will carry the long

day only when legislatures pass statutes and fund programs to force implementation. This, at least, seems the clear lesson of the studies of compliance
with Court-initiated changes in voting rights and racial equality.

4. Legal scholars have paid little attention to the psychology of political
enterpreneurship. William Riker (1984) suggest that effective political actors
behave in patterned ways, which Riker labels "heresthetic." He defines
"heresthetics" as "the method and art of influencing social decisions" (p. 2).
The heresthetic actor (and Riker specifically analyzes the founding fathers on
this scale) operates comfortably in an environment in which options keep
changing. These people want to prevail, and to do so they eschew standing on
principle. Riker's theory implies both that constitutional language is inherently compromised and that the people who become justices will not commonly be committed to principle for principle's sake.

Over twenty years ago Martin Shapiro pointed out that whether a unit of
government does or does not represent effectively, does or does not respond to
informed pressures for policy change, does or does not possess the capacity to
process information effectively, depends on the issue and the always somewhat idiosyncratic informal structures and individual skills of the decisionma-
kers involved. He preferred "to determine in each separate policy area whether
judicial policy-making contributes to well rounded representation of interests
or to popular control more or less than policy-making by some rival agency.
This approach is surely more useful than issuing blanket condemnations of
judicial action on the basis of an abstract model of democratic policy-making
that does not reflect the realities of American government" (1964, p. 45).

These unexceptional social science conclusions might lead us, with McKay,
to stop worrying about the Court except in times of political "destabiliza-
tion." But what about political instability? If the Court is safe because it is
institutionally nested in a relatively open and representative environment,
what happens when the environment itself destabilizes? If the Reagan presidency marks the end of the New Deal consensus, but no popularly rooted
ideology replaces it, what becomes of the constraints on the Court? Shapiro
(1983) holds that the increasing political uncertainty about national goals and
increasing disagreement about the criteria that distinguish good policy from
bad will associate with an unfocused and confused constitutional law. In these
circumstances legal scholars might see only one alternative, to seek to reforge
the political consensus itself.

AN INTRODUCTION
TO CRITICAL LEGAL STUDIES

Thus re-enters the Critical Legal Studies movement. What fascinates about
the movement is that its rhetorical excesses, the willingness of some scholars

to "trash" all conventional scholarship, indeed its self-designation as a "movement," confirm the thesis that scholarship is normative discourse shaped by scholarly communities in just the same way that political communities need and shape a different normative discourse. Critical scholars are divorcing one community. The revolutionary trappings of the movement simultaneously ease the pain of this academic divorce and seek energetically to create the basis of a new community. The basis of this new scholarly community advocates that legal scholars must seek to reforge the political consensus itself.

Despite the evidence in the pages of the January 1984, *Stanford Law Review*, the Critical movement does not, as the cliché goes, defy description. The Critical approach, like all radical positions in intellectual development, creates a new language and new values. To describe it in old terms, terms the uninitiated will recognize, necessarily underrepresents the virtues of new ways of thought. Critical legal students share a belief that American society wrongly oppresses the disadvantaged, stifles self-fulfillment and, by linking individual worth to material acquisitions, warps and misstates the essence of individual dignity.

The movement consists almost entirely of relatively young law professors trained and/or teaching at Harvard, Yale, and Stanford law schools. Duncan Kennedy, who denied that anything as formal as law could generate intersubjective agreement, might be said to hold the deanship but for the fact that Critical adherents, Kennedy at the front, would rightly reject such an authoritarian metaphor.

The *Stanford Law Review* symposium issue and *The Politics of Law: A Progressive Critique* (Kairys, 1982) contain a broad range of Critical writing. One quickly learns that the movement is not primarily concerned with the Supreme Court, certainly not with constitutional law. The American legal system, from the first day of law school, inculcates into practitioners in all fields a method of knowing that masks the systematic way law legitimizes materialism and capitalist power. Law, in short, operates as the social scientists say, but the dominant political order it conforms to and supports is morally corrupt.

Like the other approaches described in this chapter, the Critical view of law derives from a vision of political life. It sees no distinction between the views of Bork and Berger, on the one hand, and Ely, Perry, Fiss, and Tribe on the other. It is immaterial whether judicial protection of racial or political minorities derives from a legalistic interpretation of the Fourteenth Amendment or from political speculation that no other branch of government is politically structured and motivated to do so. What matters is that the political system, courts included, does not adequately promote the cause of human dignity. All imaginable forms for justifying the status quo are wrong. The status quo deserves not justification but condemnation. The inner city schools are, after all, still segregated and inner city blacks more dependent than ever on the whims of bureaucratic power for a meager livelihood.

Tushnet (1984a, p. 262), for example, pushes Shapiro's description (1983) of the "rootless activism" of the Burger Court to a more radical analytical plane:

> A really clever counterrevolutionary, faced with the political situation Shapiro describes, would conduct what Antonio Gramsci called a war of position. Conceding small gains to the opposition in areas not of central concern, the counterrevolutionary would attempt to secure somewhat larger gains in areas closer to the center and would conduct lighting [sic] raids to capture really important targets. . . . There *is* a counterrevolution under way, but the tactics are not what the liberals expected.

Readers should not infer from its neo-Marxist leanings that Critical scholarship threatens to undermine and overthrow the political system through the radicalization of the legal profession. All communities need to share some points of agreement so that vigorous disagreement does not threaten the deeper value of scholarly community. Marxist and Gramscian writings are that formal point in the Critical community, just as legitimacy theories anchor more conventional legal scholars. I suspect that Critical scholars care more to expand serious political dialogue than to provoke revolution.

Robert Gordon describes his scholarly community as struggling "against being demobilized by our own conventional beliefs" (Kairys, p. 289). The struggle seems inescapably necessary in light of this and the prior chapters' descriptions of theories of judicial review. Preservative, moderate, and activist conventional theories all fail elementary tests of internal consistency and external validation. They are often circular; they often inflate a part of an argument into the whole. All to some degree insist on preserving the artificial forms of legal analysis.

Milner Ball (1983, pp. 311–312) summarizes Gordon's biography of the movement:

> They have attempted first to identify the complex of beliefs that lends to contingent, value-laden decisions an air of neutrality, inevitability, and rightness and that allows decision makers to deny responsibility for the suffering their judgments create. So dominating is the ruling order of thought that the mind is disabled "even to *imagine* that life could be different and better." Critical legal thinking has accordingly sought in Marxism the means for gaining distance from and understanding of the prevailing belief system. . . .
>
> Gordon explains that critical legal scholars are attempting "to make maps of" the value systems that permeate the received structure and thereby guide and limit perception. They are also attempting to liberate thought and action from imprisonment within the false constraints of these belief systems: by showing the historical contingency of belief structures, empirically disproving claims of necessity, and exposing the incoherence of the various theories of liberalism, they hope "to unfreeze the world as it appears."

The movement seeks to maintain the community of thought that its members developed during the antiwar movement of the 1960s and early 1970s. It seeks to replace the older generation, nearly all of whom—Choper, Ely, Gunther, White, Wellington, Sandalow, Parker, Tribe, Fiss, and Grey—clerked for the Supreme Court during the tenure of Chief Justice Warren and shared that communal experience.

But what if, as Bickel thought, the Constitution leaves us only with paradoxes and contradictions? The discussion implies that we must develop the capacity to think simultaneously about rationality and indeterminacy. Does our culture equip us to do so? Machiavelli assumed man could not accept a world of becoming, that he hungers for constants, and Berger and Luckmann seem to agree. What if we cannot think simultaneously about a constitution that, as a legal document, must provide "closure" and "truth," and a constitution that merely stimulates conversations, none demonstrably true or final or constant? Critical scholars urge us to solve the dilemma by abandoning the legal model altogether. I think they are partly correct. But Machiavelli rightly reminds us of our need for constants. Again I argue in this book that aesthetic theory rather than legal or political theory can provide these constants.

THE IRRELEVANCE OF THE LEGITIMACY PROBLEM

I noted previously that the legitimacy of noninterpretive review, though it is not a trivial problem, has a straightforward solution that anyone who wishes to transcend academic shouting matches will accept. Let me now elaborate this solution.

At the conceptual level "legitimacy" can only transcend its status as a fudge word if we provide it with an analytically useful definition. If we define it etymologically, so that legitimate institutions and practices possess the characteristics of "law," then the problem resolves very simply. All quarters in the academic debate concede that the Court possesses the power to declare constitutional law, and all would seem to concede that the Court is thereby constitutionally authorized to define its own power.

This definition constrains the Court to claim that its decisions flow from something constitutional, but this something need not be words or intent or its own prior decisions. The Court might adopt *any* jurisprudential theory and, simply by adopting it, make it sufficiently "lawful" to satisfy this definition of legitimacy. The Martian visitor observed a Supreme Court that operated in just this fashion throughout American history.

Thus if the Court adopted Ely's position that the deeper structure of constitutional government necessitates vigilant restrictions on the power of government to constrain individual liberties, it would not need to prove that truth against competing claims, merely assert it. The Court similarly might announce that as conditions change the Court properly applies ancient standards analogously to new, but comparable, settings. Or, it might conversely revert wholesale to Raoul Berger's strict interpretivism. In such cases the Court might create highly controversial law, but it would not act illegitimately.

So defined, could the Court declare and simultaneously legitimate anything it chooses? With one exception, I think the answer is "Precisely so!" *Marbury*, *Dred Scott*, *Lochner*, *Debs*, *Youngstown Sheet and Tube*, the most controversial decisions imaginable, provoke our ire precisely because they all take on unquestionably the color of law. Legitimacy is not the problem; these decisions *are* lawful. That fact merely creates our difficulty, which is how to decide if they are good. The exception imagines that the Court could behave "illegitimately" if it (a) conceded the existence of a constitutional command, and (b) conceded that the Constitution obligated the Court to enforce that command in the case before it, but (c) denied its obligation to enforce the command on admittedly expedient, extra-legal, grounds. The Court would, by its own definition, not act "legally." The prospect is, of course, bothersome because the Court in wartime has come naggingly close to denying its capacity to take legal action.

But to dismiss the legitimacy problem by equating it with minimal legality too much resembles academic sleight of hand. Another definition of legitimacy, Berger and Luckmann's, more closely resembles what the Court has consistently done throughout its history. Legitimacy refers to those things that are institutionalized within a society, community, or culture. That is, those conditions and practices which members of the system accept as true and noncontroversial are legitimate. Yet nearly all forms of noninterpretive judicial review, including the most wildly creative ones, meet this test. Constitutional amendments may seek to balance the budget, or to put religion back in the schools, or grant women equal legal treatment more concrete than the current mist of equal protection clause doctrine, and Congress may seek halfheartedly to limit Court jurisdiction in school busing or abortion cases, but nobody, with the possible exception of Gary McDowell, seems serious about proposing a "back to the framers" bill or amendment.

Yet, having put behind us a century of scholarship, we have gotten almost nowhere, or, to be more precise, we have arrived at a fork in the road near the beginning of the journey. If, in the long run, the Court is politically responsive, and if two-dimensional legitimacy theories only replicate medieval scholasticism, and if the best efforts at analysis raise the image of a James Thurber cartoon of a room full of people throwing furniture at one another, then we must find some alternative frame of reference that allows us to assess the quality of the work of the Court.

Constitutional lawmaking correctly done makes statements about the normative character of the polity. It is a struggle to identify what sort of a community the United States is and what it might become. Communities are characterized in significant part by the kind of justice they do and do not tolerate. The Thurber image of scholars shouting at one another about justice demonstrates just how seriously, indeed passionately, involved people can become precisely because justice is a symbol for community. Scholars actually engage in a critically important conversation, one that the Court has stimulated. If they throw furniture, it is, I think, from frustration at learning that legitimacy is a blind alley.

In response to Ely's book, Laurence Tribe (1980) puzzled over the persistence of process-based theories of the legitimacy of constitutional law. He was puzzled by their obvious logical and evidentiary shortcomings. The puzzle resolves, however, if we stop asking which scholar has the right answer and start examining the commonality of method. From Raoul Berger to Duncan Kennedy and everyone in between, each one professes to have satisfied an aesthetic standard. Each claims to have found a "good fit" between a theory and his vision of the data that "matter." Each has been socialized differently, of course. These influences, and particularly the sociology of work itself, strongly shape each scholar's perception of fittedness. Each addresses an academic audience, and I think it is meaningful to say that many of these conflicting works are, from the academic perspective, equally good "fits." We do not hesitate to appreciate as equally good different performances of different symphonies, or even different performances of the same Beethoven symphony.

But the Court is not an academic institution, and it does not perform for law professors. A plain look at the Court tells us that doctrines of legitimacy simply do not matter very much for the audience of students, practitioners, and attentive citizens that it plays to and the political script from which it improvises. When I elaborate the political applications of aesthetic theory, I shall explain how the Court can perform convincingly before a pluralistic political audience, one whose members do *not* necessarily share the same ideologies, values, or personal goals. Pluralism does indeed complicate the process of legitimizing normative community values. I shall, however, try to persuade you that pluralistic political conditions *increase* the political demand for normatively convincing performances. Perhaps we tend to elect good performers rather than good technicians to the presidency of the United States because ideological diversity prevents us from creating visions of community except through the devices of fiction and poetry, devices that good performers routinely master.

Chapter 5 NORMATIVE ALTERNATIVES TO INTERPRETIVISM

True peace is not merely the absence of tension, but it is the presence of justice and brotherhood.

—Martin Luther King, Jr.

Philosophers help to build society as a picture of itself. A constitutional regime like ours has to have some conception of itself in order to function well.

—John Rawls

The road to good intentions is paved with hell.

—Peter DeVries

REVIEW

My analysis of Michael Perry's theory described briefly a road that he did not take. That road, the path of this chapter, examines normative political theories themselves. Before starting, however, let me emphasize two important conclusions that I hope the materials we have thus far covered allow us to draw.

First, I have insisted that constitutional lawmaking follows no consistent patterns of legal reasoning or method and that it is heavily influenced by immediate and relatively short-lived political and social beliefs. Despite this evidence, however, it is inherent in the nature of the Constitution that people who attend to it at all care strongly that constitutional decisions be somehow good. I have reviewed at some length the attempts of some scholars to go back to the Constitution and the attempts of others to justify noninterpretive alternatives not so much to criticize them as to produce evidence that scholars care deeply about the problem of constitutional goodness. The same concern for goodness drives preservative and Critical scholars alike, though they differ on virtually all other matters.

Second, each and every attempt to generate a constitutional theory has presented itself as a good theory *because* it claims to have created a good fit among the elements it treats as important. Thus the heart of the problem from the preservative perspective is that too many judicial decisions so evidently do not *fit* the meaning of constitutional words in their historical text. The heart of Wechsler's problem is that too many results do not logically *fit* with the intelligible legal premises stated in the opinion. For Perry (and I think for the Critical scholars and their political jurisprudence cousins), the problem is to account for the evidence that the legal process is indeed political. Conventional legal theories do not *fit* the political reality. I believe, in other words, that this jurisprudential common denominator, the concern for fittedness, obligates us to treat constitutional goodness as an aesthetic phenomenon.

Because I concur that the legal process is fundamentally political, let me also here summarize why preservative and legitimacy-based alternatives fail, why each has met with a barrage of sometimes almost gleeful criticisms of their internal inconsistencies and evidentiary shortcomings. I think the failings boil down to two.

The first involves the nature of logic itself. Each of these approaches cannot shake the legal habit, so central to preservative thought, that logic ought to generate a single best solution to any analytical problem. The difficulty is not simply that people cannot agree on the starting premises, though constitutional scholars obviously do not. Even if they did agree on a starting premise, social logic does not operate in a linear or determinate fashion. Robert Bork said we must follow where logic leads, like following a path in the woods. But the proper simile for legal logic resembles not a path in the woods but touring an unfamiliar city without either fixed goals or a street map. Each intersection requires a choice to continue or to turn right or left, and each intersection reveals new information about where one might like to go. This is the problem the Court faced in *Logan*. That case afforded a new and unanticipated glimpse of where entitlement theory might take us. The handicapped Illinois worker affected by a bureaucratic error did not resemble the prisoner or the spanked school child.

Second, these law professors cannot bring themselves to take the evidently political nature of the legal process quite seriously enough. The evidence unequivocally shows that the personal values of appellate judges determine the outcomes in contested appellate cases. The evidence is not the secret province of political scientists, it is part of routine "news" reported in the press.[1] I do not mean to praise or condemn this pattern here. (Indeed my deeper point, with which Wechsler agreed, holds that we cannot judge results without reading the opinions themselves.) The point is rather that the evalua-

---

[1] For example, on December 18 and 19, 1984, the *Wall Street Journal* ran a front page series analyzing how President Reagan's appointments to the federal appellate bench reversed legal trends pursued by President Carter's appointees. In passing we learn how Judge Robert Bork refused to follow the Supreme Court's recent privacy decisions in a homosexual rights case. We learn how Richard Posner, another Reagan appointee, voted to deny free legal counsel to prison inmates on the ground that, according to free market economic theory, prisoners ought to be able to attract paid counsel if their cases have enough merit to risk trying them. And we learn that in its 1983 term the Supreme Court reversed 26 of the 27 full opinions it heard from the Carter-dominated Ninth Circuit.

tive standards we seek must work with the political reality that judges of all sorts, including those whose scholarly theories deny that personal values matter, decide in terms of personal values. The judge's aesthetic task is to persuade us that the personal values he brings to the case simultaneously help constitute our political community. Again, the goal is to build into otherwise appealing political theories what they lack: standards of evaluation of the goodness of the decisions themselves.

NORMATIVE THEORY

Individuals and communities need ideologies, tools with which to make chaos appear coherent. Geertz (1973, p. 218) says communities need ideologies as much as people need prose in order to communicate. The very persistence of the concept of a constituted community and the vast quantity of literature about the Constitution's meaning and its health prove only that our culture is no exception. Thus from the normative perspective, judicial decisions should bypass all the institutional and democratic meta-analyses about legitimacy and go straight to the ideological questions themselves: What are political rights? What is the nature of man such that he desires to limit how government may use its power to shape choices and lives? In the concrete case, courts must decide whether a legislative policy or bureaucratic practice seems unintelligible in light of constitutional ideology. If no intelligible defense exists, the policy must fail. The articulation and defense of ideological principles will constitute the community. That electorally responsible politicians made a policy or approved a practice has no independent bearing on the ideological debate. Constitutional law must get on with the task of defining rights and duties. Until it does, we can have no justice, nor will we share a community, a brotherhood. On these, said the Reverend King, true peace depends.

This chapter will suggest that normative philosophy cannot help the justices resolve cases much more effectively than do theories of democratic legitimacy and interpretive self-restraint, but I do not by any means wish to reject it altogether. The final two chapters will show how the justices, practical people, may plausibly share a sympathy for normative philosophy and act upon it. They will not, however, get much direct help from philosophers. Philosophers are trained to doubt knowledge, to challenge the adequacy of another's assertion of truth. The person who seeks constitutional justice from philosophy will find disagreement, not ideological consensus. Again, the academic community seeks to discover truth, but truths are not discovered. They are part of the picture of society that philosophers and other artists help create. Perhaps this is what Wittgenstein was driving at when he reportedly wrote, "Philosophy is the disease of which it ought to have been the cure."

PRAGMATIC INSTRUMENTALISM

As jazz is America's unique contribution to the arts, it is also said that pragmatism is America's principal contribution to philosophy. Since Geertz, as well as Berger and Luckmann, would have us look within cultures for meaning, pragmatism would seem the logical place to begin. Robert Summers (1982) describes both that philosophy and the extent to which the American legal process implicitly deserves the label "pragmatic."

Charles S. Peirce, William James, and John Dewey lead the field of pragmatic philosophers. Pragmatism rejects, as classical versions of natural law would not, beliefs in a transcendent reality, a reality beyond experience. Summers (pp. 31–33) summarizes:

> . . . The world is what experience tells us. Ideas are to be tested in terms of the difference they make for possible human experience. Brute facts . . . of experience reveal a social reality that is highly plural. . . . Problems arise out of these [plural] contexts and relationships, and solutions are relative to and dependent upon them. These solutions do not and cannot, as in mathematics and in certain idealist philosophies, take the form of fixed relations between timeless essences. . . .
>
> . . . [S]omething is true if it proves to be useful in the appropriate human activity in the long run. . . .
>
> . . . This theory is predictivist and functionalist in character. . . . [T]he likely success of a use of law should be judged in terms of its probable effects.
>
> . . . Dewey generalized that "the task of philosophy is to clarify men's ideas as to the social and moral strifes of their own day. Its aim is to become so far as humanly possible an organ for dealing with these conflicts."
>
> . . . James . . . stressed that theorists should turn "away from abstraction . . . from verbal solutions, from bad a priori reasons, from fixed principles, closed systems, and pretended absolutes and origins." Instead, they should look "towards last things, fruits, consequences, facts."

Pragmatism counts as a normative theory because it defines the good and prescribes behaviors to attain it. Holmes put pragmatism's moral command in a nutshell when he urged us to "think things, not words." Unlike legal realism, which tried to describe actual judicial behavior, including its irrational, idiosyncratic, and unconscious side, pragmatism offers a test to differentiate better from worse decisions. Judges do not always behave pragmatically, but they ought to. The changefulness in constitutional law, the Court's disregard for the intent of the framers and particularly the Warren Court's commitment to the ideal of social progress, for example, seem to resemble something very much more like pragmatic theory than the fixed principles, closed systems, and pretended absolutes of the preservatives.

But Summers' book on close inspection says much more to and about legal scholarship than it does about judicial decisions. Summers allows students to appreciate the goals that law may more or less effectively serve in a modern society, for example, but in Summers' hands pragmatism does not itself suggest norms for deciding cases. As Michael Moore (1984) concluded, pragmatic instrumentalism is not really a theory of legal decision. Pragmatism foreshadows the scientific method, the logic of inquiry common to engineering and planning, not the resolution of disputes. For the Court to decide pragmatically, it would need openly to abandon the formalities of law. In drawing the boundaries separating the powers of competing units of government (for example, in the last chapter's Montana coal tax case), the Court sometimes appears to do so, but rarely with the pragmatists' devotion to the central importance of data and experience. The experimenter's or the engineer's attentiveness to the data and constant adjustment in light of consequences seem almost to contradict the idea of rights. While a few prominent American judges would have called themselves pragmatists if not extreme skeptics, e.g., Jerome Frank and Justice Holmes, pragmatism alone does not provide criteria for making and evaluating constitutional decisions because decisions rarely report an engagement with "brute facts" in anything like enough detail to permit assessment on completely utilitarian, consequential, or functional grounds. Judicial resources and traditions are incompatible with open-ended pragmatic inquiry.

Yet pragmatism, like jazz, does help constitute our culture. The "Brandeis brief" style of factual analysis is pragmatic. So, and this is most significant, is the judiciary's frequent justification of results in terms of projected social consequences of various choices. The justification for forbidding public school segregation in the District of Columbia was fully pragmatic (*Bolling v. Sharpe*, 1954). So was Justice Rehnquist's glib, seat-of-the-pants, functionalism, asserting in *Usery* that the consequences of imposing wage and hour conditions on state workers would cripple state sovereignty. Both *Bolling* and *Usery* are dramatic pragmatic performances.

I am driving at a subtle distinction that is central to my argument throughout the book, so let me restate it. Pragmatism has profoundly affected how we think about law, and I shall try to show in the last two chapters how it shapes our evaluation of the Court's constitutional lawmaking. But pragmatism does not provide a normative theory of rights or of legitimacy or of any other jurisprudential theory we have thus far covered. In fact, just the reverse. It is pragmatism's push away "from verbal solutions, from bad a priori reasons, from fixed principles, closed systems, and pretended absolutes and origins," that liberates law from the necessity of justifying itself in terms of grand theories at all. Pragmatism, it turns out, helps explain why constitutional history yields so little theory and so much constitutional change over time. Moreover, the pragmatic elements in our culture—elements that distinguish the United States from, say, modern Iran—may explain why we so easily accept judicial performances that make sense of our raw experience but that do not honor legal forms. Finally, as my quote from John Dewey (p. 9), the archetypal pragmatist, meant to hint, we communicate what we think our experience means aesthetically, through art. Thus I hope finally to show that an aesthetic theory of constitutional lawmaking is a direct extension of the American pragmatic tradition.

None of this would seem so mysterious or novel were it not that a "funny thing" happened to pragmatism's emphasis on the philosophical importance of experience itself. The emphasis on gaining meaning from experience transformed into a commitment to "objective" methods for observing and classifying experiences, the methods of science. What began as a device to free thought and action from absolutes has tended instead to reinforce an obligation to a different absolute, the absolute of "value-free" science. Much of the Court's fascination with balancing and its unconvincing use of the scientific metaphor of cost–benefit analysis in rights and liberties cases reveals this distortion of pragmatism. The logic of science has affected constitutional jurisprudence most directly through the "science" of economics, to which we now turn.

ECONOMIC MODELS OF CONSTITUTIONAL DOCTRINE

Almost in spite of itself, pragmatism encouraged people to believe that the social consequences of policy choices are knowable and, more important, susceptible to "objective" rather than "ideological" analysis. Modern microeconomic theory has, in the hands of professor Richard Posner (now a judge appointed by President Reagan to the U.S. Seventh Circuit), yielded an elaborate pragmatically rooted normative theory of law. The theory applies to legal policy regardless of source or subject matter, and it therefore has constitutional applications.

First assume that society seeks to maximize collective wealth, that is, to operate in an economically efficient fashion. Social transactions and the policies that make them possible—buying and selling of goods and labor, protecting personal property against taking by others, or the statutory prohibition of abortions, for example—make some people better off and others worse off. How are we to tell whether these transactions are socially efficient? Kaldor (1939) and Hicks (1939) suggest that a state of affairs is socially efficient if the "winners" compensate the losers out of their winnings and still show a profit.

The model is a standard justification for public policies that sustain a mix of private competitive choices (and private charity) with public welfare programs and the theoretically progressive tax systems that support them. But how can society determine the mix? Ronald Coase (1960) suggests that under three conditions: rational and cooperative behavior, no costs to making transactions, and no wealth effects, like monopolies, then private transactions simultaneously promote individual and collective welfare. Thus, according to Posner (1977 and 1981), legal policies should go no further than to mimic the market, for example, to minimize transaction costs and to compensate only insofar as the three conditions fail. In this perspective, public policy should confer "rights" on those who could win them in private competition anyway and concentrate on minimizing transaction costs in private affairs and facilitating social compensation. Thus a manufacturer who pollutes retains the right to pollute on the condition that those who suffer the pollution receive compensation.

The economic model for law and policy is what I have called a normative rather than a political theory. It is normative because it proposes substantive solutions to disputes that a societal norm—efficiency—assertedly justifies. It deems desirable and proper that policymakers of all sorts seek economic efficiency, and it states a normative justification for the supremacy of the principle of efficiency in comparison to other principles. Economic models appear to push the pragmatists's logic of inquiry to its end. Only economic models can realize the goals of social pragmatism because only the use of a standardized unit of value—money—permits building social policies from empirical observations. These models possess great appeal precisely because they claim, aesthetically, to have fit so many unconnected things together.

The criticisms of the economic approach, and its conclusion that much modern protection of civil liberties is socially inefficient, fall in three categories. First, and this is a standard criticism of much microeconomic theory, the knowledge that the policymaker must possess under the theory is not routinely obtainable. The policy cannot mimic the market consistently because lawmakers can never get information about what people would have done in a market free of transaction costs. Says Jules Coleman (1982, p. 1109n) in his extensive critique of the technical and normative underpinnings of Posner's argument, "Judgments about behavior under such conditions are counterfactual conditionals: i.e., X would have done Z if Y had obtained, but Y did not obtain. Determining the truth value of counterfactual conditionals is notoriously difficult. . . . Standard theory appears to preclude gathering the information necessary to insure that Posner's rule can be applied or, if it is applied, that its outcome is efficient."

Second, Alfred MacKay (1982) demonstrates that the economists universalize a model of human motivation that neglects a significant range of human wants altogether. Individuals, according to economic theory, desire categories of things by evaluating the characteristics of different items in the category. They order and weight their preference for these characteristics so as to make optimal choices. For example, they substitute margarine for something with very similar characteristics—butter—when the price differential exceeds the preferred value of the characteristics of butter over lower priced spreads.

No doubt this "categorical desire" explains much human decisionmaking, but MacKay notes that people also desire particular objects "without intervening lists of characteristics" (p. 444). These "direct desires" make no comparisons and admit no substitutions. Direct desire defines and motivates such wants as love, loyalty (including patriotism), justice, caring, and so on. It is the subject of divorce proceedings as well as of poetry and novels (p. 449). MacKay quotes Robert Nozick, a proponent of private choice and minimal governmental interference, as rather stumped by the implication of direct desire (pp. 449–450):

> Love is an interesting instance of another relationship that is historical, in that (like justice) it depends upon what actually occurred. An adult may come to love another because of the other's characteristics; but it is the other person, and not the characteristics, that is loved. The love is not transferable to someone else with the same characteristics, even to one who "scores" higher for those characteristics. And the love endures through changes of the characteristics that gave rise to it. . . . Why love is historical, attaching to persons in this way and not to characteristics, is an interesting and puzzling question.

The implications for constitutional law are fairly clear. In civil rights litigation, and for that matter in other forms of constitution-making illustrated by the drive for the Equal Rights Amendment, the want for justice is direct; it accepts no substitutions. Direct desire seems to characterize the desires of those who campaign for rights. Martin Luther King, Jr., and Anthony Lewis' portrait of Clarence Earl Giddeon (1964) come to mind. Such claimants do not thereby necessarily deserve to prevail. The point is rather that such people do *not* desire merely to trade their wants in private transactions. They want justice directly. If part of the Court's constitutional obligation requires it to justify to claimants why their claims lost, it will not do to tell them to trade instead for some other desire privately. In any case the reality of direct desires, even in the absence of individual or collective political efforts to achieve them, prevents utilitarian efficiency from claiming superiority as a premise for public policy.

Finally, Frank Michelman suggests, at the conclusion of his essay "Ethics, Economics, and the Law of Property" (1982), that the supposed virtues of private property and of market determinations of rights and welfare do not necessarily condemn legal or political intervention in private affairs. Suppose, for example, the premise that "every properly formed human individual places a supremely high value on secure command over his or her body, labor and product" (p. 33), or the premise that socially induced transactions, in contrast with freely chosen private transactions, produce in individuals a trustless "prisoner mentality." Such premises nevertheless "are potentially the grounds of significantly critical appraisal of the particular, detailed embodiment of private property we may from time to time observe in practice."

Michelman argues that social data, the stuff of journalistic and academic reports alike, tend routinely to raise doubts that any policy regime fully and finally reaches in practice the goals these private theories postulate. Politics must therefore keep the machinery for social improvement open:

> Suppose, for example, you think that the efficiency of private property is rooted in a species-characteristic need or craving for privacy and security of person, or for the experience of self-command over personal labor and product. Then if you observed a society in which measurable numbers of persons were selling rights over their bodies in exchange for the means of subsistence, or could live only by submitting to the productive direction of others, you would have to see that situation as problematic. Though it might turn out that there is no way, in this vale of tears, to make things on the whole any better, you would be committed to at least searching for some corrective. . . . (pp. 33–34)

Societies must, in other words, keep open and viable the institutional capacity to find authoritatively that, given any prescriptive and/or normative theory of private and public welfare, some realities don't fit the theory and must therefore change. To get back to the Court, a society is better off with an institution that, seeking to fit practice to theory, intervenes in controversial fashion, as in *Lochner*, than with an institutional scheme that denies itself the capacity to test the fit in the first place.

JOHN RAWLS AND NATURAL LAW

Economic models of constitutional law, at least as Posner treats them, are an interesting hybridized cross of natural law and pragmatism's empirical functionalism. The theory claims universality. It ignores competing claims and assigns labels to observations so that the observations appear to fit the theory. It is, like the preservative natural law approach, not intellectually skeptical. Yet this natural law-like theory strives to make operable pragmatic notions of social welfare. It has about it some of Dewey's nineteenth-century optimism, not Alexander Bickel's darker fear that social welfare and the public good are unknowable and undefinable save through Burke's political counting principle, that there is no truth in politics except political outcomes, and that we can only test the rightness of outcomes against the results of a vote count.

The chief virtue and appeal of avowedly natural law normative theories helps clarify what distinguishes legal from other ways of knowing and acting. Natural law expresses its answers as intelligibly and authoritatively right for the community. It meets Karl Barth's prescription for effective communication: to "speak with authority." The claim of legality makes conversations about legality and the political values behind legality possible. Elections supply the authority of legislative and executive acts, but impartial judges resort to the rightness of a theory of law for theirs. The desire that courts convince us of the *legal* goodness of the result motivated Wechsler's concern that decisions be based on neutral principles.

We tend to associate natural law with medieval, scholastic, and old-fashioned habits of thinking, but natural law often seems stylistically closer to what the Court does than does the style of utilitarian, welfare function analysis. Natural law assumes that, behind every written text, behind every human and therefore fallible effort to make positive law, rests an unwritten and yet superior text. Written texts—the *Holy Bible* or the Constitution—will reveal glimpses of the whole, but not the whole itself. When Justice Douglas announced a penumbral justification for striking down Connecticut's limits on birth control information and use, and when the Court held President Nixon immune from suit in tort for violating the civil rights of citizens, the Court justified the result by appeal to principles deeper than the document itself.

Thomas Grey (1975 and 1978) has argued that the framers were, for the most part, natural-law philosophers. As predecessors to pragmatism, they necessarily attempted to articulate a version of a substantively good society, but much of the federalists' (and especially Madison's) defense of the new Constitution grew directly out of their reading of political history and political experience.

This tension between the framers' familiarity with the natural law style and their glimpses of a pragmatic future exacerbates what I earlier called the "level of analysis" difficulty for hermeneutic interpreters. Perry and Sotirios Barber (1984) seem to say that the framers thought they came pretty close to expressing the nature of society in the document; therefore, we must honor their legal choices or justify straying from them. But I might argue that *Home Building and Loan* (the "mortgage moratorium" case), *Griswold* (the birth control case), or *Fitzgerald* (the presidential immunity case) are good decisions to the extent that they seek, as did the framers, to base policy on a vision of a society that is good because it adjusts policy to experience. Perry might call such decisions "noninterpretive" while I might call them interpretive on the deepest level because they struggle with deeper truths just as did the framers.

In any event, John Rawls (1971) has proposed the most widely discussed theory of justice in the last fifty years. It is very much a blend of natural law and pragmatism. Both Perry and Arthur S. Miller draw upon Rawls in justifying judicial defense of civil liberties, as have Dworkin (1978), Ackerman (1980 and 1984), and Michelman (1982). Readers already well versed in Rawls may skip this description, but given Rawls' influence, the uninitiated must master him. *A Theory of Justice* proposes "a" unitary theory of the just constitution. Richard Parker (1979) points out that the appeal of Rawls is that his eighteenth-century way of philosophizing not only justifies a good constitution; it justifies many of our actual constitutional choices.

Rawls first asks his readers to imagine the drafting of a constitution in the following "original position": All of the founders operate behind a veil of ignorance. They know neither their own personal status or wealth nor those of anyone else in their society. In these circumstances Rawls states that the founders will necessarily agree to two principles. The first principle grants equal right to the most extensive total system of basic liberties (freedom of conscience, freedom to vote, freedom to hold property) that can accommodate extending these liberties to all members of the community. The second principle permits social and economic inequalities that (a) work the greatest benefit to the least advantaged, and (b) attach wealth and status to offices and positions of power that are open to all members under a system of equality of opportunity to seek office.

The founders behind the veil would supplement these principles with priority rules of clarification and implementation. Thus: (a) The principles of justice are ranked in lexical order such that the first must be satisfied fully before moving to the second. Liberty, the first principle, can only be restricted for the sake of liberty. A restriction of liberty, through the drafting of a citizen for military duty or the incarceration of a citizen for a crime, must strengthen the system of liberty shared by all. (b) The second principle of social justice is superior to principles of economic efficiency, so that inequality of opportunity and inequality of wealth must enhance the opportunities and the wealth of those least well-off. The poor, in other words, must be better off in conditions of inequality than they would under conditions of pure equality.

Rawls then moves in stages from behind the veil, to drafting a workable constitution, then to legislating specifics, and finally to implementing legislative rules. Each stage reveals more about social conditions than the one before, but each is simultaneously bound to the agreements generated at earlier stages.

Does the U.S. Constitution seek the results Rawls prescribes? Rawls believes that the Constitution is limited primarily to the first principle, that is, the guarantee of liberty, and that the legislative stage must work out the achievement of equality. Richard Parker points out, however, that Rawls does not try to explain variations in the popularity or stability of different political regimes in historical experience. His is not a predictive theory. His book constructs a moral theory for the present. It gives considerable scope to social and political innovation and therefore accepts that today, given actual social conditions, it may be necessary to treat the inequality rules, the principle that differences must advantage the least advantaged, as part of a constitutional policy process in order to achieve them (pp. 274–275).

A Theory of Justice has not fared particularly well in the hands of other social philosophers. Rawls does not defend or justify the proposition that justice and fairness ought to be the overarching virtues of a community. Why not military strength? He does not show why the proposition that the position unanimously accepted behind the veil of ignorance is thereby necessarily the most fair structure, nor does he show why we should believe that practical people who do know their self-interest can and will nevertheless sustain a society composed of free and equal moral persons committed to a single common vision of justice. Robert Paul Wolff (1977) suggests that Rawls suffers from the same defect as the utilitarians, namely, that policymakers do not and cannot have access to the knowledge the theory requires in order to work. Indeed, I find persuasive the argument that Rawls' method asserts rather than proves functional relationships in precisely the same way the utilitarians do. Rawls has merely opted for "maximin" utilitarianism rather than some other analytical starting premise.

Richard Parker's excellent treatment of Rawls (1979) holds that these criticisms, entirely valid ones from the perspective of academic philosophy, miss the significance of the Rawls phenomenon precisely because they are academic. As Berger and Luckmann taught, academicians do not swim in the mainstream of political experience. Parker urges us to realize that Rawls has not attempted a deeply sophisticated academic theory at all. Rather, he has tried to perform for a political audience in the way Posner's utilitarian theory does not. Rawls has tried, in an admittedly culture-bound way, to reconstruct and order our own views of what our Constitution ought to mean. He has tried to build a picture of ourselves and our Constitution so that it may "function well." The significance of Rawls then, lies in how the audience of law students and the legal profession reacts. Parker asks: What if lawyers and students charged with responsibility for the state of society find that reading "the book strengthens their commitment to the Constitution by clarifying for them what they themselves believe about social justice"? What if reading the book becomes "an exciting reaffirmation of constitutional and personal values"? (Parker, p. 276). Parker finds his own students react in just this way, and he reemphasizes the breadth of the uses academic lawyers have made of Rawls. Parker finds Rawls exciting not because of his success as a theoretician but because of the enthusiasm of his intended audience.

Within a concededly relativistic framework, Rawls succeeds in Parker's view because he has expressed values that his audience cares about but had not previously organized and expressed. In his framework, ideas that had not fit together now seem to fit. He raised his audience's consciousness. Robert Nozick, who wrote *Anarchy, State, and Utopia* (1974) in rebuttal to Rawls, has received an equally enthusiastic response from a different audience, but for the same aesthetic reasons.

More important, although Parker limits his discussion of the point to footnotes elaborating the work of Bruce Ackerman (1977), Rawls appeals because his choice of language corresponds, unlike the symbolic (mathematical) analysis of economists, to the language of law, which is ordinary. Scientific and ordinary language battle for control over policy:

> With respect to the objective of legal analysis, for the Observer [the user of ordinary language], "[t]he test of a sound legal rule is the extent to which it vindicates the practices and expectations embedded in, and generated by, social institutions" (Ackerman, p. 12). The [scientific] Policymaker, on the other hand, aspires "to view seemingly disparate legal issues within a common framework

provided by a relatively small number of abstract and general principles that are assumed to permit the consistent evaluation of all the disputes the legal system is called upon the resolve" (pp. 11–12). . . .

. . . [T]he American constitutional tradition . . . bases its authority primarily on the fact that it is a reconstruction of our personal beliefs and of American constitutional values. It tries to systematize those beliefs and values but does not claim to provide a unique solution to every case. It has a strong and clear sense of the limits of abstract theory and leaves room for the important casuistical work of the application to hard cases which is the special skill of lawyers. And that casuistry is to be carried on in ordinary language. . . . (pp. 293–294)

In summary, academicians can justifiably reject natural law assertions as "unproven," or "inconsistent with other equally plausible alternative premises." But natural law models, even mutually inconsistent models such as Nozick's and the modest dignitarian theory posed by Mashaw (1983), which do not square with Rawls, nevertheless appeal because their rhetoric evokes for readers coherent visions. Rawls does care that our constitutional system functions well. In doing so he appeals to us because the norm of functional efficiency *is* very much a part of how we see our world. But Rawls appeals on a deeper level as well. Unlike Posner, Rawls constructs his theory upon a foundation that itself *is* an image of a political community: the constitution-makers who begin by deliberating behind a veil. I think, in other words, that Rawls has appealed because he has created for his audience a vision of a human group that actually achieves normative consensus. (See Ackerman, 1984, pp. 94–96.)

NATURAL LAW AND THE CONSTITUTION: TWO EXAMPLES

John Rawls' philosophy does not respond directly to the specific constitutional questions the modern Court faces. He saw his political philosophy as an extension into modern political life of Locke and social contract theory. This section describes two more specifically jurisprudential applications of Rawlsian analysis. I have chosen what I believe is the most elaborately developed prescriptive theory in two quite distinct academic communities, Ronald Dworkin the jurisprudent and Walter Murphy the political scientist. It is significant that both Dworkin and Murphy, although they start from quite different places, find it appropriate to describe constitutional interpretation with reference to the metaphor of "art." Their thought moves us toward my goal, which is to see constitutional lawmaking as a form of art. Legal decisions are no less artistic expressions than is a musical performance or the creation of a sculpture. They are not, in other words, merely metaphorically "like" art. I mean, furthermore, that the justice who composes a "good" opinion and a composer writing a "good" sonata will behave like each other, a point I elaborate in chapter seven.

Ronald Dworkin

Dworkin's *Taking Rights Seriously* (1977, revised ed. 1978) and "No Right Answer?" (1978a) oppose specifically the positivist legal model that most political scientists take for granted. For the Hartian positivist, law consists of rules and behavior promulgated and enforced by the state. The secondary rules through which people recognize the authoritative reality of the primary rules of behavior also count as law. A legal system at any historical moment affects and is affected by communal norms and political ideologies, but the fit is never perfect. The pushing and tugging of political interests and the structural imperfections and institutional agendas of courts and legislatures prevent some widely shared ideas from receiving legal recognition, and honor others long after their necessity and their political support have died.

In the positivist world, primary and secondary rules often fail to specify clear and unambiguous solutions to disputes involving new social facts and values that the law does not yet authoritatively recognize. In such cases, according to positivism, judges choose an answer to the dispute, but neither they nor anyone else will be able to justify that it is the right or the best answer possible. The solution and its justification mix legal and social values with factual assertions as the judge believes them.

Dworkin objects to this state of affairs in part on rather conventional grounds. Positivism justifies and legitimates judicial policymaking, which is undemocratic. Policy decisions that take from *B* to give to *A* belong in a representative and responsive institution. Judges do not make policy; they articulate principles, which differ from policy because they transcend pure distributional choices. Thus, when judges resolve a dispute they speak retroactively, and fairness requires judges to demonstrate that the law they impose existed "in principle" at the time the actions the parties dispute took place. Judicial decisions affect the distribution of wealth between the litigants. Judges may do so only by showing that prior law required it. Furthermore, judges do give answers. They do not declare ties. As an operational matter they care that their answer is right.

Dworkin illustrates with an example of a group of scholars studying a work of fiction, Dickens' *David Copperfield*. If the scholars assign themselves the task of answering collectively questions about David that the book itself does not answer clearly, they will each seek a right answer to the question. That answer, they will agree, will be that which best fits what the book does tell them about David (1978a, pp. 19–20). If judges or the Dickens scholars cannot agree in practice on a right answer, we will chalk that up to the limits of human rationality, but we will not nihilistically reject the belief that some answers are better than others and that a right answer is theoretically achievable.

Dworkin repeatedly insists that judges and lawyers will disagree about right answers (1978, pp. 81, 280), but that only demonstrates human imperfection.

Although it would take an omnicompetent Hercules to reach a demonstrably right answer—to demonstrate that answer X is the best fit with all the givens—judges, like scholars, still share an obligation to seek answers that fit most consistently the narrative material that governs their decision.

For Dworkin, the legal system's analog to the narrative facts given in *David Copperfield*—what Dickens *does* tell us about David—is the political tradition of a nation. This tradition contains principles that generate best-fit, and therefore "right," answers to hard cases. Dworkin rightly criticizes positivism at its most vulnerable point. Positivism does diminish the critical problem of impartiality, and it fails to deal with the possibility that a social enterprise cannot function without a belief that it possesses some objective identity. Dworkin calls for a commitment to the task of maintaining a sense of objective propriety and common purpose in law, without which things fall apart. Elements of principled reasoning and respect for articulate consistency are part of our legal tradition and its morality of justification now, and Dworkin therefore claims his jurisprudence, unlike positivism, is "truer to the complexity and sophistication of our own practices" (1978, p. 45).

Robert Grafstein (1983) believes that Dworkin's system is plausible precisely in the sense that mathematics has proven itself a viable enterprise. If people can do mathematics in the "real world," they can do law:

> We know that in mathematics any consistent set of axioms rich enough to encompass arithmetic will be unable to prove certain mathematical truths [e.g., Godel's theorem]. These truths represent hard cases in a rather extreme sense. Nonetheless, even these cases do not authorize mathematicians to look beyond mathematics for an answer—to exercise mathematical discretion—nor do they suggest that some particular statement that resists proof is for that reason unprovable. Dworkin merely insists on a parallel set of conclusions in the case of law.

Within this framework Dworkin defends Rawlsian rights, for example, the "right to equal concern and respect in the design and administration of the political institutions that govern" (1978, p. 180). However, the more interesting part of Dworkin's work tries to show how judges operating in the common law tradition can move from such fundamental constitutional principles to answer specific legal questions. Does the Constitution permit a state university to admit a portion of its entering class exclusively on the basis of race? Yes, Dworkin answers. Are laws imposing criminal sanctions on homosexual acts or the distribution of pornography constitutional? No. I paraphrase one path Dworkin follows to reach these conclusions.

In *Sweatt v. Painter* (1950), the Court struck down the policy of the State of Texas that required blacks to attend an all-black law school and barred them from the all-white University of Texas. Twenty years later, the University of

Washington Law School denied admission to a white student who was, on objective admissions criteria, more qualified than blacks whom the school admitted.

Dworkin finds the two cases distinguishable. Both schools can make ideal arguments. Texas can say that its segregation makes society more just; Washington can say that its quotas make society more just. But on these grounds Texas violates the constitutional principle of equality. Washington does not because seeking to improve the equal status and opportunity of disadvantaged blacks relative to more advantaged whites pursues the constitutional ideal.

Both schools can make utilitarian arguments. Washington can argue that increasing the number of black lawyers will reduce racial tension, which improves the welfare of nearly everyone in the community. Texas can say that the preferences for segregation are so strong that, despite the costs of segregation, the protection of Texans of both races from violent disruption through segregation maximizes their well-being.

Dworkin rejects the Texas utilitarian argument because it, unlike Washington's, depends on counting not a citizen's personal preference for his own enjoyment but an external preference for the assignment of goods to others. But, argues Dworkin, the principle of equal concern and respect cannot work in a system that lets external preferences count, for counting external preferences is a form of unequal double counting (1978, pp. 232–235). Similarly, laws punishing homosexual or other private or consensual sexual deviance seem necessarily to follow from a presumed double-counting.

Dworkin is a provocative writer, and I do not doubt that, like Rawls, he has nudged much legal thinking in a normative direction and away from false confidence in legalistic or scientific solutions to legal problems.[2]

However, Dworkin has not provoked the same "intersubjective zap" that Parker observed in the reaction to Rawls, and, the response of academic lawyers, many of whom embraced Rawls, has been hostile, from H.L.A. Hart himself through Ely to Critical legal scholars. There are, I think, two kinds of reasons why.

First, while we never flaw an argument for containing an unproved assertion—all arguments have to start somewhere—we can question whether a scholar has adequately defended his choice of a starting place. Many of what

---

[2] In response to my comments on *Soldano v. O'Daniels*, in *Reason in Law* (1984, chapter 5) Judge Kenneth Andreen of California wrote: "My guide has been Dworkin. . . . I indicated my reliance on principle in footnote 9 of *Soldano*. If this seems a timid way to call attention to my philosophy, I admit a reluctance to enter into the battle of heavyweights. . . . There is also a practical reason for avoiding extensive philosophical forays. An appellate justice writes with his colleagues in mind. Will I pick up a dissent? Or a concurring opinion? Or that ultimate put-down 'I concur in the result.'?" (Personal letter to the author dated July 12, 1984, quoted with permission.)

Dworkin takes as starting assertions cry out for justification. Dworkin does not defend the right to equal concern and respect from the elementary charge that the economic redistributions necessary to bring about true equality of concern and respect will interfere deeply with a citizen's liberty, his property, his family, and community relationships (Ackerman, 1984, p. 101).

And how does Dworkin deal with the universally accepted feature of common law that judges make law, or the confessions of many observant common law judges, Cardozo at their lead, that judges make law? Why not assume that legislatures and courts both act in part in principle and in part on policy grounds, and let the familiar political forces of separation of powers and checks and balances handle the fine points? And what of the retroactivity problem? In hard cases is it not true that *neither* side by definition could rely on the law at the outset? A hard case often "settles" law; it does not overturn previously clear commands. Finally, does not a Dworkinean judge's obligation to conform to the received tradition, including precedent cases in which judges have claimed to articulate principle and apply it in practice in the past, introduce in the psychology of decisionmaking a conservativizing element? Judges do not want to work any harder than the rest of us. Unless the *David Copperfield* model of "best fit" reasoning promises results fairly efficiently (and we shall see that Dworkin's method for asserting a "best fit" does not really generate consensus at all), judges will parse the prior cases urged upon them because these will offer the most efficient measure of the best fit.

Dworkin does not respond fully to these criticisms, but the second and deeper problem is internal. The trouble with Dworkin, as with Ely, who also met a highly critical, if energetic, academic fate, is that the parts don't fit. Dworkin is too slippery. The *David Copperfield* model of getting theoretically best answers to unknowns from the best fit to what is known will not work in practice. Scholars will disagree about what constitutes the evidence that needs fitting in the first place. For example, in the search for an answer some might argue that, since we know this novel to be the most autobiographical of all Dickens' novels, we should admit as relevant evidence about David facts about Dickens' own life. Others might refuse to consider information external to the book, and their disagreement would put us right back in the middle of the interpretivism debate.[3]

Or consider, ironically if you choose, Ely's criticism (1983, and see also H.L.A. Hart, 1979) of Dworkin's external/personal preference distinction.

1. In what sense is the Texas policy mandating segregated law schools based on external preferences? Is it not fair that in the segregated south, whites preferred personally to associate with other whites? If this counts as external preference because it is based "deep down" on racist feelings, how is the judge to know and distinguish one state from the other? (Ely, p. 963).

---

[3] For a description of judges as dramatic actors, see Charles Dickens, *David Copperfield*, Part 1, chapter 23.

2. Dworkin grants that Washington's admissions practice may also depend on the external preference that blacks should have black lawyers. If the utilitarian argument also holds that Washington's policies will reduce racial tension, how are those distinguishable from Texas' belief that segregation will do so? The only difference lies in the difference between the two ideal arguments, but at the ideal level Dworkin, on second glance, begs the question. The question is not whether racist policies are constitutional; they are not. The question is whether the equal protection clause permits affirmative action policies that disadvantage members of majority groups. Dworkin merely asserts the answer (p. 964).

3. Regarding the distinction between economic and noneconomic liberties claims (*Lochner* versus laws against sexual deviance, for example), Ely, citing Sager, points out that the era of progressive reform in the late nineteenth and early twentieth centuries, which the Court opposed, was heavily polluted with the external preferences of humanitarian reformers (p. 966). Perhaps *Lochner* correctly rebuked the bakers' hours statute because it was improperly based upon the external preferences of social reformers.

4. Unlike laws that impose racial segregation or other racially based restrictions on liberty, do not laws prohibiting homosexual contact seek to encourage assimilation into majoritarian society? If so, does not the real difference, as a practical matter of judicial decision, necessarily boil down to a judge's hunches about which policy motives were really evil "deep down"? If so, Dworkin has pulled a neat trick. He has disguised, in terms of ideal principles, a system whereby liberal judges can strike down policies based on their personal preferences about good and evil.

Ely states many more examples of chains of Dworkinian logic which, elegant in themselves, directly contradict other Dworkinian chains. This form of argument, which prompted Professor Fish to title a critique of Dworkin "Working on the Chain Gang" (1982), seriously limits Dworkin's helpfulness in the quest for sharable standards for evaluating constitutional law decisions. We must, however, return to Dworkin, for in the article that provoked professor Fish, Dworkin held that constitutional interpretation had much in common with aesthetics.

The dialogue that Dworkin and Fish began in the *Texas Law Review* has gone through at least one additional cycle. Dworkin subtitled his reply to Fish "Please Don't Talk About Objectivity Any More" (1983, p. 287), to which Fish responded in an essay titled "Wrong Again" (1983). Dworkin had originally offered an "aesthetic hypothesis" of interpretation: "[A]n interpretation of a piece of literature attempts to show which way of reading the text reveals it as the best work of art" (1982, p. 531). Interpretation for Dworkin explains but cannot change the work: "The text provides one severe constraint in the name of identity: all the words must be taken account of and none may be changed to make 'it' a putatively better work of art" (1982, p. 531). Fish's response shows the incompatibility of Dworkin's position with modern hermeneutic theory, and in passing provides another compelling literary analogue to constitutional lawmaking.

Dworkin argued that Shakespeare might have written a better *Hamlet* if he had made the protagonist "a more forceful man of action," but this does not license a performance that changes Hamlet into a forceful man. That would be, says Dworkin, like reading an Agatha Christie murder mystery as if it were a treatise on the philosophy of death. To treat Christie as a treatise on death would, says Dworkin, make all but a few sentences of the book meaningless (p. 532). To bolster the point, Dworkin offers a retooled version of the *Copperfield* argument. If we asked a group of authors to write successive chapters of a novel, each would feel increasingly constrained by what had come before, so that the author of the final chapter would have virtually no discretion at all. Judges working within a legal tradition should conceive their role in "last chapter" terms.

Fish (1983) responds that of course it is possible to read Christie as a treatise on death *without* changing it in the fashion Dworkin proposes. He would agree with director and producer Tyrone Guthrie's point, made in the epigraph for my preface, that there are fifteen different ways to play Hamlet correctly. Fish describes how in 1963 Christopher Ricks changed decades of scholarly consensus to the effect that Milton's *Paradise Lost* did not attain the level of coherent psychological plausibility that the novel as literary form later developed. Ricks showed that Milton did attain that level, but he did not change *Paradise Lost*; he claimed merely to have justified as plausible an alternative reading of the same text.

Dworkin's distinction between explaining and changing must assume that there is a concrete, indisputable, and immutable essence in the text itself. This holding runs Dworkin directly into the wall of postpositivist philosophy. If the things we think we understand come from the continual mediation of ourselves and our environments, then we cannot distinguish explaining and changing. Every explanation is a potential change.

Fish states that the distinction between explaining and changing will not hold up

> because organization, style, and figure are interpretive facts—facts which, rather than setting limits to the elaboration of a reading, emerge and become established in the course of that very elaboration. In short, that which is to be the measure of change is itself subject to change and is, therefore, not sufficiently stable to underwrite the distinction between changing and explaining. (1983, p. 302)

The "explanation" that *Paradise Lost* is psychologically coherent, like a novel, arises in part from changing experiences with novels and with changes in psychological knowledge, but these intervening experiences hardly undermine Ricks' persuasiveness. On the contrary, if interpretations persuade in part because the articulation of a new fit clarifies and sharpens a reader's understanding of self and text, then the good interpretation pays deliberate attention to both elements.

Readers who do not yet grasp Fish's merger of changing and explaining might examine a recent series of books in which a group of authors did in fact serially compose chapters in what they claimed was a single narrative world. I refer to the *Thieves' World* fantasy series, edited by Robert Asprin. In the essay "Things the Editor Never Told Me" at the conclusion of *Shadows of Sanctuary*, Lynn Abbey, one of the authors, described serial composition as liberating rather than constraining, quite the opposite of Dworkin's assumption: "Each set of stories brings new oddments of human behavior, new quirks of character that the authors wouldn't dare put in a universe for which he or she was solely responsible" (Abbey, 1981, p. 335).

The Dworkin–Fish dialogue may seem like another academic arabesque, but it is not. I prefer Fish's position, but not because it is more elegantly or consistently argued, or because I believe I could analyze *Murder on The Orient Express* as a treatise on death (though I am in fact confident that, with a loose definition of a "treatise," I could). Again, I believe the historical evidence of judicial action fits Fish far better than Dworkin. In refusing to turn back the clock in *Brown*, in rewriting the contract clause to accommodate police powers, in accepting the psychologically coercive and conformist consequences of authoritatively endorsed daily school prayers, in moving away from Justice Bradley's sense of the legal status of women, the Court changes the Constitution no more or less than Ricks changes Milton. If the Court had sanctioned authoritative prayer or the continuation of segregation in public schools, the results would combine explanation and change just as much as the actual decisions did. To reject the relevance of experience in adjudication is as potentially changeful as to accept it.

One more observation about Fish's critique: He devotes the greater part of his article to demonstrating the slipperiness of Dworkin's use of words, that "the terms of the discussion and the levels on which it is proceeding [in Dworkin] are continually shifting, although no shift is ever announced" (p. 308). This description aptly describes the argumentative style of typical Court opinions. The similarity cautions us to remember that the Court, like Dworkin, creates even in its most strictly interpretive moments.

Walter Murphy

On the second page of Walter Murphy's "The Art of Constitutional Interpretation" (1978) he writes:

> If a judge wants to persuade others, he or she should write intelligibly convincing opinions. To do so, he or she must display not only literary elegance but also internally consistent reasoning that can be explained and justified not only for the decision in a particular case but also in terms of general principles of jurisprudence.

Murphy builds a natural-law theory almost exclusively out of the historical materials of law and politics in action. Murphy does not claim to develop a systematic theory of constitutional jurisprudence. Murphy says, as much through his style as his substance, that "ordinariness," not "universality," is the most appropriate dictionary definition of the "natural" in natural law. (This, I assume, is the meaning of the words "all natural ingredients" on food package labels.)

Murphy accepts at the outset that general principles cannot be neutral in the distributive sense; "rather, the real questions are who or what will benefit and how" (p. 131). This fact makes it all the more imperative that judges work out a constitutional jurisprudence such that they can justify the allocations of benefits that their decisions inevitably influence. And to do that, judges must resolve the identity of what they interpret: a social contract, a statute for government made in extraordinary session, or "a symbol of national unity stating societal goals, restricting and distributing power, establishing procedures to set more specific goals, and creating institutions and processes to determine and enforce duties and rights, costs and benefits, and settle disputes" (p. 132).

Murphy reads the legacy of John Marshall as necessarily putting us somewhere near the last of the three definitions, but he points out that, in doing so, we answer no important questions. The framework does not tell us whether or how to lexically order the objectives of a symbolic constitution. The justices, of course, have never collectively answered these definitional and lexical questions. Individual choices range from Frankfurter's procedural functionalism, which minimized judicial protection of rights, to Frank Murphy's belief that the law "knows no finer hour than when it cuts through formal concepts and transitory emotions to protect unpopular citizens against discrimination and persecution" (p. 133).

The Court's failure to answer officially these fundamental questions reveals, says Murphy, the most obvious fact about the constitutional scheme. It does not create a democracy. Rather, it creates a "free government," or if one prefers, a constitutional democracy that marries two incompatible norms, freedom and majoritarianism. Judicial review in this context cannot be any more deviant than a U.S. Senate that is "malapportioned" or staggered congressional and presidential elections or an electoral college. "[I]t does not help and probably hurts whatever progress can be made in the art of constitutional interpretation for judges—or scholars—to pretend that the Constitution is something very different from what it is" (pp. 134–135). It is, in short, a political compromise with limited potential to generate legal absolutes.

On first thought we might expect that a compromise constitution would rule out appeals to a higher natural law. But if we define natural law as an attempt to condense and give meaning to ordinary political experience, then it is precisely the Constitution's competing aspirations that necessitate appealing to natural law. Murphy catalogs the Court's appeals to the "spirit" rather than the letter of the document in every era of constitutional history. *Ex parte Young* (1908), which effectively read the Eleventh Amendment out of the

Constitution by permitting federal courts to hear suits by private citizens against state officials as individuals for actions taken or threatened in their official capacity, highlights Murphy's chronology of "higher law" rulings (pp. 136–138).

Murphy unhesitatingly accepts appeals to the spirit rather than the letter for these reasons.

1. The founders were quite familiar with Coke, Blackstone, and the natural-law tradition in common law. References in the Constitution's Preamble "to terms such as 'liberty' and more especially 'justice' were not likely to have been meaningless to educated people during the Enlightenment, when natural law and natural rights were commonplace concepts" (p. 138).

2. Locke was of course the most immediate source of constitutional philosophy, but Locke believed quite explicitly in natural rights that existed apart from government action. Government "secures," it does not define or confer, rights. The Ninth Amendment, like the Preamble, presumably expressed for its time a fundamental commitment to natural law.

3. Modern resistance to natural law theories does not arise from technically superior historical research into the mindsets of the framers. Rather, modern realists have, postfounding, come to accept science's fact–value dichotomous framework as the only correct way of knowing. The fact–value distinction forces interpreters to discount as value anything that they cannot prove conclusively, a sure formula for judicial literalism.

4. Despite good reasons why judges might abandon natural-rights thinking, rights models have played an active role in much modern constitutional adjudication. Economic substantive due process methodologically resembles natural-law thinking, even if its substance perverted traditional natural law's preoccupation with individual liberty and dignity. Natural-law impulses underlay Justice Black's superficial commitment to literalism. He believed in incorporation, and no modern justice appears to deny the doctrine that due process includes unspecified rights "implicit in the concept of ordered liberty."

The opinions of Chief Justice Warren and Justices Douglas, Stewart, and Brennan embody, sometimes powerfully, natural-law principles, but I trust by now Murphy's mission, and mine in covering him at length, has become clear. Murphy ends where Rawls, Perry, Dworkin, and other defenders of the Warren Court end, but by a much more natural and ordinary route. I mean to endorse here the elegance of the route more than the conclusion, for the route looks directly to the world and both finds and creates there a coherent and untortured vision of the lessons of constitutional history. Murphy's reference to the art of interpretation in his title means, I think, to convey that questions of interpretation are questions of fit. The decider simultaneously discovers and creates the fit as he goes. Murphy cannot make a fit that excludes judicial protection of individual dignity. Here are excerpts from his concluding section (pp. 155–159). Note particularly how Murphy persuades his audience. He combines statements of seemingly undeniable fact with unabashed rhetorical passion:

> I . . . believe that the Constitution contains a hierarchy of values. First, substantive goals take precedence over process. Indeed, a strict positivist might note that the preamble lists only substantive not procedural goals. . . .
>
> Second, among the Constitution's substantive values, I believe the most fundamental has become human dignity. . . .
>
> Because I agree that the framers—and Jefferson, and Marshall, and Lincoln—put national unity ahead of the dignity of blacks (at least), I do not rest my case on original intent, but on the internal logic of the polity as the framers built it and as it and its values have developed since 1787. The preamble's goals of liberty and justice were not mere rhetorical flourishes, but meaningful articles of hope. . . .
>
> The Constitution's commands for intricate procedures for criminal prosecution, the Warren Court said in 1966, force government "to respect the inviolability of the human personality." "The basic concept," a plurality of the Burger Court repeated a decade later, underlying the prohibition against cruel and unusual punishments, is "the dignity of man." Affirmation of human dignity bursts out of the Thirteenth Amendment and the abolitionists' long agitation and stern preachments about natural law, natural rights, and the wrath of God. The Fourteenth Amendment's four great clauses . . . speak the same language, though in more measured tones. The Fifteenth and Nineteenth Amendments' proscription of discrimination against the rights of blacks and women to vote reaffirms their equal share in humanity. . . .
>
> The linkages with doctrines of natural law and right are obvious. The "unassailable dignity of the individual" has been at the heart of natural law and right since the early Sophists debated Socrates. . . .
>
> . . . In essence [dignity] means that the individual, as a person, is the basic unit of legal—and moral—accounting; that government must respect all persons, in Kant's terms, as ends rather than treat them as means; and that each person has equal claim to that respect, not because government so deigns but because we share a common humanity. Along with Thomas Jefferson and William O. Douglas, religious writers would chorus that that dignity must be respected because it has been given by God. It is sufficient for a nontheologian to note that to degrade a fellow human, to strip him of dignity or honor, is to degrade oneself. . . .
>
> . . . Allowing judges to interpret a constitution is inherently risky, but so is an effort to maintain a polity based on both constitutionalism and democracy. The risks involved become attractive only when one considers the alternatives.

In 1979 Walter Murphy published a successful novel titled *The Vicar of Christ*. One way to distinguish Murphy from Dworkin is that while Dworkin philosophizes about the similarities between constitutional interpretation and literary criticism, Murphy writes literature. In this respect Murphy has the advantage, for what he does comes much closer to what the Court should do in its opinions, that is, tell a persuasive, dramatically fictionalized, story.

I do not want to overemphasize the differences between Dworkin and Murphy. Substantively, they agree about which rights courts should protect. Both reach this shared conclusion by insisting that the protection of human dignity best unifies, explains, or fits together the wide range of our political experiences as a nation. The difference between them is the difference between their audiences. Dworkin wants to persuade constitutional scholars. He naturally uses the language that this audience shares, that of deductive theoretical elegance. I suspect my preference for Murphy's more descriptive and poetic style has a great deal to do with my training in, and professional identity with, political science. The elements in Dworkin's argument, for example, the external/internal preference distinction, do not seem to me to fit political experience as he claims they do. Yet I cannot help believing that Murphy's audience, more than Dworkin's, resembles the audience that attends to the goodness of the Constitution itself. The task is to restore ways in which lawyers may construct for clients political visions in which the client's actions and desires make moral sense, ways for trial court judges to convince losing litigants of the fairness of the result, and ways by which students of constitutional law may organize the moral meaning of what they read. Those ways are, I suspect, more Murphy's than Dworkin's.

THE CRITICAL LEGAL STUDIES MOVEMENT REVISITED

I wrote in the previous chapter that the Critical movement is the most significant development in American jurisprudence in fifty years.[4] In this section I want to review the common denominators that unite Critical thought. I believe Critical scholarship has much appeal, but not for its radical substance. I believe Critical scholarship appeals because it is a direct extension of the pragmatic tradition I described near the beginning of this chapter. It insists on dealing as directly as possible with the raw experiences of political life. Its attentiveness to political experience in turn allows it to develop aesthetically appealing legal theories. Above all, Critical scholars insist that if we merely describe the world around us we shall find gross *misfits* between what we observe and "facts" on which conventional legal theories rest.

---

[4] The significance of any movement depends on its audience's perception that it has changed basic paradigms. Fifty years ago legal realism persuaded its audience to treat as fundamentally true Holmes' notion that law is what judges do in fact, a premise on which decades of ensuing "judicial behavior" research in the social sciences are based. The Critical movement makes Holmes' implicit political premise explicit. Law is inseparable "from moral, economic and political discourse" (Kennedy, 1976, p. 1724). "[L]aw in a class society is a form of incomplete hegemony of the ruling class" (Tushnet, 1979, p. 1346). The Marxist elements in much critical thought no doubt limit its acceptability, just as preservatism's reliance on academically unpopular notions of linguistic and historical objectivity limits its audience. The future of Critical studies depends not on its truth but on how effectively its adherents sell it to a non-Marxist audience.

The first common denominator is the movement's attentiveness to the nature of interpretation itself. Robert Gordon and Mark Tushnet, legal historians, have helped draw attention to the importance of hermeneutics in constitutional jurisprudence. As Gordon (1981) put it:

> The old text will be rendered almost wholly archaic if it can be shown to embody a set of conceptions—about human nature, property, virtue, freedom, representation, necessity, causation, and so forth—that was a unique configuration for its time and in some ways strikingly unlike what we believe to be our own. (p. 1021)

Hermeneutic appreciation requires scholars to try to see the world independent from and liberated from any conventional frameworks. We saw in the last chapter how Robert Gordon described the movement in such terms. Roberto Unger's review of the movement put it this way: "Our conventional legal tradition exists in a cultural context in which, to an unprecedented extent, society is understood to be made and imagined rather than merely given" (1983, p. 579). Duncan Kennedy's analysis of the hidden structure of *Blackstone's Commentaries* (1979) asserts that Blackstone contrived artificial legal distinctions designed to support and justify the authority held by the Crown and the Anglican church in England. Each of these writings accepts the pragmatic prescription to move beyond conventional forms to identify the consequences of observed social conditions.

The necessity that scholars transcend legal forms and methods gives rise to the second apparent common denominator, which opponents of the movement designated as "nihilism" or "trashing." Duncan Kennedy has provoked much antagonism and soul-searching among the Harvard Law School faculty by denouncing the accepted methods of legal education wholesale. His performances have been indeed dramatic (see Kairys, 1982), but they are nihilistic only from the "non-Critical" perspective. If we privately know that legal policies are not value-free or objective in the conventional senses of those terms, then we must reject a liberal theory that requires the pretense of objectivity in teaching. The teacher whose highest goal is to remain neutral, to avoid advocating his own point of view, and who thereby tries to teach the law objectively, will only reinforce ill-fitting wisdoms (Tushnet, 1981a).

This second common Critical denominator does not trash, it takes criticism seriously. Critical analyses state a conventional argument, disassemble (or deconstitute) it to reveal its empirical assertions and causal assumptions, and then show how phenomena in the world we claim commonly to know refute the factual assertions and/or demonstrate the incoherence of the argument. It is impossible not to prefer some ends to others. We may desire that judges in some circumstances overturn offensive acts of other branches of government, we may desire restraints on judicial power, and we may desire that adjudication be impartial in the value-free sense. But we simply cannot have all three. The resolution of the problem of judicial power within our political framework requires choices based on values. It cannot be value-free.

Although not a universal characteristic of the movement, "playfulness" characterizes many of its writings. Aviam Soifer (1981), for example, offers a framework for evaluating the Court in terms of the role played by Humphrey Bogart in the celebrated movie, *Casablanca*: "We expect the Court to be tough and neutral and above the fray—but we also want it to come through in the crunch." He then proceeds to show how the Court's mechanistic reasoning in *City of Mobile v. Bolden* (1980), which upheld an electoral system in previously segregated Mobile, Alabama that substantially underrepresented black voters, fails the three pronged *Casablanca* test. To Justice Stewart's reasoning in that case he applies the label, "Dada" (p. 393).

In a similar vein (and in the same symposium issue) Mark Tushnet (1981, pp. 424–425) answered the question, "Well, yes, but how would *you* decide the *X* case?" with the following:

> My answer, in brief, is to make an explicitly political judgment: which result is, in the circumstances now existing, likely to advance the cause of socialism? Having decided that, I would write an opinion in some currently favored version of Grand Theory. For example, I happen to like the political obstacles theory, probably because it has an air of scientism and realism about it. So I would write a political obstacles opinion. . . . [But] I am not in a position to do what my theory suggests . . . and . . . the whole point of the approach is to insist that there are no general answers, but only tentative ones based on the exact conjuncture of events when the question is asked. The answer I give today would not necessarily be the one I would give were I a judge, for that fact itself would signal that political circumstances had changed drastically.

I suggest in the final chapter why "playfulness" may be essential to good theory.

Finally criticism, we often hear said, is cheap, but the Critical movement is not cheap because it asserts the positive value of fittedness as a criteria of goodness. The failure of conventional argument is not so much its conservativism as its inability to generate a product that is internally consistent and plausibly fitted to our experience, even treated entirely on its own terms. This is why I have taken some pains to show how the preservatives, Ely, Perry, and Dworkin, whose scholarly prescriptions differ widely, fail for the same reasons. It is not that each fails to correspond with the objective reality. Rather, each offers a theory that patently fails to fit on its own terms. Rawls, Murphy, and Tushnet, though they do not arrive at identical conclusions, present aesthetically more attractive theories because each on its own terms creates a better fitted, more coherent, and hence more believable vision of a constitutional world.

The Critical movement has demonstrated the emperor's nakedness. But why, exactly, has it received so much attention? Thurman Arnold anticipated many of the movement's criticisms in 1935. He was for decades senior partner of as influential a law firm as the Washington establishment knew. The movement cannot claim originality. Its roots go deep into legal realism and political jurisprudence. Nor has it yet offered politically attractive alternatives. The super-liberalism of extended autonomy, dialogue, and a structure of no structure preaches only to converted revolutionaries.

The movement attracts attention, I think, for two reasons. First it has found an audience to perform to, which is the audience of new legal educators that has abandoned the presumption that legal expertise differs from social, economic, and political discourse. Second, and more important, the Critical scholars focus their attention directly on the absence of fittedness, the palpable incoherence, in conventional jurisprudence and in much work of the Court itself. The movement insists above all on taking pragmatism seriously. One who thinks things, not words, could not possibly resolve the liberties claim of a prisoner by deferring, as Justice Rehnquist did in *Wolfish*, to the greater institutional competence of prison officials to make such judgments. The movement is deeply tied to a culture that is wary of slogans and ideologies. It is, I think, where pragmatic philosophy had to go once the shortcomings of strictly utilitarian analysis became clear.

AESTHETICS AND CRITICAL THEORY: AN ILLUSTRATION

The critical approach attends to the aesthetic character of law. Its criticisms move us closer to an aesthetic theory of constitutional jurisprudence. Because I think the contrast between conventional and critical scholarship starkly reveals differences in the internal consistency of the fit these two approaches create, I describe at some length a scholarly exchange, here between Owen Fiss, a sophisticated conventional theorist, and Paul Brest, a Critical scholar.

Owen Fiss falls into fewer traps than most of the liberal interpretivists. His 1982 article, "Objectivity and Interpretation," begins, "Adjudication is interpretation. Adjudication is the process by which a judge comes to understand the meaning of an authoritative legal text and the values embodied in that text" (p. 739). But Fiss is not a naive preservative. He knows the hermeneutic truth that interpretation moves toward knowledge through an interaction between interpreter and text. Although judges can and sometimes do interpret social conditions—the differential distribution of wealth between black and white Americans, for example—instead of the legal texts, judges should not do so. They should limit themselves to interpreting legal texts, not economic and public opinion data. For Fiss, the only alternative to this mode of interpretation is the nihilistic rejection of any truth or value in adjudication or politics.

Nihilism, according to Fiss, permeates the Critical movement, and unnecessarily so. Critical scholars condemn what is instead inevitable in law. Judges must say what the law is, must claim to reach right answers. Fiss treats the Constitution as no less interpretable than other documents. It is more general and comprehensive than a sonnet or a contract, but no more so than an epic poem or the Internal Revenue Code, whose interpretability no one doubts (pp. 742–743). For Fiss, constitutional interpretations, like any other interpretation, are objective, not because they are "wholly determined by some source external to the judge," an impossibility, but because judicial choices are "constrained" (p. 744). Procedural disciplinary rules developed by the courts themselves, and the rules the larger interpretive community recognizes as authoritative, constrain discretion sufficiently that we may call it objective, for the objective decision openly seeks to conform to these audience standards for judgment. Judgment is bound to its culture.

Fiss believes that the audience that constrains is primarily the audience of fellow judges, all of whom are pledged to uphold the rule of law (pp. 747–748). They may disagree in their interpretations. Indeed, given the interactive, double-bind nature of interpretation, their disagreements should not disturb us. The game permits disagreements without doubting objectivity.

This model of objectivity allows us to distinguish legally acceptable results from "correct" results. *Plessy* and *Brown* may both have been acceptable in their time, yet only one is correct. Judged by the internal procedural rules constraining legal decisions, the former passes, even if it fails badly by the moral, political, and religious standards society might apply to the problem.

Law, like moral theory, prescribes behavior, which is why we easily slip from the legal to the external or moral viewpoints. Sometimes the two overlap, as they do in Rawls' original position. Negotiating behind veils of ignorance mirrors closely the internal requirement of judicial independence, the judge's obligation to listen, his personal responsibility for the decision, and the requirement that he justify the decision in terms of a principle that applies beyond the case itself. But unlike moral decisions, legal decisions are binding. They have force and authority behind them, which is why judges must limit themselves to deciding within the legal system's rules.

Occasionally, as in the implementation of *Brown*, the Court may have to act prudently and instrumentally, but it is critically important for the law to refrain from calling such instrumental implementation "law" at all. Better to deny that this phase of lawmaking has precedential force than to fake the legal issues through warped and unfaithful readings of the text itself (pp. 760–762). Critical nihilism

> calls into question the very point of constitutional adjudication; it threatens our social existence and the nature of public life as we know it in America; and it demeans our lives. . . . It must be combated and can be, though perhaps only by affirming the truth of that which is being denied—the idea that the Constitution embodies a public morality and that a public life founded on that morality can be rich and inspiring (p. 763).

Paul Brest's response (1982) asks whether Fiss makes sense with himself, and whether the sense he makes fits what we know about the legal and social world. If not, and according to Brest he does not, Fiss fails the aesthetic test. I quote directly (pp. 766–773) to underscore the centrality of the criteria of internal and external fit in Brest's critique:

Professor Fiss . . . acknowledges that adjudication requires the interpretation of inherently indeterminate materials. . . . But Professor Fiss argues that objective interpretation is nonetheless possible.

Central to Professor Fiss' argument is the concept of an "interpretive community," put forward by the literary theorist, Stanley Fish. . . . Fish aligns himself with a group of post-structuralist literary theorists, including the so-called "deconstructionists," who—to oversimplify but not understate—regard interpretation more as a process of fabrication than of discovery. But Professor Fiss removes Fish's concept from its destabilizing surroundings and fashions it into a bulwark. . . .

I am puzzled by the sources or materials that Fiss would allow a court to use for constitutional interpretation. His judge must "read the legal text, not morality or public opinion, not, if you will, the moral or social texts. . . .

The Court has commonly interpreted social morality . . . in articulating public values [citing interpretations of the prohibition against cruel and unusual punishments and *Brown*].

. . . His Court's task is to articulate "public values," and our "understanding of such values—equality, liberty, property, due process, cruel and unusual punishment—is necessarily shaped by the prevailing morality."

How can a court perform the essential constitutional task without interpreting the social as well as the written text? Perhaps Professor Fiss means that the social text, while inevitably and even appropriately present, ought not to be the *conscious* object of interpretation. But . . . [s]uppressing consciousness of social values, far from constraining the judges' discretion, gives them free rein—unchecked by self-scrutiny and the criticism of others.

. . . Constitutional interpretation is fraught with indeterminacies of two sorts. First, even when we have a general notion of the aims of a constitutional provision—the conditions it seeks to bring about or the mischiefs it seeks to remedy—we confront uncertainties about the appropriate *level of generality* on which to articulate those aims. Does the equal protection clause . . . only prohibit discrimination against blacks, does it protect minorities other than blacks, does it prohibit race discrimination against whites, does it prohibit unfair discriminations based on characteristics besides race? Second, our texts, histories and traditions are seldom univocal, but often include competing and conflicting values. . . .

Such indeterminacies inhere in any interpretive enterprise. They pervade constitutional adjudication: The issues are brought before courts precisely because the written text is not determinative and the social text is ambiguous—because society, and its individual members, are conflicted. Consider, for example, the issues in *Bakke* and in litigation over the death penalty and abortions.

. . . Legal interpretation seeks to resolve ambiguity. A court faced with a constitutional challenge to an anti-abortion law may not stop after it has identified our moral, social or psychoanalytic conflicts around the issue. It must decide the case. . . . Even a finding of indeterminacy is, in effect, a final judgment delineating the bounds of what is and is not (legally) known.

The institution of constitutional interpretation is comparatively monolithic. . . .

When combined with the authoritativeness of legal interpretation, the demographic composition of our "interpretive community" presents normative problems in a democratic polity. The members of the legal interpretive community are mostly white, male, professional, and relatively wealthy. However humble their backgrounds, they are members of a ruling elite.

. . . [W]hen Professor Fiss' judges interpret "our" values they speak with an authority that can affect the lives of murderers and victims, of women and their unborn children, of black applicants who benefit from preferential admissions programs and whites who are excluded from them.

This might seem less of a problem if constitutional interpretation were the kind of technical process that determinist commentators assert it should be. But hopes for scientific objectivity in legal interpretation are on a par with the fantasy of a single, objective reading of *Hamlet* or of Balinese culture. Therefore, one must confront the question of the relationship, if any, between the composition of the dominant legal interpretive community and the outcomes of its interpretations. . . .

Indeed, I imagine that not only particular interpretations but the *interpretive rules themselves* respond to our backgrounds and experiences. The very notion of constitutional adjudication as hermeneutics—a notion shared by both Professor Fiss and his commentators—is "sophisticated," not just in the sense of being complex, but in what the Random House dictionary gives as the first definition: "altered by education, experience, etc. so as to be worldly-wise". . . .

. . . I imagine . . . that the very sophistication of our rules perpetuates the tradition of the "mysterious science of the law" by making constitutional law inaccessible to laypersons. This in itself confirms and reinforces the power relationship, while insulating the community's interpretations from external scrutiny. . . .

Stanley Fish [*Is There a Text in This Class*, 1980, p. 370] concludes his lectures on literary interpretation by inquiring into the "practical consequences" of his thesis:

"Since it is primarily a literary argument, one wonders what implications it has for the practice of literary criticism. The answer is, none whatsoever. . . . The reason for this is that the position I have been presenting is not one that you (or anyone else) could live by. Its thesis is that whatever seems to you to be obvious and inescapable is only so within some institutional or conventional structure, even if you are persuaded by the thesis. As soon as you descend from theoretical reasoning about your assumptions, you will once again inhabit them and you will inhabit without any reservations whatsoever". . . .

Most of this seems equally applicable to legal interpretation. . . . [T]he lesson I carry away from contemporary literary and social theory is that the line separating law from politics is not all that distinct and that its very location is a question of politics. I do not think this is nihilism. Rather, I believe that examining the "rule of law"—even at the risk of discovering that it is entirely illusory—is a necessary step toward a society that can satisfy the aspirations that make us hold to the concept so tenaciously.

WHY NOT END THE BOOK HERE?

To this point I suspect I have convinced you only that scholars do not agree with each other. If all is preference and paradox, if law is neither naturally nor artificially objective, I should invite you to select that evaluative approach—from preservativism to nihilism—which suits your ideologies and inclinations best, and stop. Why not accept the fact that the Court will follow political ideologies and that beyond the political dynamics that keep the Court in political check most of the time, everything is personal preference?

I think the short answer is simply that too little fits together at this point to leave us comfortable. Paul Brest closes with the reminder that we hold tenaciously to some moral vision of constitutional meaning, one that transcends political jurisprudence. I have argued that this tenacious holding to a concept is a desire for an aesthetic experience of political goodness. In passing this far, we have encountered a variety of references to the legal art, dramatic metaphors, and so on. But I have not explained an aesthetic theory or showed with any precision how it can contribute to jurisprudential understanding. I have flourished before you some definitions of community that depend on maintaining political conversations, but I have hardly convinced you why that is so, or shown how the fittedness of a judicial opinion or an academic theory affects the quality of our political dialogues.

Besides, some patterns in jurisprudence demand further explanation. Despite scholarly disagreement on almost every point of logic and method, scholars triangulate to a startling degree on the importance of the respect for individual dignity. Ely, Choper, and Perry all do so. Rawls, Dworkin, and Murphy do so. Gadamer, Habermas, and the Critical scholars do so. The triangulation requires some explanation. Why not, instead, a triangulation on the importance of maintaining the nation's military might?

If the Court performed in ways that seemed uniformly incoherent or partisan or rigid we might stop, but we want to judge both the justices and the decisions against some shared normative understanding, an understanding that elevates some justices above others, some decisions above others. We have, after all, learned a constitutional history in which great judges and the Court itself have at times "performed" nobly. These noble performances have not "obeyed" the rules of the legal craft, they have expanded our political understanding.

I shall try to complete these pictures in the final two chapters. I shall close here with a transitional thought. Most of the jurisprudence we have covered assumes in one guise or another that a constitutional decision is "good" only if it convinces us that it is "correct" and that therefore we must *agree* with it. Critical theory denies this truth, but its alternatives do not explain our tenacious aspiration to the "rule of law." Part of appreciating the aesthetic approach in law or anything else requires us to separate our feeling that something is good from our agreement with its goodness. This is no great trick, actually. We may see a play or movie depicting the thrill of masculine involvement in battle, or the power of community opinion to perpetuate racial injustice and dislike the message at the same time we know we have experienced a good performance. The Court may, similarly, reach a result we disagree with yet still convince us that it has performed well.

Chapter 6 LAW AND
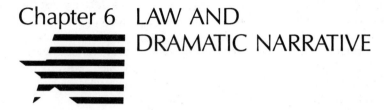 DRAMATIC NARRATIVE

What we need in education more than anything else is genuine, not merely marginal, faith in the existence of moral principles.

—John Dewey

[T]he function of art is to make life better. The depth to which an artist may find current experience to be sunk in discord and confusion is not his special concern; his concern is, in some measure, to lift experience out.

—George Santayana

The Prophets used much by metaphors to set forth truth.

—John Bunyan

THE MODEL WE CANNOT ACCEPT

Paul Brest left us at the end of chapter five with an unsolved puzzle. We hold tenaciously to a model of normative constitutional order despite the existence of a value-free political model that better fits the historical evidence of judicial practice. Let me restate that political model one more time.

Constitutional history repeatedly confirms that the Court usually defines the problems it will hear and the solutions it offers in the same terms in which the larger political community frames and debates them. In the early period, the public problem was federalism, and the Court, in part by the accident of the personalities involved, chose a nationalistic path. It gambled on the future then, in the sense that the justices made plausible guesses based on some version of then-current theory about how federalism ought to work, and it won. In the industrialization postbellum, the public problem inevitably became the nature of private property and the extent to which government could modify private distributions of wealth. The Court eventually took its cue from a dominant and plausible enough theory of the time, social Darwinism. This time the gamble failed. Then it turned its attention to the problem of individual autonomy, a natural consequence of the growing prominence of the concepts of liberty and equality in democratic political ideology.

It is too early to tell whether this latest gamble will pay, and if so how much, but that hardly matters. Rather, throughout this history we find no evidence that the Court has stated or maintained any consistent jurisprudence of

135

constitutionalism. Nor do we find, with the exception of the early twentieth century, any pattern of Court policymaking that is, when weighted against the other sources of human triumph and misery (wars, pestilence, and the Chicago Cubs' failure to make the World Series), anything worse than the consequences of normal political pulling and tugging. The Court never strays very far from politics. It is and always will be politically controlled, both by the external forces of electoral politics and the internal structural necessity to generate coalitions of justices in deciding specific disputes.

From the academician's perspective, the Court will nearly always say things that look narrow, illogical, incomplete, and compromised. But that is just the point. Academicians are trained to criticize. They judge the Court by rules of a game the Court does not play. When the Court says particularly silly things, the legal community responds. And when the Court prescribes pills some interest groups cannot swallow, they will resist. If there is enough resistance, the Court will back down. The Court blew over like a feather in the death penalty cases, so one can hardly presume the Court politically remote and inflexible. If political, economic, and social evidence deflate the urgency of fears about the Court's political illegitimacy, and if the philosopher's disarray shows the hopelessness of the search for unified constitutional theory, why should we expect the justices to do any better?

The political model implies that our study of Court and Constitution can at best only reveal clues about changes in political ideology. For example, Mark Tushnet (1984a), believes Burger Court decisions since Watergate show increasing enthusiasm for an "imperial presidency." He concludes his description of "imperial presidency" cases, *Nixon v. Fitzgerald* prominent among them, with an analysis of *Dames & Moore v. Reagan*, the Iranian hostage accord case, which approved an exercise of presidential power to alter private property arrangements "indistinguishable in its essentials from that disapproved" in *Youngstown Sheet & Tube Co. v. Sawyer*, the steel seizure case.

> *Dames & Moore* shows how the considerations of judicial politics . . . interact with substantive concerns. For, in addition to a rather greater enthusiasm for the imperial presidency these days, *Dames & Moore* differs from the *Steel Seizure Case* primarily in that the Court in 1981 could not possibly have gotten away with invalidating the Iranian Hostage Accords while the Court in 1952, facing a politically weakened President who had—horror of horrors—trampled on the prerogatives of property, could get away with what it did. (p. 1268)

To avoid any misunderstanding in what follows, let me state here that I do not reject the "goodness" of this political model. Its description of the work of the Court over time seems accurate. Within its framework, it fits the evidence. Moreover, it provides a better fitting framework than conventional constitutional jurisprudence, which has never been so cacaphonous, so lacking in common assumptions, so seemingly remote from agreement on the elementary questions in the field: What is a text? What is a constitutional text? What is interpretation? Is interpretation in constitutional law or in any area a meaningful and useful concept? A jurisprudential alternative, if there is one, must recover a normative theory of evaluation within, not despite, this political framework. I have suggested that it is necessary to do so because we resist thinking otherwise. We somehow need a normative framework.

WHY WE NEED A NORMATIVE FRAMEWORK

Duncan Kennedy (1976) linked the eternal demand for a normative framework to our desire for individual freedom, which we can only achieve in reference to group action. But groups depend on the use of force and coercion, and we must moralize that power to retain the conviction that we are free:

We can achieve real freedom only collectively, through *group* self-determination. We are simply too weak to realize ourselves in isolation. True, collective self-determination, short of utopia, implies the use of force against the individual. But we experience and accept the use of physical and psychic coercion every day, in family life, education and culture. We experience it indirectly, often unconsciously, in political and economic life. The problem is the conversion of force into moral force, in the [face] of moral indeterminacy. (p. 1774)

The epigraphs for this chapter sketch this book's solution to the problem as Kennedy, Brest, and other Critical scholars have stated it. We need genuine faith in the existence of moral principles but we do not (and in any event cannot) satisfy this need by arguing academically about which moral principles are true and which are false. Art satisfies the need for faith by repeatedly ordering the meaning of experiences. It is not the "correctness" of any one specified order but the act of persuasive ordering itself that preserves the faith. As in any religious activity, these acts must regularly recur. The parties to a litigated case frame the issues for the Court so as to dramatize and illuminate a problem in political experience that has "sunk in discord and confusion." Judges must lift the experience out of its confusion, that is, perform what Santayana calls "the function of art," and thus attempt "to make life better."

In other words, we may not need Wechsler's neutral principles in law, but we do need to believe that the opinion has ordered raw experience convincingly. Political jurisprudence, and Tushnet's example of its practice, undercut directly that desire. Again my point is that, assuming Tushnet is entirely correct about *Dames & Moore*'s political inevitability, it is still within the Court's power to convince us that the result is "good." If the Court succeeded, we can only say it succeeded because it "performed well."

The aspiration that drives the search for a "theory," a common ground that will simultaneously explain the Court's proper constitutional function and provide criteria for evaluating the quality of individual constitutional decisions, is not particularly mysterious. Scholars and practitioners aspire to a "genuine faith"—in the Hippocratic Oath in medicine or Newtonian physics in engineering—because people cannot choose or act without some theory to impose an order on material chaos. And political life, says Kennedy, must provide a mechanism to convert brute force into moral force. If constitutional law is to play any role in the moralizing of force—and it claims to deal with precisely that problem—then constitutional scholars have a double reason to aspire to a normative theory.

This and the final chapter state the argument that aesthetic theory satisfies the aspiration. I have "genuine faith" in something—like a constitutional theory or the goodness of a specific court decision, a Sunday sermon or a performance of Beethoven's Ninth Symphony—when I believe the parts of the thing fit with each other and with some model of what it ought to be like. You may disagree with my specific judgments, but when you do you will argue that the fit is not so good. Nevertheless, we will share respect for fittedness. But how can we share a model of what the "thing" ought to be? I believe that pragmatism in American culture provides a basis for agreement. It sensitizes us to the relevance of raw experience to the "fits" we create. Current jurisprudential criticism of the Court shares a sense that the Court is out of tune with the authoritative appeal of pragmatism in our culture. Engineers and physicians are not so out of tune, which is why critical movements within these professions are lower keyed.

The evidence for this aesthetic theory may be too close to our noses to see clearly, so let me emphasize that good performances—those of the script-writers, director and cast in a classic film like *Casablanca*, a Ray Charles or Cleo Lane vocal, a winning gymnastic routine at the Olympic games, a great campaign speech—"happen" to us all the time. When these happenings occur, we know they have occurred primarily by sharing the experience of rightness with our fellow members of the audience. The persistence of the preservative and other conventional jurisprudential searches in the face of their futility, like the persistence of religious practices and beliefs in a scientific age, means the search is intrinsically important. The fun is the chase. Keep the chase alive, and life will remain graceful. Pragmatism, according to Richard Rorty, has "sketched out the possibility of a freer, more romantic, more playful, form of philosophical life" (1983, p. 34).

Conversations do not proceed without goals and ideals. I have alluded earlier to incoherence in court opinions and shall say more about it before we are through. Fred Rodell (1939, p. 98), wrote, "[T]he alleged logic of constitutional law is equally amorphous, equally unconvincing, equally silly whether the decisions the Court is handing down are 'bad,' 'progressive,' or 'reactionary,' 'liberal,' or 'unliberal.' " The Court in the latter part of the twentieth century too often speaks such gibberish that the conversations cannot proceed at all. I have in mind the example of *Logan* and the collapse of the jurisprudence of rights, and of *Chadha* and its professed ignorance of political realities, which I shall discuss at length at the end of this chapter. The nihilism that Fiss condemns might, unfortunately, be a considerable jurisprudential improvement over what we have now.

Richard Rorty's proposal for a freer and more romantic form of jurisprudential life calls for a redefinition of objectivity, or rather a recovery of the pragmatic definition, which is to deal more directly with the objects of our experience. It is, I think, highly significant that a very prominent current development in the theory of legal practice—the Harvard Law School Negotiation Project, which teaches people how to negotiate disagreements through the identification and expression of their fundamental interests—claims to be objective in just this way: it exhorts us to listen carefully to one another (Fisher and Ury, 1981).

My final chapter describes the specifics of an aesthetic theory of jurisprudence. This chapter completes the groundwork by (a) describing an elegant article by Robert Cover, a scholar very much part of the Critical movement, which links constitutional jurisprudence to the nature of normative narrative; (b) extending the discussion of modern hermeneutic philosophy introduced in chapter three; (c) noting the intriguing similarities between the structure and goals of dramatic theater and the structure and goals of Supreme Court lawmaking.

"NOMOS AND NARRATIVE"

In 1979 Owen Fiss, an advocate, as we have seen, of the recovery of objectivity in constitutional law, wrote (pp. 16–17):

> In my judgment, the resurgence of *Carolene Products* does not stem from doubts about the special capacity of courts and their processes to move us closer to a correct understanding of our constitutional values, but from the frail quality of our substantive vision. We have lost our confidence in the existence of the values that underlie the litigation of the 1960s, or, for that matter, in the existence of any public values. All is preference. That seems the crucial issue, not the issue of relative institutional competence. Only once we reassert our belief in the existence of public values, that values such as equality, liberty, due process, no cruel and unusual punishment, security of the person, or free speech can have a true and important meaning, that must be articulated and implemented—yes, discovered—will the role of the courts in our political system become meaningful, or for that matter even intelligible.

Fiss does not here add another voice to the choir calling for a reconstruction of natural law. He emphasizes instead the need for a strong commitment to "substantive vision." Note that substantive vision thus becomes a value in itself. Why?

In the *Harvard Law Review*'s annual "Foreword" for 1983, four years after Fiss' 1979 "Foreword," from which I just quoted, Robert Cover provided an elegant explanation. In essence, Cover argues that, if Berger and Luckmann correctly describe reality as socially constructed, and if those constructions are inevitably normative, then constitutional law necessarily contributes to the construction. But the Court has lost touch with the symbolic and dramatic character of that process. Myths, narratives, epics, and stories are the dramatic bases of social construction in societies.

I must let Cover's first two paragraphs speak before continuing my less elegant summary:

> We inhabit a *nomos*—a normative universe. We constantly create and maintain a world of right and wrong, of lawful and unlawful, of valid and void . . . . The rules and principles of justice, the formal paraphernalia of social control, and the conventions of a social order are, indeed, important to that world; they are, however, but a small part of the normative universe that ought to claim our attention. No set of legal institutions or prescriptions exists apart from the narratives that locate it and give it meaning. For every constitution there is an epic, for each decalogue a scripture. Once understood in the context of the narratives that give it meaning, law becomes not merely a system of rules to be observed, but a world in which we live.
>
> In this normative world, law and narrative are inseparably related. Every prescription is insistent in its demand to be located in discourse—to be supplied with history and destiny, beginning and end, explanation and purpose. And every narrative is insistent in its demand for its prescriptive point, its moral. History and literature cannot escape their location in a normative universe, nor can prescription, even when embodied in a legal text, escape its origin and its end in experience, in the narratives that are the trajectories plotted upon material reality by our imaginations. (pp. 4–5)

In any civilization that takes law seriously, law becomes central to the community narrative. We call our document a constitution because we ascribe to it power to constitute or make the society in which we live. More important, by articulating clear models of moral behavior, narratives teach us how to live in our normative world. When the Court announces the end of *de jure* public school racial segregation, when it announces that the state cannot prohibit a woman from choosing to abort her pregnancy in the first trimester, when it sanctions capital punishment, it alters the normative points of reference we use when we act and when we communicate with each other. That some approve and some reject the outcome is immaterial to the fact that the decision changes the bases of the social construction of reality. The narratives are not utopian. They instead link and integrate "the 'is,' the 'ought,' and the 'what might be' " into a whole in whose reality we necessarily believe (p. 10).

Histories of the development of religious communities (Cover uses rabbinic and biblical illustrations) immediately reveal difficulties. On one hand normative world-building is pedagogical and hence personal. Its "word," its unquestioned statement of precepts and narratives, educates and directs the growth of each individual in his community. Obedience in small groups often follows automatically from personal understanding. "Discourse is initiatory, celebratory, expressive, and performative, rather than critical and analytic" (p. 13).

Yet these tightly made communities, because they take precepts so seriously and cannot admit to modification, necessarily fracture into sects: groups who interpret the precepts in opposing ways and who develop competing and inconsistent narratives. In the United States, we share the text and precept of the Fourteenth Amendment's equal protection clause, but the narratives that give it meaning vary, as we have seen. Given the reality of disagreement, the narrative over time can claim to govern only through the force of authority. Obedience comes from fear, not understanding (p. 18).

> The conclusion emanating from this state of affairs is simple and very disturbing: there is a radical dichotomy between the social organization of law as power and the organization of law as meaning. This dichotomy, manifest in folk and underground cultures in even the most authoritarian societies, is particularly open to view in a liberal society that disclaims control over narrative . . . . Even when authoritative institutions try to create meaning for the precepts they articulate, they act, in that respect, in an unprivileged fashion.

If we are to escape the conclusion that the Constitution, by stating the precepts of liberalism yet enforcing them with authority and the threat of force, is at war with itself, the escape will come through an endorsement and a delimitation of the creation of narratives for private communities. The First Amendment's protection of religious liberty would seem an obvious place to seek such an endorsement, and *Bob Jones University v. United States* (1983) raised the question directly.

In this case the Internal Revenue Service had denied the University tax exempt status because university policy forbade interracial dating. The university claimed that its reading of its private biblical narrative required it to follow this practice. The Internal Revenue Service did not act in this matter under direct statutory language from Congress. Internal Revenue had adopted the policy denying exempt status to institutions practicing racial discrimination on its own initiative, using only general statutory language for support.

The government of course has power to destroy the small community. It might well have destroyed the Amish community if it required the conventional education of Amish children. In *Wisconsin v. Yoder* (1972), it chose not to do so. Cover argues that the American *nomos* is not only filled with examples of private religious communities—the Pilgrims, the utopians, the Mormons, for example—but its well known legal narratives have endorsed the principle of group autonomy much more generically. Property law, corporate law, and contract law, the latter bolstered in some constitutional sense by the contract clause, all serve the same end as does the free exercise clause of the First Amendment. They endorse the value of the liberty to create private legal worlds.

The Mennonite brief in *Bob Jones* presented the issue starkly. It stated, "Our religious beliefs, however, are very deeply held. When these beliefs collide with the demands of society, our highest allegiance must be toward

God, and we must say with men of God of the past, 'We must obey God rather than men,' and these are the crises from which we would be spared" (p. 27). It is precisely this fundamental moral issue, the tension between a public and political commitment to removing racial stigma and a private and specific desire to preserve community narratives, that the Court in *Bob Jones* ducked. The Court merely asserted a compelling governmental interest in eradicating racial discrimination in education. It chose to sit firmly on one of the dilemma's horns.

The critical issue is not the simple clash between two slogans—freedom of religion versus freedom from racial discrimination. The problem is that the IRS, a bureaucracy, has acted without legislative sanction to disrupt a private *nomos* despite a legal culture that purports to value highly this freedom of private association. The Court cited Congressional silence since the 1970 IRS ruling, but *Bob Jones* and *Chadha* were decided only a few days apart. If legislative *action* under Article I has no formal constitutional force under *Chadha's* invalidation of the legislative veto, it is difficult indeed to find in legislative *silence* justification for bureaucratic actions that pull directly against a fundamental element of our legal narrative. The Court granted to IRS the power to deny the exemption at the same time it explicitly refused to decide whether Congress could have granted such a tax exemption itself. *Chadha* certainly left the impression that Congress could not do so silently. Thus Cover concludes:

> [T]he force of the Court's interpretation in *Bob Jones University* is very weak. It is weak not because of the form of argument, but because of the failure of the Court's commitment—a failure that manifests itself in the designation of authority for the decision [to Internal Revenue]. The Court assumes a position that places nothing at risk and from which the Court makes no interpretive gesture at all, save the . . . statement that an exercise of political authority was not unconstitutional. The grand national travail against discrimination is given no normative status in the Court's opinion, save that it means the IRS was not wrong. The insular communities, the Mennonites and Amish, are rightly left to question the scope of the Court's decision: are we at the mercy of each public policy decision that is not wrong? If the public policy here has a special status, what is it? Can Congress change the policy? . . .
>
> . . . The insular communities deserved better—they deserved a constitutional hedge against mere administration. And the minority community deserved more—it deserved a constitutional commitment to avoiding public subsidization of racism.
>
> . . . The Justices . . . were unwilling to venture commitment of themselves, to make a firm promise and to project their understanding of the law onto the future. *Bob Jones University* is a play for 1983—wary and cautious actors, some eloquence, but no commitment. (pp. 66–67)

Cover criticizes the Court for failing to address the fundamental tension between two central values, the autonomy of primary communities and the removal of racial stigma. Cover seems simultaneously, and with stronger conviction, to criticize the Court on stylistic grounds. The Court sinned by faking it, by avoiding its responsibility to lift experience out of confusion through the creation of a normative vision that harmonizes the competing claims. Cover might prefer an articulate defense of the university's position, or contrarily of the sufficiency of IRS power to act as it did, than the cautious posturing of the decision itself.

THE JURISPRUDENTIAL IMPLICATIONS OF MODERN PHILOSOPHY

We are now positioned to begin to grapple more directly with an unresolved tension that has thus far lurked below the surface of my argument. I have more than once condemned the belief that "objective" or logically deducible constitutional interpretations exist. I have urged, in the alternative, that communities are continuously reconstituted by political acts (among them those of courts) that create momentary visions of coherent normative order. I have argued, consistent with the evidence across constitutional history, that these visions need not conform to any single legal or political value system. These visions, for example, about the political status of women, change as political values change. We should call these judicially created visions good because they encourage our faith that our normative world is real and meaningful. Our faith is sustained less by the perceived correctness of the result than by the coherence of the result, for coherence permits conversation, and it is ultimately a faith in our ability to converse morally that holds us together.

We should not expect much consistency among constitutional cases across time. Indeed we cannot expect great consistency among cases at any one time. A pragmatic, as opposed to a religiously fundamentalist, political culture draws our attention to the meaning of the raw experiences represented by each case, experiences that are to some degree unique. This line of my argument insists that we keep our eyes on the quality of the performance, defined by the elements of concrete cases, in the opinions that decide them. We can imagine finding opposing opinions in one case equally good if each gives us a persuasive starting point for conversations about what is politically good.

But here is the tension: In spite of the difficulties with objective theories of constitutional interpretation, we have seen in passing a remarkable degree of scholarly agreement that the Constitution is somehow about the respect for and protection of individual dignity. Maybe the protection of dignity amounts to an objective constitutional theory after all. In this section I want to pursue further the possibility, first introduced in the preliminary discussion of hermeneutics in chapter three, that the protection of individual dignity matters so widely not because the Constitution legally commands it but because conversations about political goodness cannot proceed without it. Put another way, if aesthetic theories are theories of political communication, then the concern for dignity is less a legal command than an aesthetic prerequisite, related, as we shall see, to a performer persuasively "wooing" his audience.

Communities exist by definition when people seek to share knowledge and understanding through communication. Effective political communication requires that each citizen be free to participate and that his participation be valued equally with every other citizen. This section returns to recent developments in social philosophy because its leading edges converge in agreement on the first two sentences of this paragraph. More specifically, contemporary social philosophy converges in (a) rejecting scientific, empiricist, and all other methods of gaining knowledge that claim to produce community norms through the application of the techniques possessed only by experts and professionals; (b) asserting that all understanding is personal and felt and tied to an individual's practical experiences; (c) holding therefore that equal respect for all persons is central to the nature of the community itself.

Understanding is judgmental, creative, and imaginative, and never finished; hence the political conditions that foster the never-ending enterprise of understanding must always be tolerant and open-ended. Indeed, the concept goes back to Aristotle himself, who, opposing the claims of professional superiority by the lawmakers of his own time, held that in political matters, only practical knowledge, not theoretical or technical knowledge, should count in debate. In practical matters, the opinions of all citizens deserve to be heard.

Berger and Luckmann, and Stanley Fish, in Paul Brest's quotation at the end of the last chapter, made the same point. Scholars tend to operate outside the practical world that unites speech and action. To escape Fish's conclusion that philosophy is really irrelevant, philosophy must turn from its own concern for ultimate truth to an investigation of the conditions that foster practical understanding among men. (See Winch, 1958, and Mansbridge, 1982.)

The impact of modern philosophical developments on practical knowledge has begun to appear since the Second World War. Thomas Kuhn's popular debunking of the myth of scientific objectivity, Lewis Thomas' poetics of biology and medicine, and the Critical Legal Studies movement itself all seek to relate modern philosophy to practice. These developments owe a great deal to the spirit of Dewey and James, for they seek to overcome the self-indulgent tendencies of academics and to relate knowledge to action. One medical analogy, the move toward holistic treatment of patients, is a particularly striking practical application of this idea, for it holds at its core that physicians must *listen* to their patients as much as they talk to them. (See Oliver Sacks' *Awakenings*, 1976, and *A Leg to Stand on*, 1984.) Medicine, like law, might be moving toward making the integrity of conversations the primary human value that systems must serve.

Richard Bernstein's recent *Beyond Objectivism and Relativism* (1983) describes these philosophical convergences, and I draw on his lucid treatment of what is in the original sometimes obscure. Bernstein describes, more or less in order, the work of Gadamer, Habermas, Rorty, and Arendt. Many of

Gadamer's basic assertions encompass the work of all four, and Bernstein gives Gadamer the plurality of his space.

According to Gadamer, understanding "happens" through a constant interplay or mediation in the mind of the interpreter of the universal and the particular. The interplay does not follow, nor need it follow, rules or authoritative methods, nor does it necessarily accept without challenge anything previously given. This method of understanding "is a form of reasoning, yielding a type of ethical know-how in which what is universal and what is particular are codetermined" (Bernstein, p. 146). Moreover, the process is never detached from the self of the interpreter and what that person is becoming. Just the opposite. The way people develop understanding is central to their identity and their growth.

This model of understanding parallels conventional constitutional practice in several respects. It explains, or might explain, the diversity of sincerely held constitutional positions, e.g., the differences between Justice Brennan's and Justice O'Connor's understanding of the scope of Fourteenth Amendment due process. Neither seems bound by any legal authority nor to any one method for achieving or defending one's understanding. If understanding never stops and is always conditioned by what has come before, the lack of constitutional consistency should not surprise us. The ideals or universals, perhaps the value of autonomy, or of majority representation, or organizational efficiency, that each justice combines with the particular facts given in the case are necessarily personal.

Gadamer holds that, when honestly and openly done, men can in some circumstances generate from their independent personal experiences common answers to practical questions, questions of feasiblity, possibility, and even correctness (p. 152). In this regard Gadamer appears to approach Dworkin, who believes that within a community of interpreters, the Dickens scholars, for example, the material constrains understanding substantially. But Gadamer finds intersubjective hermeneutic agreement much harder to attain than Dworkin. Thus Gadamer would not necessarily conclude that the failure of the justices to agree on matters shows an irresponsible failure to take their interpretive role seriously. He is thus closer to Stanley Fish's position.

Yet, as Bernstein points out, "There is a significant gap in Gadamer's fusion of hermeneutics and *praxis*. This is not just an innocent omission but a glaring substantive deficiency, if one is concerned about contemporary political life" (p. 159). He continues:

Without some sort of theoretical understanding and explanation of the structure and dynamics of modern technological society, there is always the real danger that *praxis* will be ineffectual, merely abstract. Let us not forget that *praxis* requires choice, deliberation and decision about what is to be done in concrete situations. Informed action requires us to try to understand and explain the salient characteristics of the situations we confront. (p. 160)

Gadamer, in other words, supposes that understanding occurs in dialogue and community but only because the participants share a theoretical starting point. If the Court fakes and flinches at the point where it should seek to understand and explain the salient characteristics of situations, it may be because the justices lack even a common starting point. The justices may not agree on what they are interpreting in the first place.

Gadamer makes central to his argument the conviction that understanding happens primarily through "true conversations," that is, conversations among free and equal people where "each opens himself to the other person, truly accepts his point of view as worthy of consideration and gets inside the other to such an extent that he understands not a particular individual, but what he says" (p. 162).

While Gadamer, in comparison to Habermas, seems traditional because he believes interpretive communities can extract truth from history, Gadamer asserts one radical hermeneutic truth that is not far from Habermas: "No higher principle is thinkable than that of the freedom of all, and we understand actual history from the perspective of this principle: as the ever-to-be-renewed and the never-ending struggle for this freedom" (p. 164).

Gadamer does not develop the political implications at any length, but the jurisprudential questions seem clear. Do the justices give evidence of engaging in "true conversations" among themselves? With the attorneys at bar and the litigants they represent? If conversations and dialogues are critical to understanding, and understanding powerfully shapes identity itself, the opinions that send judicial messages surely matter. Do these opinions encourage dialogue? The Critical theorists would answer no, but the potential is there, and sometimes it does happen.

In the modern philosophical dialogue described thus far, Habermas seems to play pragmatist opposite Gadamer's romantic. Gadamer argues that if practical understanding, the beliefs we act upon in conducting our daily affairs, is a constant movement between the self and external universals and particulars, then practical understanding arises in dialogue. The sanctity of dialogue, depending as it does on the freedom and integrity of its participants, in turn makes the value of human freedom real, universal, and elemental in practical affairs. But, asks Habermas, what about the social conditions that prevent or distort the conditions of true dialogue? We saw in chapter three that Habermas advocates changing the material conditions that block communication. He buttresses his political prescription by insisting that the practice of communication itself presupposes the possibility of intersubjective agreement. Therefore, communication presupposes the universality of the procedural forms and conditions of "communicative reason" (p. 191). The ideal government is therefore one that works to minimize the constraints, material and otherwise, that limit private and public dialogue alike.

Habermas ultimately does not defend the discovery of a unitary theme any more effectively than does Gadamer.

Both, although in different ways, have argued that we can take our historical situation and our existing social practices seriously and at the same time develop a critical perspective on them that is informed by an understanding of our history and oriented to an open future. (p. 196)

Richard Rorty (1979) plays a more dramatically pragmatic role than does Habermas. All modern philosophy has sought universals, but the universals are not there, and can not be there for the very reasons the hermeneutic theorists reject positivism and historicism in the first place. The universals of freedom and equal participation are themselves the last vestiges of philosophical elitism, a movement that uses a "privileged vocabulary" to justify the belief that philosophers (whether James Madison or Karl Marx does not matter) properly prescribe the foundations of culture.

Rorty endorses the "willingness to talk, to listen to other people, to weigh the consequences of our actions upon other people" (p. 198), but these virtues, and pragmatism itself, are valuable only within our cultural traditions, that is, within a culture whose primary role model is Socrates. Rorty insists that he has no method for arguing that such a community is any better than a ruthless and self-serving autocracy in a different culture.

But Rorty turns the collapse, the "death," of Western philosophy into a blessing. By abandoning the universal impulse, by turning away from the preoccupation, indeed the "obsession" (p. 203) in specific instances to get the right answer, we are liberated to cope with the contingencies of life. And coping with contingencies in this fashion may "renew" our sense of community:

Our identification with our community—our society, our political tradition, our intellectual heritage—is heightened when we see this community as *ours* rather than *nature*'s, *shaped* rather than *found*, one among many which men have made. In the end, the pragmatists tell us, what matters is our loyalty to other human beings clinging together against the dark, not our hope of getting things right (pp. 203–204).

Rorty's Socratic virtues may only be part of our community, but by relieving the obligation to claim universality, they become as values less arbitrary, and more objective. Thus by his very rejection of the philosophic impulses of Gadamer and Habermas, Rorty ends up with a practical prescription not far from theirs. In the process, of course, he would urge the Court and constitutional scholars to worry less about getting the right answer and more about the interplay of social ideals and the pragmatic consequences of political action on the formation of communities that allow us to cling together against the dark. I trust you see the similarity to Cover's analysis, especially the importance that the Court address the claims of religious minorities like the Mennonites directly, and the diminished legal authority Rorty would impute to expert, professional, and bureaucratic status, e.g., to the Internal Revenue Service in *Bob Jones University*.

But applying this analysis to the constitutional work of the Court immediately poses a major problem. If all understanding, including our understanding of our community and other things political, depends on a continuous dialogue, if political being and political action are shaped by speech itself, then that dialogue necessarily accepts the participation of all on equal grounds. It is necessarily democratic in the full sense of the term, and professionalized interests, like lawyers and scientists, have no special claim to power. Yet if this is true, the professionalized Court should play at best a relatively minor role. If so, why do the American political tradition and practice tell us we must look to the Court and the Constitution for the checks on political power and authority? Constitutional law as we know it seems a contradiction of the terms of the dialogic community the philosophers envision.

There is, however, an alternative, one in which acts of public judgment try to model or create in action the community envisioned. Bernstein points out that in Hannah Arendt's analysis of none other than Kant, judging is one of the most important activities in the envisioned world:

> [W]here Kant deals with aesthetic judgments (which are frequently thought to be the furthest removed from politics), [Arendt finds] his "unwritten political philosophy." What she has in mind is Kant's analysis of "reflective judgment," the mode of judging particulars that does not subsume particulars under general rules but ascends "from particular to universal." Such judging requires an "enlarged mentality" . . . that enables one to "think in the place of everybody else." "The judging person, as Kant says quite beautifully, can only 'woo the consent of everyone else' in the hope of coming to an agreement with him eventually." This wooing itself is a form of rational persuasion that is characteristic of politics . . . .
>
> Kant was particularly incisive in basing judgment on taste, taste which is a discriminatory sense and is not to be identified with "private feelings." On the contrary, taste is a kind of *sensus communis*: it is a "community sense," the sense that fits us into human community . . . . It is a mode of thinking that is capable of dealing with the particular in its particularity but which nevertheless makes the claim to communal validity . . . . (p. 217)

To play this role effectively, a judge must have an audience. The judge who seeks to speak rightly to or for the community must enlarge his thinking, by transcending individual biases, preferences, and limitations, but he needs the presence of the community and the anticipated need to justify the action to that audience in order to operate in this fashion at all. Judgment itself teaches by example the principle that power and authority are incompatible with persuasion and the testing of truth through "communal argumentation" (p. 223).

Man's dialogic nature (Gadamer), the value of practical discourse (Habermas), our cultural heritage of the Socratic virtues (Rorty and MacIntyre), and the critical role that public judgments, as acts of speech, play in creating a community of discourse (Arendt), do converge into a political prescription. It is not necessarily a more radical prescription than Lon Fuller's "natural law" prescription to keep the channels of communication open, nor even than the rather conventional textbook model of democracy as a system that works because it handles conflict openly under conditions of reason and persuasion.

Bernstein concludes that American politics must and indeed does presume to seek this end, and that minimizing the barriers to achieving it is as vital a practical problem as our system faces. But Bernstein is pessimistic. Each of his four philosophers has to presume that some perhaps primitive patterns of community life exist prior to dialogue and provide at least kindling to fire the dialogue. But does the pluralist nation-state possess such common starting points? What if the objective forces of science and professional expertise undermined the enterprise?:

> But what, then, is to be done in a situation in which there is a breakdown of such communities, and where the very conditions of social life have the consequences of furthering such a breakdown? More poignantly, what is to be done when we realize how much of humanity has been systematically excluded and prevented from participating in such dialogical communities? (p. 226)

[And]

> When Aristotle sought to clarify what he meant by [public dialogue], he could still call upon the vivid memory of Pericles as the concrete exemplar of the individual who possessed the faculty of discriminating what was good for himself and for the *polis*. But today, when we seek for concrete exemplars of the types of dialogical communities in which practical rationality flourishes, we are at a much greater loss. Yet we can recognize how deeply rooted this frustrated aspiration is in human life. (p. 230)

It would be entirely appropriate for readers at this point to apply the convergent conclusions of Bernstein's four philosophers to the Court in the following manner: "In order to promote political dialogue, the Court must aggressively defend First Amendment freedoms, and it must place a heavy burden of justification on all government actions that systematically produce, whether intentionally or not, inequalities in the distribution of wealth and of claims of right." I do not mean to denigrate this triangulation with Rawls and with the conventional, legitimacy-based, constitutional scholarship of Choper, Ely, and Perry. It would be entirely appropriate to note that Justice Stevens, the justice most obviously concerned with the meaning of words and with the coherence of an opinion, has moved steadily since his appointment in a "liberal" direction. However, that application, proper though it may be, misses the main lesson the philosophical convergence teaches. Creating and nurturing community is a practical and political task. If we are really serious about moving away from the loss of community, the issue for the Court or any political institution is strategic. The Court will in this analysis successfully woo by starting where its audience is. This is why Kant links political judgment to aesthetic judgments about taste. Merely to "declare" the law contradicts the wooing on which dialogue can build. It is the opinion that woos. The court becomes, in this view, a performing body whose visions of communities are created with audiences. I believe that constitutional history contains examples of good judicial performances, and that these examples may offer an antidote to Bernstein's pessimism. Let us therefore look more closely at law as theater.

LAW AND THEATER

In chapter three (p. 65, note 6), I quoted Mark Twain's description of a meaningless universe. The universe is a chaos of elementary particles. This is Rorty's dark against which we cling together. Man protects himself from the dark by creating in communities the experience of order and meaning. The conviction that life has order and meaning is essential to the survival of the race, but it is an illusion. The concept is neither new nor merely academic. It is the central theme in all of Wagner's mature nineteenth century operas. Joseph Gusfield (1981, p. 168) quoted a 1922 essayist in *The New Republic*:

> We want to know more about our relation to the world. But we emphatically do not want the raw material of life; we want life made emotionally intelligible—and that can only be effected by a process of simplification and arrangement.

The methodological problem for law thus is to discover how it may contribute to the arranging and simplifying of raw material. The materials this chapter has described urge that law protect and nurture community, but that cannot end the matter. The legalistic and conservative program of the preservatives is driven by the same fear of darkness. It appeals, as does fundamentalist religion and did Hitler's Nazism, because the apparent simplicity of preservative assertions of order and value potentially enlarge the community that might embrace them. The fundamental task of law, as for politics and religion and the institutions that validate popular beliefs, is to identify and practice the techniques for creating rather than discovering values

A person can neither make moral choices nor engage in deliberate action without relying on some theory. Theories permit us to see a chaotic world coherently. Theories thus create a view or a vision of a world. Theater and performance accomplish the same end. Compare *The American Heritage Dictionary*'s derivation of the two words:

> theater [. . . from Latin *theatrum*, from Greek *theatron*, from *theasthai*, to watch, look at, from *thea*, a viewing]
> and
> theory [late Latin *theoria*, from Greek . . . *theoros*, spectator, from *theasthai*, to observe, from *thea*, a viewing. See *theater*.]

I have dotted the discussion to this point with metaphorical references to art and theater by other authors. In this section I begin to explain the significance of these references, of the subtitle of this book and of the epigraph from Morse Peckham at its beginning. We commonly think of those in the illusion-making business as artists, and we call their technology "performance." A "good performance" creates a shared belief in a reality. The good performance does not merely identify visions previously "present" in the mind of a listener. People go to performances in many different moods and with many inconsistent expectations. The good performance creates in that audience a belief that it shares a communal experience. Performances thus teach in a weak sense if they recall to mind a community vision once shared but temporarily forgotten. They teach in the strong sense when they create and make plausible new ideas and new visions of possibilities in community. Creating visions of community order are the defining characteristics of public performance. "Doing justice" is a subset of this phenomenon. So is televised evangelism. So is the presidency of a performer, Ronald Reagan, who teaches in the weak sense, above, and so was the presidency of John F. Kennedy, whose popularity derived from his ability as a performer to teach in the strong sense. If, by pardoning Richard Nixon, Gerald Ford lost his bid for reelection in 1976, it was because he prevented a theatrical solution to Watergate that would allow us to share the experience that justice was done in the case.

In his *Stanford Law Review* article, "The Play's the Thing" (1975), Milner Ball reviewed the similarities between courts and theaters. Both occupy formal, symbolically important spaces. Both have audiences. Both seek to persuade, in part through poetic devices like metaphor. Ball reviews various dramatic types—morality plays, saturnalia, theater of the absurd—and then argues that judicial theater is "a distinct type of theater, . . . highlighted by ordered exchanges, nonprogrammatic individuality of outcomes, and contest or play" (p. 100). Judicial theater encourages impartiality, redirects aggressions, and describes, implicitly or directly, images of legitimate political community. (Compare Bennett and Feldman, 1981.)

In more recent writing (1981 and, with D. Robert Lohn, in 1982), Ball points out more powerful similarities. I include two important footnotes (1982, pp. 855–857). These footnotes suggest that performances constitute community concretely—the case of New York City—and jurisprudentially—the proposed improvement on Dworkin's terminology.

> Lakoff and Johnson suggest that a person arguing with you could be understood as giving you her time in a joint effort at mutual understanding. They ask us to think of argument as cooperation, without reference to attack or defense, gain or loss of ground. "Imagine a culture," they say, "where an argument is viewed as a dance, the participants are seen as performers, and the goal is to perform in a balanced and aesthetically pleasing way." Imagine appellate advocacy, we say, to be a performance where legal argument is devoted to achievement of an affecting, just performance.
>
> In a performing, theatrical—as opposed to martial—setting, the advocate will find it as inept to assault the other side as to assault the judge. If appellate advocates are actors representing (taking the parts of) their clients and the judge or panel of judges is the audience, then an attorney may view herself as engaged in a joint enterprise with the other advocate with whom she is pursuing a common cause, i.e., a performance (which is played also to the public at large as well

as to the judges). The action then becomes dialogue rather than diapolemics, and the kinds of arguments offered will be drawn from a wholly different environment than that of battle and verbal warfare. We may identify this environment as one of cooperation and professional mutuality.

Theater lends itself to a sense of collegiality. One recent essay, for example, observes that theater elicits the reality of offering and receiving among the actors and between the actors and the audience.[a] This reality of connectedness may also be imagined as animating successful courtroom performances.[b] Within the context of such a reality, a brief that seeks to destroy the other side will fail—not for weakness, but for irrelevance. It is wholly out of place and not in keeping with the task at hand.

We hasten to point out that, if the brief is not a salvo, neither is it an abject surrender. There is need for strong individual performance in the joint effort of an appellate argument. A weak or stupid brief does not invite a good response and will have as depressing an effect as a poor, lifeless performance by an actor in an ensemble.

We are also constrained to note that one of the advantages to the conception of appeals as theatrical performances is that it frees legal argument from the constricting limitations of warfare and frees it for experimentation.

I am particularly aware here of the danger that the very academic language that I use to try to identify the phenomenon may kill it. Readers will only appreciate the point if they put the book down now and reflect on their own experiences. These need not be with live theater, or even with anything dramatic in the conventional sense. Performance is a generic concept; it is not limited to the dramatic plots of "Hill Street Blues" or "The Seventh Seal" or "The Caine Mutiny Court-Martial." These dramas have taught me much, but I would not have experienced order and meaning by reading their scripts.

Public performances of all sorts play a central role in public and private, large and small, plural and uniform, open and insular communities. The

---

[a] The essay proposes that, although a city is "ambition and hubbub, buying and selling, greed and haste," it remains the case that "the real stuff of the city, that which makes it alive rather than dead, civilized rather than barbarous, a place of nourishment rather than of deprivation, is . . . the reality that comes of offering and receiving." *The Talk of the Town: Notes and Comments*, New Yorker Mar. 15, 1982, at 33. This reality, the essay notes, is most vividly called forth through musical or theatrical performances "that take place in a room of some sort." *Id.*

[b] The success of the performance of a play or piece of music can be measured, it has been suggested, "by its ability to elicit connectedness." *Id.* A performance elicits the nexus of offering and receiving "by being, first, true and second, articulately true, so that people present not only recognize the truth of whatever is expressed . . . but also hear it." *Id.* This standard for theater (being true and articulately true) is translated into the standard for judicial theater that it do justice and be seen to do justice.

Another word for connectedness is love. The love that it is the particular responsibility of judicial theater to evoke is civic affection. As this country's only state-supported theater that is at the same time a branch of government, the courts have a distinctly political assignment unlike both private theater and the state-supported theater of other countries.

It may be more traditional and acceptable, but less accurate we think, to talk about "according dignity," instead of "having affection," and about the court as "forum of principle," instead of the court as "theater of affection." Ronald Dworkin, for example, finds citizens' dignity to be vindicated by the forum of adjudication as a matter of principle. See R. Dworkin, Taking Rights Seriously 216–17 (1977); Dworkin, *Seven Critics*, 11 Ga. L. Rev. 1201, 1249–50 (1977).

celebration of communion is the central act in the Roman Catholic church and its immediate descendants. Families have their own unique rituals that enhance the experience of family membership. Kabuki and Noh seem indestructible parts of Japanese culture. There is speculative talk these days about the potential capacity of popular music to unite the aspirations and moral convictions of youth throughout Western civilization.

If the human condition is chaotic and meaningless, and men therefore create visions of order and meaning to survive, these creations are performances. There is no other way. And in the case of all performances, creations must constantly recur. The power of communion is its repetition. The message of a play or movie, Barney Greenwalt's drunken condemnation at the close of "Court-Martial" of the adversary spirit the legal system encourages, or the image of salvation through simple faith at the close of "The Seventh Seal," will last only if our experiences regularly reaffirm them, or if we see the shows repeatedly.

In this perspective the existence of a constitution, quite apart from its contents, acknowledges by the act of constituting that political institutions must continuously recreate visions of order and meaning at a level of national community. In our particular scheme of things, judicial review had to happen and will persist because the courts are better structured than other institutions to engage in the performative acts on which constitutional recreation depends.

The claim here is a modest one. The metaphorical linkage between court and theater does not determine the script, nor does it distinguish good performances from bad. It only claims that we can best assess the claims of legal scholars and the work of the Court itself if we use the criteria for assessing the quality of scripts and performances. Milner Ball asks the legal process to make manifest the ideals of love and affection that our culture inherits from the *Bible*. That is one defensible script, but we are also a pragmatic and technologically rooted culture. A script that gives life to the values of empirical inquiry and cautions skepticism about causation may be just as defensible. Indeed, I think this is the script the Court now tries to perform. But it does so very badly. To perform that script well, the Court would have to eschew its glib recitation of whatever legal formula seemed handy. It would have to convince us that it had engaged the raw experiences that the dispute before it exemplifies. It would have to do precisely what it did not do in *Bob Jones*.

Still, all behaviors are not performances. A Court that dramatizes the values of pragmatism behaves differently from the medical research team that seeks to identify the cause of Legionnaire's disease. A Court that makes manifest the principle of loving thy neighbor, (the principle that Ball holds should have disposed of the *Bakke* case, and in the university's favor) behaves differently from the person who forgives his neighbor who runs over and kills the family dog. Why?

Public narratives, of which legal, theatrical, musical, and religious performances are all subsets, claim to reach some form of normative or moral closure. The theater of the absurd does so as much as do morality plays. *Waiting for Godot* and *A Man for All Seasons* create equally vivid, if deeply inconsistent, messages. The claim of closure need extend no further than the intended audience. A satire reveals truths about the object of satire only to those familiar with the object. But it must go that far. Holy Communion claims to act as a symbolic or metaphorical equivalent of a complex truth that all communicants are invited to share. To outsiders, however, Communion no doubt seems a trifle silly, if not slightly cannibalistic.

Performance seeks to create in an audience of diverse members an experience of shared moral closure. That process is inevitably symbolic, metaphorical, fictional (in the sense that fidelity to empirically demonstrable events and objects is not the primary value in the process), and poetic. Perhaps the best philosophical explanation of the dramatic and poetic nature of persuasive performances comes from Michael Oakeshott.

In *Experience and its Modes* (1933) and "The Voice of Poetry in the Conversation of Mankind" (1962), Oakeshott holds that the only meaningful definition of truth is totally individualized. "Truth" for Carter can be no more or less than the sum of Carter's experiences, all of which are in some degree unique to Carter and not transferable to or sharable with others. Group life—communicating to anyone but ourselves—requires that we arrest our experiences. In thinking about our experiences we must categorize, exemplify, and therefore falsify our experience into "modes."

Oakeshott finds four modes for arresting experience, for organizing our experience and our thinking into forms that permit communication: "Practice" (the activity of acquiring and keeping possession of that which people desire); "history" (the description and explanation of the past in the language of the present); "science" (measurement and prediction); and "poetry." Oakeshott defines poetry more generically than the art form of rhymes, epics, and e.e. cummings. Poetry makes images and delights in them. Poetry "moves about them in a manner appropriate to their character."

Of these four categories only the poetic mode suits performance. Practice is individuated economic behavior. It is subjective and "self-ish." It has no capacity to generalize norms to communities. History and science, by virtue of their strengths in describing—their obligation to comprehensiveness and their embrace of tentativeness and susceptibility of disproof—do not and cannot claim to produce normative closure. The careful scientist and historian even hedge their empirical predictions heavily. The performance that in its moment reasserts the reality of a normative vision inevitably creates the image or vision and delights in it. Oakeshott's poetic mode resembles Kant's wooing, and playfulness plays an important role in wooing.

In performance—indeed in all forms of thought—Oakeshott believes that the claim to reach truth through interpretation is a logical impossibility. At best we arrive at meaningful interpretations only through the "thick-textured" and painstaking methods of Geertz and Gadamer. True interpretation occurs only in science precisely because it appreciates the rich, inherently ambiguous, and open-ended nature of the questions and the data that bear on them. Geertz and Gadamer warn constantly against the premature presumption of closure. Legal reasoning, at the constitutional level, at least, does not and cannot interpret. If it claims to do so, the effectiveness of the claim depends on the Court's creating and delighting in a simplified and fictionalized image of interpretation, a "play" of interpretation, that appeals to the audience.

SOME PRELIMINARY APPLICATIONS TO CONSTITUTIONAL JURISPRUDENCE

The next chapter proposes how to assess the goodness of constitutional scripts and court performances. It develops in more detail a jurisprudence of performance. Here, at least to alleviate the abstractedness of this chapter, is a first cut at the constitutional applications this approach implies.[1]

1. Conventional jurisprudence holds that the Constitution's status as "supreme law of the land" and the communal norm of the rule of law require the Court to follow rules strictly or abandon the very *nomos* of our national community. I argued previously against this position for two separate reasons. Hermeneutic theory and the thrust of Critical legal scholarship show it cannot be done. The rules are indeterminate and the jurisprudence for making them determinate is in chaos. But even if this argument fails, the justices have never practiced this theory and we have no expectation that they will. Recall that this book searches for a theory that accommodates what I have said the metaphorical woman from Mars would see. The performance model seems to fit what the Court has done in history. The creation of a coherent vision and the evocation of a *nomos* cannot be bound to substantive rules. One cannot create and celebrate or delight in images of racial justice, the sanctity of private property, or the propriety of the death penalty by asserting no more than that a rule commands them. This stops the conversation of mankind dead in its tracks. The Court must perform an authoritative justification of the normative meaning of the rule in order to keep the conversation going.

2. Students of the Court over time seem, like sports fans, to agree that they can distinguish "great" and "mediocre" justices. The rankings are not unanimous, but the clusters are. How can we account for this consensus in light of: (a) the absence of any formal or standardized measure of judicial greatness, and (b) the obviously inconsistent philosophies of many of the "greats"? Justice Frankfurter did not, after all, consistently agree with Robert Jackson.

---

[1] I develop these ideas in my article, "Die Meistersinger von Nurnberg and the United States Supreme Court," (forthcoming) in *Polity* (Spring, 1986).

I suspect the great become so because each persuades us that he possesses a coherent view of community. The great have all been great writers, often off the bench as well as on, which is to say they have performed persuasively with words, which are the tools of the legal craft. John Marshall, Holmes, Cardozo, Brandeis, Frankfurter, and Jackson are better known for the poetic force of their opinions than are Lurton, Butler, and Whittaker.

3. If we told nine performers to prepare a character, a "dramatic persona," and then to maintain it throughout an extended improvisation, we might then observe, on the "stage," much collective nonsense and much consistency of individual characterization all at once. This is, I think, a plausible characterization of the modern Court. Neither rules, precedents, nor constitutional theories seem to cause results or unite the justices. Rather, individual justices use these tools selectively to create and justify their personal visions.

4. Increasing political pluralism would seem inevitably to widen the visible divisions and distinctions among the players in this drama. If individuals quest for a constitutional "idea that appears to be complete in itself" (Oakeshott) in a pluralist world, the compromises they must reach to generate majorities will become inevitably more compromised, arbitrary, and incoherent.

5. Not all performances are good ones, and the working conditions on the Court may, in conjunction with political realities, make good performances less frequent. Still the Court gives us unconvincing and incoherent visions of community far too often. Our philosophers and many Critical theorists have already identified the problem. The "good" constitutional decision, that is an effective performance, must woo its audience by shaping the experiences common to the members of the audience. The very effectiveness of the political dynamics that keep the Court aligned with its audience just now prevent the justices from appreciating the aesthetic essence of their role. The Court's failures of vision mirror the failure of vision in our time. Joseph Gusfield (1981, p. 194) put the point this way:

> Science is the idiom of our age. It is the language in which command is cast as the compulsion of external nature. Authoritative law that rests its claim to legitimacy and acceptance on the technical reasoning of the realm of science denies any moral status. It denies that a moral decision has been taken, that a political choice among alternatives has been made.

The justices' individual visions and the Court's collective visions tend toward incoherence because our culture discredits the poetic voice in conversation. In an age of flexibility, cost–benefit analysis, and scientific objectivism, virtue recedes from view. If the voice of science appears to capture the normative essence of community, then judges come to assume that any justification couched in the language of science, the ritual recitation of balancing, for example, will do. Perhaps it would do, but it will do only to the extent the Court creates a vision of a normative world in which it does so rightfully. But that very culture prevents us from recognizing or accepting the critical role performance necessarily plays. It convicts dramatic fictions on the indictment that they are "unscientific." Worse, it offers significant disincentives for taking seriously what normative discourse is all about, or why norms, not scientific studies alone, constitute communities.

6. We cannot and should not expect high levels of consistency among cases, or fidelity to grand jurisprudential theories over time. The grand theory that some scholars seek, whether it is preservative or neo-Marxist, will kill the creative expression on which the illusion of legal closure in the case and on which the conversational development of the narrative over time depend. One of the virtues of Cover's piece is that he limits his analysis to a case. In a theatrical model of jurisprudence, the case, or perhaps the justice, suffices. The experience of a community of shared norms is always short-lived. Coherence is retested, lost or regained, in every performance.

Consider, finally, how each theory of constitutional justification, from preservative to aesthetic, might apply to the following case. Note particularly how one of the most conventional categories of all—activism and restraint—confuses rather than clarifies the analysis of the case.

Immigration and Naturalization Service v. Chadha (1983), the "legislative veto" case, struck down a power, reserved by statute, by which Congress could terminate the service's suspension of the deportation of an immigrant alien. The Court's opinion unequivocally nullified all of the more than 200 veto provisions in other statutory schemes. The chief justice's justification for the majority appears at first glance as a strictly interpretive effort. It purported to reach a conclusion made inevitable by the logic of the constitutional text, yet the decision virtually doubled the number of judicial nullifications of Congressional acts over nearly two centuries of review.

Chadha, an East Indian with a British Commonwealth passport, was raised in Kenya. He emigrated to the United States from Kenya on a student visa, which expired. Having previously declined an option to become a citizen of Kenya, Kenya would not accept him, and Great Britain was not inclined to admit Indians from Kenya. For this reason the immigration judge, a civil service bureaucrat working within the Immigration Service, upheld Chadha's request for compassionate suspension of deportation. Very shortly before the expiration of the statutory period, in which either house of Congress could, under the statutory terms of the veto, terminate Chadha's suspension without debate, the House voted down Chadha's suspension.

These facts would seem to frame the legal issue along these lines: Can Congress, as a condition of the authority created in the judge to suspend deportations, include a veto provision? Can Congress attach to a function it creates and defines as "judicial" provisions for overturning the result on unexamined legislative grounds without violating the principle of separation of powers? However, the majority held simply that any exercise of a legislative veto constituted a legislative act. Under a literal reading of Article I, every exercise of legislative power must win approval of both houses and submit to a possible presidential veto. All legislative vetos are legislative acts because they have "the purpose and effect of altering the legal rights, duties and relations of persons . . . outside the legislative branch," wrote Chief Justice Burger.

By a formal, legalistic test of the sort the preservatives presumably prefer, that analysis might quality as "good constitutional law." A closer inspection, however, will uncover evidence not only that *Chadha* states bad policy, but that it is bad law even in legalistic terms. Peter Strauss (1983, pp. 789–801), from whom I drew the description of this case, above, discredits *Chadha* for the following reasons, and many more.

1. Altering the legal rights of someone outside the legislature cannot define "legislative" action. Executive actions, e.g., the Grenada "rescue operation," do so all the time, but they are not subject to Article I. So do judicial decisions. Furthermore, either chamber may subpoena citizens as witnesses in investigations, thus affecting their rights, duties, and relations, (particularly if they do not cooperate) *without* the approval of the other house or submission to a presidential veto. A judge who applies a rule to a concrete case must always, as Gadamer noted, identify a universal behind the rule. In *Chadha* the Court's universal directly contradicts the examples of legislative action on which its universal premise rests.

2. The majority's expressed logic is entirely circular. If the veto is valid, so that Chadha's right to remain is from the outset a right to remain only if Congress does not act, then its action has not affected Chadha's rights, duties, or relations in the first place. The majority's logic does not fit its own definitional starting point.

3. Under the conventional legal distinction in administrative law between legislative and judicial acts, the House would seem to have taken a judicial act. It does not state general policy for the future. The veto speaks to named persons and rules on the basis of past facts. The Court does not explain why it rejects this conventional distinction in defining legislative acts. Also, universally accepted principles of administrative law permit Congress to delegate its lawmaking authority to regulatory agencies within statutory schemes that are no more precise or limited than the act in question here, yet the Court makes it plain its veto decision does not threaten that accepted practice.

4. The Supreme Court itself proposes the judiciary's Federal Rules of Civil Procedure by laying them before the Congress. They become law unless Congress within a stated time blocks their adoption, yet the Court insists that its reasoning in *Chadha* does not threaten this arrangement.

5. Of 230 exercises of the veto between 1930 and 1982, nearly half had occurred in deportation cases. Congress had also disapproved presidential budget alterations 65 times. In 24 instances the Congress had rejected aspects of executive reorganization plans proposed by the president. Less than 30

exercises of the veto set aside regulatory policies. These different uses serve very different administrative and political functions. Some strengthen the adjustment of important policy questions between White House and Congress. Some fine tune enterprises, like budgetmaking, for which Congress and the president share continuous joint responsibility, some make decisions on individuals, like Chadha, and some oversee bureaucratic lawmaking. The Court could have reached the result in *Chadha* simply by noting that vetoes affecting individuals must conform to the minimal guarantees of procedural fairness common to all adjudicatory decisions. This statute does not embody those protections against potential tyranny or irrationality. The Court does not acknowledge any need to assess the varying political functions of different statutory schemes in which the veto plays a part.

The "problem" that Chadha took to court raised a basic moral question that is very much part of the convergence of modern constitutional law and theory. He, like the religious sects Cover described, experienced the threat of the arbitrary use of official power. The Congress made a "judicial" decision about him in a manner that would violate elementary due process if a court had made the decision. We must, as Duncan Kennedy noted, moralize such uses of power. The Court's opinion could have addressed that moral issue directly and resolved it. In doing so, it would have contributed to the continuing dialogue about the lines that separate individual freedom and collective power. By ignoring the central moral issue in the case, however, the Court abandoned an opportunity to clothe political power with moral meaning.

From either a lawyer's perspective or from the perspective of anyone who studies national policymaking, nothing in the majority opinion seems to fit together. It ignores legal doctrine, standard analytical methods, and uncontestable facts of political life equally. What kinds of assumptions must the chief justice and those who joined his opinion have made about their constitutional role in order to reach this result? They cannot assume only the outcome matters, that opinions are irrelevant gloss: *This* opinion struck down hundreds of clauses not in direct litigation, and without the benefit of full argument. A different opinion reaching the same result on due process grounds would have left vetoes that adjust the continuing balance of power between Congress and the executive intact.

The Court's projection of the legal consequences, e.g., that other functionally identical forms of informal lawmaking remain valid, undercut whatever moral force "sticking to the words of the Constitution" might have because the Court provides no way to distinguish acceptable from unacceptable legislative forms. The palpable "misfittedness" of the case at every level prompted Mark Tushnet to presume that the Court's real and hidden motives were purely political. I quoted earlier his speculation that the Burger Court seeks every opportunity to enhance presidential power. That discussion (1984a, pp. 1268–1269) continued:

The [*Chadha*] decision is one for which there is, so far as I can tell, no defensible justification in constitutional theory . . . . But *Chadha* accomplished two things. First, the response to the decision anticipated the "no counterrevolution" thesis. It went roughly like this: "People were afraid that the Burger Court lacked dedication to constitutional principles. The legislative veto case shows that they were wrong. Admittedly, we're not sure why the legislative veto is unconstitutional even after reading the opinions, but by God it does show that they care about 'The Constitution' " And second, the decision endorsed a theory of the presidency that stresses the prerogatives and powers of the office. Thus the Court satisfied two constituencies: those favoring an imperial President and those espousing a "strict construction" perspective.

I am inclined to attribute the decision less to hidden political agendas and more to the failure of legal and political scholarship to dispel the myth that legalism and literalism promote the "legitimacy" of the judicial process, and to the failure of our culture to teach every schoolchild that logic can prove either everything or nothing. Congress can so easily accomplish the ends the veto provided by other informal means, which the opinion endorses, that the political consequences seem trivial.

Nevertheless, Tushnet dramatizes a critical point. The Court can only defend its impartiality if it provides a credibly coherent explanation of its choices. Just as we may question the "good judgment" of an actor or musician who gives a palpably bad public performance, so decisions like *Chadha* force us to conclude that something somewhere went wrong.

Justice John Paul Stevens has recently advised college students who aspire to the law that the study of poetry is essential preparation for law school (Gopen, 1984). Poetry is the craft of fitting verbal metaphors together such that they evoke visions and recall experiences behind the words. The poet's pen that, according to Shakespeare, turns airy nothings into shapes and gives them local habitations and names does not appeal to us because it finds "lost names" for us. Rather, we delight in the poet's thinking and thus creating the habitation and the name together. Style invites participation in creating meaning. The creative style not only invites our participation in a larger community; it encourages us to attain meaning and order in our private thoughts. This is what protects us from the dark. *Chadha*'s political consequences should bother us much less than the possibility that it represents the best efforts of sincere and powerful men to tell a truth about the national community. Such thinking at best leaves us in the dark; at worst it creates a black hole.

Chapter 7   AESTHETICS IN CONSTITUTIONAL LAW

[A] judge must think of himself as an artist . . . who, although he must know the handbooks, should never trust to them for his guidance; in the end he must rely upon his almost instinctive sense of where the line lay between the word and the purpose which lay behind it; he must somehow manage to be true to both.

—Learned Hand

I am a relativist who nevertheless maintains that there is a distinction between right and wrong theories, interpretations, and works of art. I believe neither that a literary work is determined by the intent of the author nor that all interpretations are equally right . . . .

—Nelson Goodman

What do you think about these things? I have offered only guesses.

—C. S. Lewis

SUMMARIES

This book searches for a framework by which we, a small minority of citizens who actually read and care about the Supreme Court's constitutional decisions, can evaluate the goodness of these decisions. The search has rejected many familiar possibilities. Let me summarize briefly which frameworks we have rejected, and why.

We start with the premise that the Constitution somehow concerns itself with political goodness in the United States. We start here not because the Constitution commands it but because we have come to take for granted that we ought to treat it that way. If modern social and political philosophers are correct, we also assume at the start that individual knowledge and beliefs develop in interaction with cultures and are bound tightly to them. Hence we reject at the outset any framework based on statements of the universal rights of man. Our perceptions of such rights must derive from our culture.

When we look at American political culture, however, we note immediately its pluralism. Therefore we also reject the possibility that the Court ought to discover and articulate majority consensus on what is politically good. There is no such consensus.

I have, however, argued that underneath our differences about what is politically good there exists a common pattern in the way we think. This is pragmatism. We do share a respect for common sense, for caring about the meaning of raw experience, and for adjusting policies and beliefs according to the meanings we ascribe to raw experience. We are a relatively changeful people.

Pragmatism in turn forces us to reject many of the conventional constitutional theories. Preservativism and all related theories that claim the Court can find meaning in the text and its history run aground on two pragmatic rocks. First, they deny that attention to the meaning of raw experience, and hence common-sense changefulness, have a place in defining what is politically good. Second, they ignore our raw experience with the Court itself which, over time, has never consistently performed within any legalistically defined framework of adjudication. In varying degrees all of the political alternatives to interpretivism—Ely, Bickel, Choper, Perry, and so on—also defend themselves on legal rather than pragmatic terms and hence fail as well.

Careful attention to the raw experience of constitutional lawmaking reveals it as an inevitably political phenomenon. Our observations would push us strongly toward the conclusions of political jurisprudence and the Critical movement except for one thing. They do not provide an evaluative framework. At this point we appear caught in a paradox. We observe a desire for some evaluative framework. All the rich and passionate jurisprudential literature we have covered exists because its authors care deeply about the importance of sharing a framework for constitutional goodness. At the same time we observe that none of them fits persuasively with what we observe in the daily workings of law and politics.

I have suggested that by viewing constitutional lawmaking as an aesthetic process, one in which the author of an opinion has an opportunity to create a momentary vision of political goodness much like a musician, an actor or a visual artist, we can break out of the paradox. If we do this we necessarily give up any expectation that the Court will obey conventional legal norms of textual or doctrinal consistency apart from the role consistency may play in good performances. But then the Court does not follow such conventions anyway. Furthermore, as the Martian observed, most of us experience constitutional cases as relatively unique events. The "jurisprudence of unique cases" casts some doubt on the importance of consistency and predictability at all costs.

I shall shortly try to explain more thoroughly how aesthetic theory may apply to constitutional opinions, but let me first review the most important elements of aesthetic theory that I have already covered.

People do need to believe in the goodness of their group experiences, but that belief is not sustained primarily by the group's reconfirming any specific norm or moral value. The belief is sustained when the group succeeds in making values seem important enough and comprehensible enough to discuss. The prospect of satisfying communications with one another explains why we cling together in groups against the fear of personal death and moral meaninglessness. A performance is aesthetically good because it persuades us that acts of ordering the chaos are doable and meaningful. This is why the essence of a good performance is that the elements of the vision it creates appear to us to be well-ordered or well-fitted together. Hence a majority and a dissenting opinion in the same case may both be constitutionally good if both create different but well-ordered political visions.

All aesthetic acts are acts of political communication in the sense that an artist seeks to persuade an audience. The nature of the relationship between performer and audience is a critical element in aesthetic events, and I shall say more about the Court's audience shortly. We have, however, seen that in political communications the performer must convince the audience that the norm on which he acts is not merely his own but is simultaneously part of the political experience his audience shares. Again, the performer's success in this regard depends on how well he fits the elements of his argument together, not on whether he hits upon the "right" norm. This is why Richard Parker's point about Rawls is so important. The way Rawls fit the admittedly culture-bound elements of his argument together clarified norms. This shock of recognition enhanced, though perhaps only for a short time, our respect for them. The performer woos his audience not by pandering to its whims but by taking experiences and values the audience knows and fitting them together in new and therefore revealing ways.

The Court's constitutional performances must address the question of political goodness. If we conclude that the Court speaks only to an audience of legal scholars, we would then necessarily judge judicial performances in what I have called "conventional" jurisprudential terms because the elements of textual and historical interpretation, fidelity to precedent, and so on, are the elements with which this audience is familiar. To persuade you to reject that solution, I must persuade you that the Court must perform for a wider audience. I hope the fact that I write for an audience of political scientists will help me persuade you, but that, of course, depends on whether you are in fact a student of politics.

AN EXTREME EXAMPLE

Before I turn to aesthetics directly, let me present an extreme version of my argument thus far. It is a version I do not in all respects actually accept. However, the more persuasive you find it, the more easily you will accept what follows it.

The Supreme Court may declare as constitutionally binding law any policy it wishes. It may abolish the presidency and the Congress. It may order the enslavement of the white race to the black race. It may order an invasion of Mexico. It may reverse a century of law and hold that the Fourteenth Amendment protects only the right of black Americans to be free of *de jure* discrimination, and so on. No imaginable decision is automatically foreclosed or forbidden by "the law." *However*, the constitutional discretion just described is subject to the following constraint: Each justice must conscientiously attempt at all times to meet the aesthetic requirements of a good performance. Thus the rightness or goodness of any constitutional decision conceivable depends on the characteristics of the performance the Court gives when it justifies the decision. A reader should assess the quality of an opinion by asking how effectively the Court has created in its performance a coherent vision of a community. Readers who can relate their reading of the Court's opinion to no community they have directly experienced or can imagine experiencing, will presumably assess the performance negatively, or not at all. However, the performance may create in the reader a vision of community that transcends his personal experiences.

Whether and to what extent those who respond or attend to a decision choose "legality" or any other norm as an ingredient which the good performance must attend to is up for political grabs. Whether the practical consequences of the decision can be predicted, and whether, if predictable, they should count, are also up for grabs. Above all, the nature of the community in question is also up for grabs. This is especially important, for it is the nature of a community that the constitutional case must shape. Moreover, the nature of the community is not necessarily foreclosed by history or precedent, for the community is always potentially changing, and what it becomes depends on the persuasiveness of the visions presented.

The only thing not up for grabs in this hypothesized world is that constitutional decisions are about the constituting, the making, of communities. This entails a commitment on the part of judges and those who pay attention to their decisions to communicate their beliefs and interests to one another as persuasively as their resources permit. Thus, the Court's obligation to identify its audience and to perform as persuasively for it as its resources permit is not up for grabs. As in any creative effort, the Court must attend closely to its audience.

If all this seems quite reckless, please recall that if we see any Court opinion as only one in an endless series of efforts to give meaning to raw experience, if we abandon our habit of evaluating the Court's work in legalistic terms, then the opinion becomes less threatening. It is not really final. Its political reception will determine what it finally means.

An illustration will no doubt help here. Suppose a ruling in a class action suit brought by unemployed white laborers in the Southwest. Appellants assert that the obvious failure of the federal government to prevent the illegal immigration of cheap labor from across the Mexican border deprives them of their jobs without due process of law. The Court agrees and orders the federal government to cut off all illegal immigration immediately. The only effective action to enforce the order as stated would, assume, require military occupation of a substantial strip of the Mexican frontier.

I have stated a mild case here, for each element of the hypothesized justification has a basis in some precedent. The order, which formally leaves the choice of implementation up to the commander in chief, does not contradict anything linguistically explicit in the Constitution. But how might the Court justify its result to an audience if it took its obligation to perform well seriously?

Take the audience reaction first. We can imagine members of some communities—the white laborers, for example—applauding not only the results but some reasons the Court might give: "A nation without secure borders is not constituted as a nation. Appellants as a class have established their standing. They have alleged direct injury proximately caused by governmental failure to meet a legal responsibility. Therefore the order is consistent with the most elementary of the Court's constitutional responsibilities." Or, "The rule of law in our society is paramount. We must take the law's logic where it leads. This Court cannot therefore condone the blatant failure of a government constituted under the rule of law to tolerate a continuous pattern of lawbreaking."

The difficulty, of course, is that constitutional decisions seek to constitute not the community of Southwestern laborers, or white laborers, but the national community. The national community includes the employers of cheap labor, soldiers who must risk their lives in potentially open warfare, businessmen with financial interests in Mexico, and so on. To perform effectively for them collectively, the Court must have some basis for believing that its appeal to the due process clause and the rule of law will persuade. I cannot say it would not persuade, but I doubt that it would. Why not? Because the justifications do not fit with (and in this case probably cannot be made to fit with) other moral values and factual hunches about consequences of such a decision on interests and values nationally conceived. The obligations I have set for the Court in this extreme example therefore greatly limit the Court's scope of action. To perform well a performer must anticipate those things to which his intended audience will relate and demonstrate their fit within his vision. The aesthetic constraint of fit, explained in more detail subsequently, solves in this framework the problem of unrestrained discretion that conventional theory assumes the rule of law must solve.

My theory holds that any public political act—a speech, a Court decision, a statute—is an aesthetic or artistic act. The theory that politics is performance would seem rather obvious, maybe even tritely so, if I used these terms to describe the dynamics of presidential politics, or television programming, on our conception of ourselves and our community. Ronald Reagan performs well on these dimensions. He talks directly to voters in their language. He claims the power of common sense and of shared national traditions. His political career is a triumph of performance over expertise. Similarly, the hypothesis that we become what television tells us we are has won millions in sociological grant money because theater *is* a standard part of human culture.

I am, of course, arguing that constitutional jurisprudence has for some time been fundamentally wrong, that is, disconnected from politics. Jurisprudence, along with modern philosophy, has become the province of the expert, but experts talk to each other. It is precisely this quality that leads to its fundamental errors. The Vietnam disaster best illustrates the capacity of pragmatic and politically responsible people to make gross, egregious errors if they come to believe they must think and know by according to the model of "expert theory." Searching openly and continuously for practical "understanding," which is part of the political art, is no less a part of a pragmatic culture. Indeed the pragmatists' influence on Rorty and Habermas contributes to their distrust of science. The very categorizations that theoretical thinking make possible simultaneously make pragmatic change more difficult. Stanley Karnow's *Vietnam: A History* (1983, p. 19) quotes General Maxwell Taylor on the point:

> First, we did not know ourselves. We thought we were going into another Korean War, but this was a different country. Second, we did not know our South Vietnamese allies. We never understood them, and that was another surprise. And we knew even less about North Vietnam.

The Court has been much less disconnected from the art of politics than most jurisprudential scholars have. However, the modern Court is in danger of mimicking the mistakes of Vietnam policy. These pragmatic men seem increasingly influenced by an unworkable version of empirical scholarship. If politics is persuasion, persuasion performance, and performance aesthetic, then mimicking the "objective" rhetoric of cost-benefit balancing and the like without explaining why our experience makes it right to do so will not persuade.

AN OUTLINE OF AN AESTHETIC THEORY

To readers unpracticed in the language of modern philosophy, the first exposure to an aesthetic theory may produce anesthetic effects. Take, for example, Nelson Goodman's answer to the question, "When is art?" (1978, pp. 67–68).

> . . . [T]here are five symptoms of the aesthetic: (1) syntactic density, where the finest differences in certain respects constitute a difference between symbols—for example, an ungraduated mercury thermometer as contrasted with an electronic digital-read-out instrument; (2) semantic density, where symbols are provided for things distinguished by the finest differences in certain respects—for example . . . ordinary English, though it is not syntactically dense; (3) relative repleteness, where comparatively many aspects of a symbol are significant—for example, a single line drawing of a mountain by Hokusai where every feature of shape, line

thickness, etc. counts, in contrast with perhaps the same line as a chart of daily stockmarket averages . . . ; (4) exemplification, where a symbol, whether or not it denotes, symbolizes by serving as a sample of properties it literally or metaphorically possesses; and finally (5) multiple and complex reference, where a symbol performs several integrated and interacting referential functions, some direct and some mediated through other symbols.

I hope to show that this paragraph contains clues to a way of thinking about constitutional lawmaking that allows more confident assessment of decisions than does conventional theory. But I hardly expect the average reader to understand the paragraph at first reading.

The world that makes this kind of theory possible looks like this. All knowledge and understanding is symbolic. Without language of some kind, nothing exists. To say, as I did previously, that the universe is a chaotic whirl of elementary particles is itself symbolic. I cannot even think the thought of universe and particle without words and the metaphors that words relate. (The universe links in my mind with the Montana "Big Sky," and particles with those motes in the air that one sees only in shafts of light.)

Thus we make worlds by using symbols, by fitting them together so that the symbols appear orderly. "In the beginning was the word, and the word was made flesh." And, because we have different languages and experiences, symbols fit for different people in different ways. Hokusai's symbolization of a mountain ridge done in the language of a line drawing may mean nothing to a person who has lived forever in flatlands.

So we make countless worlds from symbols, and the question is how we make them, how we know or come to believe in their reality, and how we may believe we share, given these principles, the same world. Verbal languages do link people who share the vocabulary. Any myths fostered by the institutions of power in communities promote common belief. The need to maintain community, to coordinate labor to insure physical survival, itself depends on maintaining at least the pretense of making a common world. This explains why sacrilege is in primitive cultures punished by death, and why modern public education drills students in the mechanics of "proper" grammar and punctuation year after year. This painful grammar drilling (recall elementary school not long ago was called grammar school) and the pain of primitive religious obedience are cross-cultural analogs.

Worlds are frames of reference. One frame of reference holds that the earth never moves. Another holds that the earth moves around the sun. Giotto's frame of reference is Van Gogh's, and Van Gogh's is not Einstein's (Goodman, 1978, pp. 2–3). But there is something peculiar in all this, for despite the multiplicity of worlds, we do not hesitate to assert that there is a rightness about Giotto's and Van Gogh's and Einstein's worlds, even though we cannot test them against a "real world" that we already know, or reduce them to a common world. We do not try to say, "Aha! Einstein's and Van

Gogh's and Giotto's worlds are all good; therefore the real world must be such that it has all three in common." Rather, the three possess the common structural capacity to persuade us that its world is coherent in its own terms.

For Goodman, the "trouble with truth" (pp. 17–18) is not that it does not exist. It is quite permissible to say a version of a world is true for those in whose frame of reference a version—a work of art, a musical performance, a political speech, a scientific experiment—

> offends no unyielding beliefs and none of its own precepts. Among beliefs un-yielding at a given time may be long-lived reflections of laws of logic, short-lived reflections of recent observations, and other convictions and prejudices . . . . Among precepts, for example, may be choices among alternative frames of reference, weightings, and derivational bases.

From this perspective note that the person who claims to "search for truth" is either confused or dishonest. We are surrounded within our cultural framework by obvious truths, so defined. The "search for truth" searches for a system of structuring observations and fitting disparate data together so that the resulting structure encourages us to see it as consistent with our underlying beliefs and precepts. "[I]f worlds are as much made as found, so also knowing is as much remaking as reporting . . . . Discovering laws involves drafting them. Recognizing patterns is very much a matter of inventing and imposing them" (p. 22). This is why Cardozo calls the judicial process "creative," and equates law with life. Again, the Critical movement's important collective contribution is its insistence that we have no choice but to treat law in this fashion.

Constitutional decisions are a subset of political speech. Speeches make worlds from the symbols of words, just as artists use paint and line and mass symbolically. A dented automobile fender in an art museum symbolizes something. The scientists' numbers stand for something else. Now the question becomes, how do verbal symbols persuade people that a message is consistent with their beliefs? Let me answer in three stages.

First, the performance must use symbols in such a way as to raise the perceiver's consciousness, to shock the perceiver into accepting the possibility of a new understanding, a recreation, or reordering of symbols they already know.[1] Placing the smashed fender in the museum presumably does just that. A "good political speech" (e.g., the Mytilenaian debate before the citizens of Athens, as reported in Thucydides and analyzed in depth by Orwin (1984), or

---

[1] Goodman, who insists that the same evaluative standards apply to science and art, wrote (1984, p. 192): "When a scientist first relates heat to motion, or the tides to the moon, our world-views are drastically altered. And when we leave an exhibit of an important painter, the world we step into is not the one we left when we went in; we see everything in terms of those works. That illumination from science and illumination from art are thus akin has been obscured only by the absurd misconception of art as mere entertainment."

Elizabeth I's speech to the army at Dover, or Macaulay's speech to Parliament, or Mario Cuomo's 1984 keynote address to the Democratic Party convention) uses symbols—of family, of collective reason or of patriotism—that raise consciousness about communal matters.

Second, the criteria for the persuasive organization of symbols in any creative performance (political, scientific, oral, or visual) include those Goodman listed in the previous quote, one that I hope you now begin to understand. A syntactically and semantically dense political speech builds a conclusion from a combination of messages that we can "tell apart."[2] The replete speech is efficient. We see how each message belongs in the whole. Replete speeches exemplify if we perceive in a message about war beligerant language, loving language in messages of peace, economic language in messages of self-interest. The complex speech is metaphorical. "Family," in Cuomo's address, refers to household, neighborhood, and nation.

Third, if the persuasiveness of a performance thus depends on matters of fit, both the internal fit of the parts and their fit, in turn, to the things they refer to, how is the audience to see, to know, to believe in the fit? The answer to this question completes the bridge between aesthetics and law. The fit is determined by practice, by what the audience already accepts as authoritatively permissible. The stories of painters and composers appreciated only after their deaths illustrate the point. The artist who creates a new radical vision will almost surely fail the tests of authoritativeness in his own time. He persuades post hoc because his work becomes its own authority. Here, however, art and politics take separate paths from the bridge. Political performances persuade in the present. Judges and other politicians, if they care to persuade, must pay close attention to, and claim to work from, moral beliefs, ways of categorizing observations, and forms of logic, (all of which the artist may, at least on the surface, dispute) that the audience can understand.

Near the beginning of this book (p. 11) I cited Goodman's belief that tradition, authoritativeness, and "fit with practice" explain the goodness of an aesthetic work. Here we must be very careful, for Goodman does not necessarily bring us back to the preservative world in which judges discover right answers in the law. Different audiences have different traditions and practices, so the analysis again requires us to ask for which audience the Court performs. Goodman's performers retain freedom to choose some elements from many the audience might find authoritative and to combine them creatively. Goodman actually comes close to equating good performance with

---

[2] Goodman (1984, p. 136) holds that no test is syntactically dense and that all texts are equally dense semantically. Since these are his terms, I am unqualified to disagree with his usage, but I believe he limits symbols to words. I may distort the concept, but I think texts—at least political speeches—do differentiate on this dimension if we use strings of words, not words themselves, as the units of symbolic analysis.

effective selling: "[What] needs to be shown is not that [the argument] is true but what it can do. To put it crassly, what is called for in such cases is less like arguing than selling" (p. 129).

THE ART OF POLITICAL SPEECH

In an essay titled "The Decline of Oratory," (1984, pp. 15–19) Henry Fairlie begins by citing the advice of King Akhtoy to his son: "Be a craftsman in speech, for the tongue is a sword to a man, and speech is more valorous than fighting." Fairlie's review of the art of political rhetoric across history covers many examples of effective persuasion, two of which I quote below, and he concludes that "Only today, and especially in America, does oratory have no place in politics." As if to confirm the point, Elizabeth Drew (1984, p. 82) quoted an adviser to presidential candidate Walter Mondale, "We have to make it clear that the question isn't salesmanship—who gives the best speech." Mondale, who appeared to heed this advice, lost big.

Fairlie's essay tells us that great oratory depends on the immediacy of the audience.

> The audience is as much an actor as the speaker. It charges the speaker with energy—there it is before him, and he must respond to it as well as it to him . . . . Heckling was an essential part of oratory . . . .
>   But how can an audience heckle, how can it play its part, in the arenas where politicians speak now? There are the batteries of microphones, which themselves separate speaker from audience; there are the loudspeakers, which make the rapport between speaker and audience unequal; there are the banks of cameras, which sometimes physically block audience from speaker.

Fairlie's article might be taken as a paean to the dialogic community that Habermas et al. prescribe, but the striking thing is that his illustrations repeatedly show how the political oratory succeeds by reforming the materials an immediate audience already possesses. The first of his two illustrations is quite simple.

> During the election campaign of 1960, John Kennedy sent Lyndon Johnson into the South. Johnson was to meet the South's angry criticisms of the Democratic Party's platform on civil rights . . . . From small town to small town across the South, he went, on a whistle-stop tour on a train called "The Yellow Rose of Texas," facing the sullen crowds of rednecks—"mah people," as he later put it to me. And head-on he spoke to them, as Stewart Alsop once characterized it, "with the tongues of angels." How would you feel, he demanded of them, if your child was sick, and you could not take him to the hospital in this town, but had to go twenty miles away? How would you feel if you were shopping and your child was thirsty, and you could not give him a cold soda at the counter in the drugstore? And again and again, he won the sullen audience.

The illustration is far more interesting than an aesthetic theory that may kill it by explanation. But the theory is apt. He built explicitly on the experience of parenthood shared in his audience, but we can imagine from this description how Johnson's style—courage and straight talk—expanded the authority with which he spoke to that audience.

Fairlie argues that all orators must act, but to reinforce reason rather than mask it:

> In times past, the acting was to reinforce the eloquence, the eloquence was to reinforce the reasoning. It must be realized that the object of great oratory was to appeal to the reason of the audiences. Few orators in any age combined close reasoning with majestic eloquence more masterfully than Macaulay when he was in the House of Commons . . . , as in this speech arguing (as early as 1833) that civil and political disabilities should be removed from the Jews: "The honorable member for Oldham tells us that the Jews are naturally a mean race, a sordid race, a moneygetting race . . . . Such, Sir, has in every age been the reasoning of bigots. They never fail to plead in justification of persecution the vices which persecution has engendered. England has been to the Jews less than half a country; and we revile them because they do not feel for England more than a half patriotism. We treat them as slaves, and wonder that they do not regard us as brethren. We drive them to mean occupations, and then reproach them for not embracing honorable professions. We long forbade them to possess land, and we complain that they chiefly occupy themselves in trade. We shut them out from all the paths of ambition; and then we despise them for taking refuge in avarice . . . . Let us do justice to them. Let us open to them the door of the House of Commons. Let us open to them every career in which ability and energy can be displayed. Till we have done this, let us not presume to say that there is no genius among the countrymen of Isaiah, no heroism among the descendents of the Maccabees."

Lyndon Johnson might, of course, have given Macaulay's speech from the rear of "The Yellow Rose of Texas" in 1960, but would it have persuaded? Macaulay appeals to the audience's presumed training in the classics, its respect for analytical reason, and its presumed knowledge of the evidence of history, a mix of experiences that differs greatly from that which Johnson's audience possessed. Note in both cases that the speech presumes it proper to use language to change behavior by raising the vision of the audience to see higher moral ideals.

Similar examples occur in constitutional decisions, for example, Justice Jackson's "If there is any fixed star in our constitutional constellation [the gaze is raised!], it is that no official, high or petty [we are equal under law] can prescribe what shall be orthodox in politics, nationalism, religion, or other matters of opinion or force citizens to confess by word or act their faith therein" (*Barnette*). The cadences are those of political oratory. Those unfamiliar with Justice Brandeis's concurrence in *Whitney* should alter that condition at once. Contrast Jackson or Macaulay to the rhetoric of the 1984 presidential campaigners. Gary Hart: "Only better is better" and "We must move beyond the solutions of the past which do not work." Walter Mondale: "A president is our leader" and "To get the economy moving again will take people." Reagan: "People must be part of our planning" and "Our national parks are the envy of the world." The contrast is aesthetic.

All political speakers, including appellate court speakers, perform well by contributing to their audience's confidence that the community can harmonize, accommodate, and fit together the experiences and beliefs that have come under tension in the moment. In a pragmatic culture this means harmonizing (a) the rules the audience may deem to bear on the dispute, (b) the facts of the dispute itself, (c) beliefs about the empirical nature of the community, and (d) normative claims that exist in common discourse (Carter, 1984, p. 290). Pragmatism and the aesthetic theory it generates thus boil down to a theory of communication and persuasion, a theory that describes the conditions in which communication and persuasion can be said to have happened. Thus far, however, this theory cuts down little jurisprudential underbrush, for we have seen that the theory pays equal attention to performer and to audience. We have not yet identified or described the audience for which the Court should perform, and hence we have not yet seen how the Court can perform well.

THE CAUTIOUS VERSION OF AESTHETIC JURISPRUDENCE

An audience is a group of people who pay attention to someone who seeks to persuade the group of something. The Court's audience consists at least of the parties to the case, the attorneys who have argued it, and those people who are similarly situated to the parties and their attorneys relative to the issues in litigation. The Court must speak persuasively to them. For example in deciding *Chadha*, it must take seriously its responsibility to persuade Chadha, the Immigration Service, and the legislators who have endorsed the legislative veto that its decision harmonizes the four factors which I listed at the close of the last section. This is precisely what the *Chadha* majority's legalistic opinion did not do. Some audiences may be small, others large. The audiences for *Brown* and *Roe* were very large.

Much of the jurisprudential debate we have reviewed really asks whether the Court must limit its audience to the legal profession. Some plausible arguments suggest it should. They yield a cautious aesthetic jurisprudence.

First, as a practical matter, the implementation of decisions is in the hands of lawyers. If translation into community norms is necessary, the lawyers, given clear messages, will complete the translation for their clients in communities. Second, appellate courts must communicate to lower courts, and the Supreme Court to all federal and state courts. Appellate courts do not make campaign speeches or dramatic orations from the benches in Parliament. They issue commands, and technicians must understand them if they are to be obeyed.[3] Third, targeting lawyers and judges as the only relevant audience

---

[3] Justice Hans Linde of the Oregon Supreme Court (1984) describes the practical difficulties of litigating state constitutional claims in the shadow of the U.S. Supreme Court's doctrinal swings.

solves what might otherwise be an insurmountable problem. Out there beyond the lawyers is a pluralist nation, one that may contain no overarching values at all. Even if we lay aside all the inadequacies of survey research and claim to know with confidence those values that are shared nationally, we will find values that, if taken seriously, undercut the purpose of law to limit the will of the majority in the name of individual liberty and equality.

Thus a "cautious version" of aesthetic jurisprudence would confine the aesthetic analysis to the world of law. To readers looking for an evaluative test, aesthetic theory would say, learn the forms and norms of legal reasoning, then judge the quality of a decision by the extent to which you feel persuaded that the decision fits the elements of legal form together. None of this rules out decisions with powerful social consequences, nor does it rule out applauding decisions that speak with moral power. But the applause will come from the artistic usage of the tools of legal analysis.

This cautious approach does not automatically return us to strict interpretivism and square one. The legal tradition does not depend on textual language; it does not authoritatively require a hermeneutic recreation of the framers' intent. It recognizes that precedents do not solve cases. Hard cases are hard precisely for these reasons. Lawyers do not take the rules of law seriously.

The position approximates that of Professor Fiss in chapter five. Objectivity in law persuades the legal audience by demonstrating judicial fits within the boundaries of legal forms. We have seen that aesthetics itself does not produce one right answer. As Charles Fried (1981, p. 57) put it:

> [Philosophy proposes] an elaborate structure of argument and considerations which descend from on high but stop some twenty feet above the ground . . . . [Lawyers and judges] are the masters of the "artificial Reason of the law." There really is a distinct and special subject matter for our profession. And there is a distinct method down there in the last twenty feet. It is the method of analogy and precedent. Analogy and precedent . . . are the only form of reasoning left to the law when general philosophical structures and deductive reasoning give out, overwhelmed by a mass of particular details . . . . The law is to philosophy, then, as medicine is to biology and chemistry. The discipline of analogy fills in the gaps left by more general theory, gaps which must be filled because choices must be made and actions taken.

The failure of legal arguments to provide right answers is therefore no reason not to take a closer look at legal methods, and particularly at reasoning by analogy.

To reason by analogy from a legal precedent does not require following it. Indeed, the routine assumption that citing cases for a position, or distinguishing them, lends authority to an argument is powerful evidence that legal reasoning takes its aesthetic task seriously. It would be hard to think of a more simple method to demonstrate internal and external fit than to show correspondence, verisimilitude, and consistency among the decisions themselves.

James Murray (1982) shows how the majority justified its position in *Virginia State Board of Pharmacy v. Virginia Citizens Consumer Counsel, Inc.* (1976) in this fashion. Here the Court struck down a state statute that prohibited a pharmacist from publishing or advertising the price of prescription drugs. In doing so the Court granted purely commercial speech First Amendment protection. The decision did not, however, pluck a theoretical moral justification for free speech out of the air. The Constitution might, of course, protect free speech only insofar as speech promoted discussion of the fullest range of opinions about matters of public policy. In his dissent, Justice Rehnquist plucked that theory. In doing so, however, he ignored five specific analogies that the majority found beyond dispute. Murray summarizes them:

> First, protection under the first amendment encompasses the rights of the listener as well as those of the speaker. Second, speech does not lose its first amendment protection because the "speakers" spend money to project it. Third, the first amendment even protects speech that is "sold" for profit or involves solicitation to purchase products or to contribute money. Fourth, the proponents of purely factual matters of public interest may claim protection. Finally, the first amendment protects the parties' interests even when their interests are purely economic. For example, both contestants in a labor dispute express themselves and, in so doing, they are protected. Each of the above propositions supports the application of the first amendment to commercial speech, although no single one of them completely encompasses commercial speech. (p. 857)

Murray notes that such reasoning by analogy is itself morally neutral. It does not mean the majority was right "on the law"; their use only allows us to differentiate the majority from Justice Rehnquist's dissent, for he chose not to counter the argument with alternative analogical fits of his own.

It should be added that in *Virginia Pharmacy*, the Court did not stop with the analogies. The majority also invoked the principle that advertising contributes knowledge valuable to individuals, in this case particularly those on low budgets. And it countered Justice Rehnquist's plucking directly: "Even if the First Amendment were thought to be primarily an instrument to enlighten public decisionmaking in a democracy, we could not say that the free flow of [commercial] information does not serve that goal" (425 U.S. at 765). Information about commercial operations may directly inform public policy debates about the need for regulation of commerce. The Court, in other words, appealed to at least a lawyer's version of an important community norm—freedom of information and informed choice. Thus the degree of analogical fit demonstrated in the majority opinion persuades the legal reader, whether he agrees with the outcome or not, that the Court has created a "good" opinion.

Robert Bennett (1984) has recently developed additional criteria for evaluating the goodness of fit within a legal framework. For Bennett the "legitimacy or objectivity of a decision has to do more with its development from a preexisting tradition and natural growth from an institutional soil than with its approval by authority" (p. 475). Judges do seem quite sincere about the legal system's own rules of impartiality. Judges commonly step down in cases that give even the appearance of personal involvement. Even unrestrained discretion does not produce really personal, that is selfish, choices; the choices are rather about public values, and sentences like "I think this is an uncommonly silly law," from judges who uphold "silly" laws regularly occur.

More important, Bennett suggests that the Court may operate in terms of a "path dependence" cognitive dissonance model. Even a judge who personally drafted a provision of a constitution and then unilaterally decided many cases under it over time would find himself psychologically bound to respect the precedents he had created, and to gain meaning from the order in which he created them. The author's original intent even here will change to accommodate what he has created over time, so that if at the end of a chain of cases result X seems incompatible with the original intent, even the framer himself will choose X. Judges who do this, or something similar, give persuasive judicial performances (pp. 481–483).

Bennett argues that if we accept these constraints, we necessarily must question whether a decision that appears as a blatant imposition of a value choice, e.g., the abortion decision, actually does so. *Roe*, according to Bennett, can be said to follow a consistent and rich line of precedents that over time increasingly protected individual choices on matters of procreation and child-rearing. In this regard *Roe*, which Ely condemns as unobjective, is more objective than the reapportionment cases of the 1960s, whose thrust Ely approves (pp. 486–487).

Justice Linde (1984) underscores the practical importance of Bennett's and Murray's standard of objectivity (pp. 180–181):

> Still, even when you have an appealing claim, I cannot recommend adopting the nonoriginalist theory of judicial review in an actual argument to a court. Your argument had better be linked to some premise that can be said to be constitutional law apart from the desired result in the case itself. Is this demand for a link to the constitution only a professional charade? If nonoriginalist arguments are good constitutional law, why should you not ask a court simply to apply the enlightened moral consensus or societal values of the day to the merits of your case and cheerfully argue that nothing in the text or the history of the constitution is important for that purpose?
> If you were to do that, you might lose even the most appealing case, and not for failing to play the professional game. The link to a constitution is essential for anyone to deal responsibly with the problem that the contemporary theorists ignore, the problem of federalism in constitutional rights . . . .
> . . . The United States Supreme Court, whatever motivates it on the merits, necessarily must insist that such a claim arises under something in the Constitution of the United States, for this alone give the Court jurisdiction under article III of the Constitution. If a state court, in turn, is to strike down a law enacted in

its own state without asserting that such a law would be void throughout the nation, the court must have a basis in its own state's constitution.

Justice Linde gives aesthetic advice, but in a disguised form: The case does not have a right answer. Either side can win. Constitutions structure and limit the legal powers of government; therefore, the lawyer must persuade the judge of a fit between the conclusion and the law.

Yet there is something odd about this cautious argument. Justice Linde warns against arguing nonoriginalist theory on one hand, and then he says the advocate must claim a premise "that can be said to be constitutional law apart from the desired result in the case itself." But the two are not opposites. Perhaps Linde is confused about his terminology. This book has described many examples of nonoriginal constitutional law. A premise can be linked to the constitution in opposition to its text and the literal evidence of the intent of the framers simply by invoking its deeper spirit. Linde tells lawyers how to perform for their audience of judges, but any competent attorney on either side of any case can easily perform this way. He *does* ask lawyers to play a professional game of charades. The lawyer must presumably proffer precedential support, but that is just as "constitutional" as speculating what the framers would think today. The desegregation cases, the reapportionment cases, the abortion cases all have precedential support. So did my hypothetical court-ordered invasion of Mexico.

Thus Linde really suggests two points. The first point, like those of Murray and Bennett, underscores my position that appellate argument and decision *are* aesthetic acts. Rhetoric assists argument, and effective practitioners know that. Near the end of his essay, Justice Linde points out that judges realize that their hunches about public values and assumptions about social facts come from their own heads, but simply disguise the fact by changing the words of the message into something that sounds neutral.

> If a court is convinced that a law is unreasonable, it may say that the burdens imposed by the law are not justified by any practical purpose it serves, or it may say that the law is unfair or arbitrary or an intolerable invasion of liberty or privacy, without thinking of these as two different kinds of reasons. (p. 193)

The only substantive issue Linde's argument touches is thus a minimalist one. The script must be about the nature and use of governmental power. A Court that announces that the Constitution imposes a moral obligation on children to care for their parents in their parents' dotage, or any other private obligation that has not become the focus of governmental policy, will not persuade a legal audience. But any other script might.

This raises the second point. Cautious applications of the aesthetic approach do not give any evaluative purchase for most constitutional decisions. Unless a dissent asserts the majority has directly misquoted an opinion it cites, or has ignored uncontroverted factual evidence in the record, only a lawyer who has specialized in the law of the case can assess its quality. For the rest, all cases that cite some precedents in any plausibly analogic fashion are equally satisfactory constitutional law. The bulk of modern political science analyses of the Court implicitly start from precisely this conclusion. Legal forms do not seriously limit judicial choices. Therefore, political scientists analyze the policy consequences of judicial choices, e.g., of the exclusionary rule. Political scientists know the Court will have only guessed at the consequences, but they know the Court can change its mind, and beneath the aesthetic rhetoric, and not visible in opinions, the consequences of choices can feed back into judicial revisions of doctrine.

Some opinions do fail the cautious approach test: *Dred Scott* does. Justice Rehnquist's dissent in *Virginia Pharmacy* might, although dissents, since they do not carry the burden of communicating legal commands, are harder to judge by these standards. Consider two more examples.

In *Mullaney v. Wilbur* (1975) the Court had held unconstitutional state provisions requiring defendants to carry the burden of persuasion that they acted "in the heat of passion" in a killing. In *Engle v. Issac* (1982), petitioners claimed that their criminal trials were flawed because they had to carry the burden that they killed in self-defense. They insisted that the self-defense issue was not logically distinguishable from the heat of passion defense. The Court refused to set aside the state convictions because the attorneys had not raised the issue at trial. The trials occurred after *Mullaney*, so the attorneys could reasonably be expected to have done so.

The decision consolidated three cases, and one of the three, Issac's, was complicated by the fact that while his appeal was pending, the Ohio Supreme Court interpreted a state statute to require the prosecution to carry the burden on self-defense. The statute predated Issac's trial, and the Ohio Court stated its rule applied retroactively. Still, Issac lost in the state courts because his attorney had not raised the objection at trial. In federal court on habeas corpus, Issac's lawyers argued that for the state to refuse to give Issac the benefit of is own retroactive decision just because his attorney did not anticipate the issue *before* the retroactive ruling violated due process, an argument supported, though not conclusively established, in several precedents. The U.S. Supreme Court held against Issac on "parallel" ground that Issac had not raised these precedents or the legal question in his habeas petition. The trouble was, as Justice Brennan pointed out in dissent, and quoting from Issac's habeas petition, Issac clearly *did* raise the issue. Worse, the lower court opinions in Issac's case had pointed out the fact. Mark Tushnet's speculations about the case point out that the majority could have reached the same result without resorting to reasoning that leads to only one jurisprudential principle, "if you have the votes you can lie" (1984, p. 633). Tushnet has no doubt that the decision flowed from the majority's "law and order" value system. What bothers him is why the Court chose lying rather than reasoned argument to reach its conclusion. The suspicion is that the Court might no longer perceive any connection between justification and audience.

Schall v. Martin, the 1984 opinion upholding New York State's statute permitting preventive detention of juveniles prior to any adjudication of delinquency, may fall into the same category. The federal trial court made detailed factual findings that showed that (a) a substantial fraction of those detained had at no time in their lives been adjudicated delinquent; (b) a substantial number of juveniles are released after arrest and then, days or weeks later, rearrested and detained under the preventive detention provision without any evidence of misconduct in the interim between initial arrest and rearrest; (c) a majority of detained juveniles are, following their trials, immediately released, either unconditionally or on probation or parole. The implication is that the detentions served in fact as short-term punishment without trial, a consequence forbidden under standard due-process doctrine. The trial court found the statute unconstitutional as administered on these facts. The result, of course, invites the state to redraft a tighter statutory scheme.

Rule 52(a) of the Federal Rules of Civil Procedure binds the Court to such findings unless they are clearly erroneous. The intermediate appellate court did not disturb the findings, but the Supreme Court, through Justice Rehnquist, dismissed both lower court factual findings and reversed:

> But even assuming it to be the case that "by far the greater number of juveniles incarcerated will never be confined as a consequence of a disposition imposed . . . , we find that to be an insufficient ground for upsetting the widely-shared legislative judgment that preventive detention serves an important and legitimate function in the juvenile justice system. (104 S.Ct. at 2414)

The majority rejects the findings of two lower courts without any showing that they are clearly erroneous. The reason offered, that many state legislatures have approved preventive detention as a matter of statutory policy, evades the factual allegations about its administration in New York City.

The concern here parallels the earlier discussion of *Logan,* of *Chadha*, and of the difficulty in much modern jurisprudence that the Court, even by the most cautious and limited definition of its audience, sends out noise, and the frequency of noisey opinions may be increasing. Noise may communicate messages at rock concerts, but it is harder to construct a jurisprudence of noise, particularly for an audience of lawyers and judges.

In short, if we conclude that the Court need only perform for a professional audience, and if that audience asks the Court merely to demonstrate a fit between the decision and minimal standards of legal reasoning, lawyers still have reason to evaluate some opinions, particularly those of Burger, Rehnquist, and O'Connor, as very poor performances.

TOWARD A WIDER AUDIENCE

The cautious application of aesthetic theory classifies Court decisions in binary form. They are acceptable if they persuade a legal audience that the judges have played the lawyers' game. Otherwise they are unacceptable. Yet for some reason, this cautiousness does not satisfy. It does not account for Brest's observation that we hold tenaciously to some deeper normative vision of constitutional order. We aspire for something grander, something that integrates political communities, not just legal communities, something that explains the popularity of constitutional law courses in colleges and universities, the press coverage of Supreme Court decisions, and the normative debates that "major" decisions inevitably seem to provoke. More important, judges may have an obligation to speak to the audience that personally cares about the outcome: the parties (usually they are not lawyers) and those similarly situated to them.

Readers who see constitutional law as a vastly overrated element in national life, either because the Court actually affects a tiny fraction of significant public policy problems (defense policy, military spending, and budget balancing, to name only three that the Court does not substantially affect) or who believe that the Court's results make little practical difference in the way people think or live (the effects of *Brown* and the exclusionary rule, particularly on the lives of the urban poor, are certainly debatable), may feel content with the cautious approach. But if Brest's question presumes that the Court contributes in symbolically important ways to maintaining faith in political goodness, then some widening of the audience and the beliefs that the "good" opinion must successfully harmonize or fit together is necessary.

I fear that at this point most readers will try to generate a normative alternative that resembles a common, but quite false, stereotype of art and theater. Allan Hutchinson and Patrick Monahan concluded a conscientiously skeptical review of the Critical movement with the observation that Critical theorists want to "promote 'street theater,' the spontaneous involvement of people in everyday situations" (1984, p. 244). They believe that the movement seeks revolution, not reform, and that it implicitly adopts as its motto Otto Brahm's manifesto for the new theater:

> The banner slogan of the new art . . . is the single word Truth; and Truth it is, Truth on every path of life, which we too strive for and demand. Not the objective truth which eludes those who stand in battle; but the individual Truth which is freely created out of the most personal conviction . . . .
>
> We disavow every formula, and do not presume to chain life and art, which are in eternal motion, to the rigid constraint of rule . . . .
>
> No turnstile of theory and no sacredly held examples from the past will restrain the infinity of development which is the essence of the human race . . . . (1984, p. 244)

As a prescription for persuasive theater this is, of course, drivel. The forms of theater that strive to achieve these goals fail because they do not embody fits and coherence that Berger and Luckmann, on one side, describe as central in social life and that Goodman, on the other side, prescribes as essential to aesthetic evaluation. This bad stereotype suggests a constitutional law that ringingly declares the rights of man, whatever they are, to a nation populated by citizen-scholars. Justice Douglas' jurisprudence sometimes resembled such street theater. He did not appear to care much about the craft of creating fits, which explains the reservations of many students about his work. It would seem wiser to identify why Otto Brahm's art fails, and in so doing identify the characteristics of successful theater, poetry, art and music, that is, why Johannes Brahms' art succeeds.

From this point in my argument, only examples can clarify and persuade further. I need to show you cases that appear "good" because they are pragmatic, good because they look beyond legal forms to the experiences of citizens, fit those experiences into a coherent normative claim, and then communicate that claim back to us in a comprehensible language. I have mentioned a number of recent cases which I have criticized for failing to persuade (at least to persuade me) that the majority opinion took seriously its responsibility to seek an aesthetically satisfying fit. Here is an example that, I think, succeeds.

In *Sweatt v. Painter* (1950), Sweatt, a black U.S. postal worker, applied for admission to the University of Texas law school. His application was automatically rejected because state law required the school to admit only whites. Chief Justice Vinson delivered the following opinion. Note his attention both to the incontroverted facts in the case and his insistence that the practical or "political" character of legal education and practice properly influences the result. Note that in doing so, that is by eschewing legalistic justifications, he speaks directly to the citizens who care about the result: law school administrators and black citizens denied access to educational opportunities that Texas granted to whites.

> The state trial court recognized that the action of the State in denying petitioner the opportunity to gain a legal education while granting it to others deprived him of the equal protection of the laws guaranteed by the Fourteenth Amendment. The court did not grant the relief requested, however, but continued the case for six months to allow the State to supply substantially equal facilities. At the expiration of the six months, in December, 1946, the court denied the writ on the showing that the authorized university officials had adopted an order calling for the opening of a law school for Negroes the following February. While petitioner's appeal was pending, such a school was made available, but petitioner refused to register therein. The Texas Court of Civil Appeals set aside the trial court's judgment and ordered the cause "remanded generally to the trial court for further proceedings without prejudice to the rights of any party to this suit."
>
> On remand, a hearing was held on the issue of the equality of the educational facilities at the newly established school as compared with the University of Texas

Law School. Finding that the new school offered petitioner "privileges, advantages, and opportunities for the study of law substantially equivalent to those offered by the State to white students at the University of Texas," the trial court denied mandamus. The Court of Civil Appeals affirmed. Petitioner's application for a writ of error was denied by the Texas Supreme Court. We granted certiorari because of the manifest importance of the constitutional issues involved.

The University of Texas Law School, from which petitioner was excluded, was staffed by a faculty of sixteen full-time and three part-time professors, some of whom are nationally recognized authorities in their field. Its student body numbered 850. The library contained over 65,000 volumes. Among the other facilities available to the students were a law review, moot court facilities, scholarship funds, and Order of the Coif affiliation. The school's alumni occupy the most distinguished positions in the private practice of the law and in the public life of the State. It may properly be considered one of the nation's ranking law schools.

The law school for Negroes which was to have opened in February, 1947, would have had no independent faculty or library. The teaching was to be carried on by four members of the University of Texas Law School faculty, who were to maintain their offices at the University of Texas while teaching at both institutions. Few of the 10,000 volumes ordered for the library had arrived; nor was there any full-time librarian. The school lacked accreditation.

Since the trial of this case, respondents report the opening of a law school at the Texas State University for Negroes. It is apparently on the road to full accreditation. It has a faculty of five full-time professors; a student body of 23; a library of some 16,500 volumes serviced by a full-time staff; a practice court and legal aid association; and one alumnus who has become a member of the Texas Bar.

Whether the University of Texas Law School is compared with the original or the new law school for Negroes, we cannot find substantial equality in the educational opportunities offered white and Negro law students by the State. In terms of number of the faculty, variety of courses and opportunity for specialization, size of the student body, scope of the library, availability of law review and similar activities, the University of Texas Law School is superior. What is more important, the University of Texas Law School possesses to a far greater degree those qualities which are incapable of objective measurement but which make for greatness in a law school. Such qualities, to name but a few, include reputation of the faculty, experience of the administration, position and influence of the alumni, standing in the community, traditions and prestige. It is difficult to believe that one who had a free choice between these law schools would consider the question close.

Moreover, although the law is a highly learned profession, we are well aware that it is an intensely practical one. The law school, the proving ground for legal earning and practice, cannot be effective in isolation from the individuals and institutions with which the law interacts. Few students and no one who has practiced law would choose to study in an academic vacuum, removed from the interplay of ideas and the exchange of views with which the law is concerned. The law school to which Texas is willing to admit petitioner excludes from its student body members of the racial groups which number 85% of the population of the State and include most of the lawyers, witnesses, jurors, judges and other officials with whom petitioner will inevitably be dealing when he becomes a member of the Texas Bar. With such a substantial and significant segment of society excluded, we cannot conclude that the education offered petitioner is substantially equal to that which he would receive if admitted to the University of Texas Law

School. . . . We cannot, therefore, agree with respondents that the doctrine of *Plessy v. Ferguson*, 163 U.S. 537 (1896), requires affirmance of the judgment below. Nor need we reach petitioner's contention that *Plessy v. Ferguson* should be reexamined in the light of contemporary knowledge respecting the purposes of the Fourteenth Amendment and the effects of racial segregation.

We hold that the Equal Protection Clause of the Fourteenth Amendment requires that petitioner be admitted to the University of Texas Law School. The judgment is reversed and the cause is remanded for proceedings not inconsistent with this opinion.

Reversed.

The opinion fits together the equal protection clause, precedents, the particular facts of the funding of legal education in Texas in 1946, the social facts about the nature of legal practice, and the fundamental norm of equality of opportunity. But it does not do so as a purely logical matter. It is a typical example of practical legal reasoning. Other fits reaching the opposite conclusion might have worked. For me, at least, this fit works because it builds directly on its reading of the experiences of citizens in a world of political power. It moralizes power. Like Lyndon Johnson's southern speeches in 1960, it claimed to harmonize a world that the members of its audience—law school administrators and black citizens of Texas in this case—shared.

CHARACTERISTICS OF GREAT PERFORMERS

One of the things I have recovered from history is that people whose works win applause from diverse audiences over time—Homer, Shakespeare, Lincoln, Rembrandt, Brahms, and Mark Twain—each satisfy some form of the aesthetic model. La Rochefoucouald said, "It is more important to study men than books." The legal tradition contains its heroes, and inspection of their lives and work reveal common aesthetically satisfying patterns. The characteristics of the process by which people create "great art" predict in part the greatness of the product. The aesthetic theory invoked here is in no way specific to "art" or entertainment.

Consider first Benjamin Cardozo. His classic *The Nature of the Judicial Process* (1921) held that adjudication in its highest reaches is creation, and that "a conscious or purposed growth" in law should be "directed to the attainment of the moral end." To use Cardozo as an illustration, in light of his professed philosophy, might seem to load the deck, but it does not for two reasons. First, Cardozo earned his reputation as a state judge and a common-law judge. In his relatively short time on the Supreme Court, he produced relatively few great constitutional opinions (he was a junior justice and received few great opinion assignments), and he was ill for the last three years.

Second, I use not his own writings but a description of his working style written by one of his law clerks, Joseph Rauh (1979). Consider the following excerpts from Rauh's memoir published in volume one of the *Cardozo Law Review* (pp. 6–10):

> Around dinner time Saturday night following the conference, a messenger would arrive at the Cardozo apartment with Chief Justice Hughes' assignments for the writing of opinions in the cases just decided. When the law clerk arrived at the Justice's apartment at 9:00 a.m. Monday morning, the Justice would cheerfully produce a longhand draft, maybe even a second draft, written on a pad of lined paper, of the opinion assigned to him just thirty-six hours earlier. The draft opinion already contained most of the relevant Supreme Court, federal, and New York precedents. Almost plaintively the Justice would suggest that "after the opinion is typed, would you mind looking at it and maybe you could add a few citations from other states. It wasn't the case you and I would have chosen, but it has some interesting points at that." . . .
>
> It was at this stage that the law clerk might make some contribution. If he uncovered some relevant precedents, the Justice usually added them to his opinion with a profusion of thanks as was his custom for even the smallest of favors. When I found a few serviceable statutory precedents from colonial statutes for the Social Security case, the Justice acted as though I had just discovered nuclear fission.
>
> Before the end of the first week of the recess, Justice Cardozo had completed his opinion-writing and usually his dissents as well, and his law clerk made himself the special scourge of the Clerk's office looking for briefs and records in the cases to be argued at the next sitting of the Court. By the time the two week argument period rolled around, Justice Cardozo knew every brief and record almost as well as counsel who prepared the cases and knew how to argue them a great deal better. In addition, he had read all the certiorari and jurisdictional papers and was more familiar with them than his law clerk—though the latter had just reduced most or all to a short memorandum.
>
> The second week of the recess was the law clerk's delight. The opinions had been written—unless a draft circulated by another Justice required a dissent or a comment—and all pressure was off. The Justice would repeatedly visit the law clerk's office in the apartment and, using the law clerk as a sounding board, discuss one of the cases to be considered at the next two week argument period. Being privy to the deliberations of this exemplar of "critical detachment, intellectual courage, and unswerving disinterestedness . . ." was nothing less than an extraordinary postgraduate law course. While still a clerk, I made my own analysis of the Justice's process of deliberation and with due apologies, repeat it here: "The Justice's mental processes seem to radiate about some invisible central median of fair dealing and impartial judgment. Almost subsconsiously he veers to the fair result and only extremely compelling reasons can turn him aside. As he argues out the various points in a case, dissecting each legal point, one is likely to think that the legal doctrines were the sole thoughts in the Justice's mind. But a few hours or a day or days later when he again brings up the case, and has reached the opposite and fairer result with a line of reasoning equally impregnable, one realizes that he was headed toward that result all the time, simply having stopped on his road to explore and explode the obstructions which stood in the way of the fair result. The Justice may outwardly change his mind several times

before argument, or change it upon the argument, though seldom afterwards. Yet I have a feeling that all the time he was going in the direction that he thought the fairest."

. . . Like a child reporting to a parent on the day's activities at school, Justice Cardozo felt the need to unburden himself of the goings-on in the conference room. Whether in the car riding home from the Supreme Court building or in his office at the apartment afterwards, Justice Cardozo gave the ready listener a full account. He would start with a summary of the Chief Justice's recitations of each case, the highlights of what the others had said, and then a discussion of the vote. The Justice always thought it humorous that the Justices spoke in turn according to seniority, but voted in reverse order, so that "junior Justices would not be affected by their seniors." The Justice took particular delight in reporting the details whenever the Chief Justice or Justice Roberts, under the pressure of President Roosevelt's Court-packing plan, would reverse themselves. Nonetheless, he preferred to indicate his feelings in only the gentlest of terms. . . .

The Justice had an intense interest in current political and cultural activities and kept up on them through newspapers, radio, and even the Congressional Record as much as anyone in town . . . . He appreciated and understood music as well as other fine arts. He loved Gilbert and Sullivan, although he must have become a little tired of Iolanthe, to which his law clerks subjected him repeatedly.

If the Justice had a motivation other than the desire to serve his countrymen, it could have been a subconscious striving to live up to his idol, Justice Holmes. As he himself told Justice Holmes in a letter, "I revere and admire you to the point of adoration. I believe in all sincerity that you are the greatest Judge that ever lived, though, of course, it may be that in the stone age or beyond there was juridicial genius or achievement beyond our ken today." Justice Holmes responded: "I always have thought that not place, or power or popularity, makes the success that one desires, but a trembling hope that one has come near to an ideal. The only ground that warrants a man for thinking that he is not living in a fool's paradise, if he ventures such a hope, is the voice of a few masters, among whom you hold a conspicuous place."

Modesty kept him from quoting the second sentence, but I noticed that he almost always paused to glance at the Holmes letter hanging in the law clerk's office when he came in to talk about a case, and when he spoke of Holmes, it was always with reverence. Only once did I hear him admit Holmes had erred, and then with the words: "Even Homer nodded, you know." . . .

Now consider the excerpts from a description by one of his clerks of California's Roger Traynor. Again individual character, work habits, and thought patterns, not the substance of legal or policy doctrines, matter (Anderson, 1983, pp. 1066–1070).

Justice Traynor's permanent assistant and colleague was Don Barrett, who had served the justice for many years as a senior research attorney. Don could anticipate Justice Traynor's views and could implement his thoughts and concepts on the basis of a few terse comments, in a manner totally mysterious to the novitiate. . . .

By a stroke of good fortune I lived in Berkeley in the same part of the Bay Area as the justice and Don. The three of us commuted daily across the Bay Bridge to and from chambers in San Francisco. It was tacitly understood that either Don or I would always drive lest the justice, while musing over some fine point of law, overlook some worldly traffic problem. Traffic conditions were often bad; the trip was frequently slow; and in the relaxed condition of the outward and inward voyages, the justice would unburden himself concerning matters before the court. Thus, I was privy to the justice's thoughts and views to an extent not usually available to a law clerk who communicates with a judge only under office conditions.

While Justice Traynor never forgot that every lawsuit is of great importance to the parties and counsel, the unfortunate reality was that relatively few of the cases offered the opportunity for significant legal writing. Justice Traynor's eagle eye was sure to spot the candidates to join *Rylands v. Fletcher* and *Palsgraf v. Long Island Railroad Co.* in the annals of jurisprudence. As Don nimbly made our way down Ashby Avenue, we could hear Justice Traynor musing, "I was looking last night at the petition in such-and-such a case and I believe one might make a contribution." Don and I knew our cue and would politely inquire. The justice would then use this opportunity to think out loud and set forth his initial views and analysis of the case.

Justice Traynor had an uncanny ability to subject the most complex legal problem to a straightforward logical analysis leading his listener or reader to a foregone conclusion and leaving one wondering how the problem could have ever seemed so complex and insoluble. While the path from initial analysis in the commute car to a polished final opinion was long and weary, the initial analysis and solution rarely required major change. . . .

One day Justice Traynor would be the strong advocate of his initial position and question the inability of his assistant to draft a meaningful exposition thereof. On another day Justice Traynor would have—or at least pretend to have—the strongest doubts of the merit of his initial position, marshal damning arguments against the position, and challenge his beleaguered assistant to endeavor to refute the cogent and persuasive arguments that he put forth. Since Justice Traynor was as skillful and adept in criticizing his initial position as he was in developing that position, it was no easy task to respond . . . .

Certain frailties of the law clerk species were evidently recurring, anticipated, and to be remedied at the first opportunity. Early in my tenure I submitted a draft of an opinion with a passage surmounting a most difficult point by blandly stating the desired conclusion and briskly moving to the next issue. The draft came back with the comment that "pole-vaulting" was impermissible. I was sent forthwith to the law library, not to return until the problem had been fairly faced and a draft prepared that squarely dealt with the argument. It was a relief later to discover that many other pole-vaulters had suffered the same fate. To this date I find myself noting in the margin of an advance sheet, "pole-vault."

Another recurring clerical sin, particularly when the assignment was the preparation of the first draft of a dissenting opinion, was to take the opportunity to introduce into the draft some cutting comments respecting the faulty reasoning process of the benighted holders of the contrary view. All language of this nature would be lined out with a red pencil when the draft came back from chambers and there would be a gentle comment during the return commute that personal attacks upon one holding an opposing view tellingly revealed one's inability otherwise to refute the argument.

Justice Traynor insisted upon clarity and simplicity of expression. The final versions of his opinions invariably met those criteria. He felt that a reader should immediately be able to understand the legal principles in the opinion and readily follow the substantiating arguments. The desire of the typical beginning law clerk to make a legal problem as complex and obtuse as possible was soon suppressed . . . .

Proposed majority opinions were distributed to all members of the court after oral argument and conference. The assent of a member of the court to a proposed opinion was manifested by signing the opinion. The author of an opinion had some latitude in determining the order of circulation of an opinion for signature. I remember much musing by the justice during the commute ride as to whether a proposed opinion likely to draw opposition should go first to Justice A who would surely sign and not thereafter be seduced by fallacious arguments, or to Justice B who had a dubious facial expression during conference and should be won over early, or to Justice C whose signature would surely convince Justice D. The analysis was similar to the construction of the batting order by savants such as Gene Mauch or Casey Stengel. With hindsight I wonder if in fact the order of circulation actually made the slightest difference, but Justice Traynor loved the game. It was great fun. . . .

In the rather striking parallels between these two descriptions I think we find examples of the traits of good legal performers. They engage directly with the raw material of the world. "[U]ltimately men and minds must prevail over methods, and where they do not the insights and judgments will lack savour and intellectual authority." So Philip French wrote summarizing the lives of Edmund Wilson, F. R. Leavis, and Lionel Trilling (See Shechner, 1981, p. 32). Traynor and Cardozo pay little attention to the way other judges theorize about the legal problem. Their problem is to examine how the law may be made to fit with their understandings of the social conditions in which the case nests. This intellectual independence explains the rapidity of work. It also explains their thoroughness. They believe passionately that the opinion communicates through the clearest possible prose, a fit between the facts and the law itself ("no pole-vaulting") and with social conditions.

The performer lacks self-consciousness. He believes he is discovering more than creating ways of fitting existing raw material together. A common criticism of the decline of modern music, and much abstract and nonrepresentational painting, is precisely that artists have become self-conscious. They begin to try consciously to "be creative," presumably to communicate their stature to other artists. Note that in the craftmanship of Cardozo or Traynor one gets no hint of preoccupation with grand legal theorizing.

Finally, obvious character traits pop out of these descriptions. Industry and dedication seem apt clichés. But these men also seem playful and deeply civil and deeply modest, which is to say that they are aware of the abiding problem of love in human affairs. I assume that these traits translate into an empathy for specific human failings and difficulties, and it is this skill that allows the great judge to shape the normative world of a wider audience.[4]

---

[4] For further discussions of the aesthetic nature of Cardozo's and Traynor's jurisprudence, see Richard Weisberg, "Law, Literature and Cardozo's Judicial Poeties," 1 *Cardozo Law Review* 283 (1979) and G. Edward White, *The American Judicial Tradition* (New York: Oxford University Press, 1976), chapter 13. White concluded, "Traynor communicated a sense that judging was ultimately an art, resisting precise characterization" (p. 301).

"FOR GOD'S SAKE, DON'T THINK OF IT AS ART!"

Some pages back I noted Nelson Goodman's frustration that we have come to think of art as a form of entertainment, not as a synonym for political communication and persuasion. I hope at the very least to have persuaded you, when you evaluate constitutional opinions, to see the fittedness they create as central to their goodness. Indeed my main point is that we already do that. Only the frame of reference changes. If you remain an adherent of preservativism or Marxism or Fried's artificial reason of the law or any other frame of reference after you finish this book, I hope you will see that in applying your perspective to the Court's work you will ask how well or badly the opinion fits together and makes sense of the elements you believe a sensible decision requires. Art is, as Dewey suggested, that method of simplifying our raw experience so that we can find some meaning in it. Aesthetic theory is a theory of "beauty," but only if you accept Keats' conclusion that beauty and truth collapse into a unity. You may reject my definition of the Court's proper audience, but doing so does not require you to reject the aesthetic nature of jurisprudential analysis itself.

Having said that, however, I must add that I think the aesthetic approach takes us further. I believe the political nature of the Constitution requires the Court to presume it speaks to an audience beyond the legal professional. More important, I think the aesthetic approach reminds us that, even under the most starkly pessimistic assumptions concerning the meaninglessness of life, good performances in fact move audiences to share a vision that goodness has been achieved. I think it possible for a white Texan who favored racial segregation to join in Sweatt's appreciation of the opinion in his case, even if it does not change his views on segregation. The Texan won't appreciate the *Sweatt* opinion because he thinks of it as art. The conventional definition of art trivializes it. He will appreciate it because it creates a moral conclusion from the raw material of a world the opinion has convinced him he already knew.

TRIANGULATIONS

If I am truly committed to an aesthetic assessment of the work of the Court, I will submit the theory itself to its own test. I have tried to fit our experience of the Court through constitutional history to the model, and thus defend the model's capacity to generate a persuasive fit. I have tried to dot my narrative with references—like Learned Hand's and Walter Murphy's—to the artistic character of law, and I have noted aesthetic parallels, e.g., how Richard Parker explained his students' favorable reaction to Rawls in terms of Rawls' success at fitting their experiences together coherently, or Hannah Arendt's discovery of Kant's jurisprudence in his aesthetic theory. (Robert

Nozick, incidentally, describes all philosophy as "an art form." See *Philosophical Explanations*, pp. 645–647.) However, to persuade you to take this theory seriously, I must, like the justices, try to persuade you that it is not "mine," that I have not created something from nothing but rather have fitted existing pieces of a puzzle together. This is very much what I believe these pages have done, but my telling you that won't prove it. Therefore, this section extends the justification for this approach by noting other inquiries that may converge on mine.

1. I have argued that constitutional opinions, in order to persuade, necessarily dramatize, simplify, and fictionalize the raw material of the case. Joseph Gusfield's study of the development of public policies against drunk driving (1981) similarly concludes that generating public policy consensus requires the dramatic fictionalizing and simplification of reality. Scientific studies were designed and conducted within an unquestioned moral framework in which the intoxicated driver was presumed evil. Data were gathered so as to block verification of competing hypotheses, i.e., that the redesign of cars could prevent deaths more effectively than "cracking down on drunk drivers." W. Lance Bennett (whose elaboration of the meaning of "civil religion" is highly relevant to my analysis) concluded that Gerald Ford's pardon of Richard Nixon hurt the nation by preventing a dramatic conclusion to the Watergate crisis (1979).

2. I have argued that the justice who seeks to persuade will not succeed by mimicking the views of an audience. (There will be no one discoverable view to mimic in any case.) Rather, he must defend *his* view through the demonstration of its capacity to harmonize beliefs in tension. I have argued that the "rightness" of the "good opinion" derives not from any proof that it find the right answer but rather from speaking in such a way as to enhance conversation. A number of recent articles in academic journals in the field of rhetoric ("speech communication," in modern jargon) reject classical objectivism and pure relativism in very much the same terms. Croasmun and Cherwitz (1982) reject the concept that effective speech "agrees" with an audience consensus. Effective speech instead appeals argumentatively for the possibility that collective, and therefore objective, agreement is achievable. It does not declare truth but invites the audience to participate dialectically in a common search for objective meaning. The speech does so by dramatizing visions of consensus. Brummett (1984) similarly finds "consciousness-raising" to be an important ingredient of effective communication.

3. Music theory in the last twenty years has moved toward the conclusion that social pluralism defeats all aesthetic theories of musical structure and composition. Evaluative standards distinguishing the quality of performances, however, remain viable. Thus Schwartz (1983, p. 103) states: "Performance is perhaps the only certainty we have in music."

4. It is significant that literary criticism and jurisprudence now explicitly join each other in dialogue. The pieces in the *Texas Symposium*, particularly those of Levinson and Fish, oppose the notion of objective interpretive truth in either law or literature. Readers familiar with Melville's great jurisprudential story, *Billy Budd*, may want to compare the incompatible but powerful analyses of that story by Hannah Arendt (*On Revolution*, 1963, pp. 77–83) and Richard Weisberg (1982). Weisberg, not so incidentally, concludes that Captain Vere's doctrinal formalism and his preoccupation with imagining possible negative consequences of his choice, instead of staying close to the immediate context of Billy's case, describe the fundamental failure of the modern Court. In a common-law system, and of course in the world of artistic performance, each work and each performance stand on their own.

5. I have suggested that an impressive amount of triangulating has targeted the centrality of the value of individual freedom and dignity in western civilization. I believe that the Court must treat some version of this value as "lexically prior" in constitutional law in order to perform effectively for a national audience. This value, at least from my viewpoint, requires the Court to communicate its decisions to the parties and those whose interests the case symbolizes. In practice this means, although the Court rarely does so, that the Court must, when rejecting a constitutional claim based on a dignitarian argument, at minimum state hypothetical evidence, and the presumptions affecting its weight, on which the losing dignitarian claim would have prevailed. If dignity is lexically prior, and if the Court's role is to enhance conversations about values, the Court must do at least this much to promote dignitarian conversation in the face of an "anti-dignitarian" decision in the case at hand. Notice that under this standard much balancing rhetoric would not suffice. Regarding triangulation on dignitarian rights generally, readers should bear in mind that Canada, in 1982, adopted a "Charter of Rights and Freedoms" that explicitly forbids discrimination on the basis of race, national or ethnic origin, sex, age, and mental or physical disability. It explicitly endorses affirmative action programs. It contains a version of the exclusionary rule, and it endorses judicial review with these words: "Anyone whose rights or freedoms, as guaranteed by this Charter, have been infringed or denied may apply to a court of competent jurisdiction to obtain such remedy as the court considers appropriate and just in the circumstances."

6. If my argument strikes you as transcendent, though I do not intend it as such (it is usually unclear to me what "transcendental" arguments are transcending), you may for triangulation wish to review Timothy Terrell's "Flatlaw: An Essay on the Dimensions of Legal Reasoning and the Development of Fundamental Normative Principles" (1984), holding that persuasive arguments may be beyond reason itself, and Harold Berman's recent book describing the religious foundations of legal systems throughout the world.

For Berman "the spirit of the whole creation was about the reformation of the world" (1983, p. 30). Therefore, if the Western legal system has lost its sense of transcendent possibilities, it is necessarily breaking down.

7. Finally, let me speculate briefly about self-consciousness in art. Perhaps the most common criticism of modern music and of the visual arts is that they have become self-conscious. This seems true of modern theater, too. Of the fourteen plays running "on Broadway" during my last visit to New York, on September 3, 1984, nine were plays about performing, plays about plays and about the lives of actors and theater people. I suspect the excessive emphasis on legal form represents a similar ill. Art across time is not self-conscious. It serves church or patron or some object of goodness quite unrelated to the professional advancement or prestige of the artist. In the failings of modern jurisprudence we may see the weaknesses in modernism itself. Each scholar-artist (Carter included) must state a personal, "creative" theory in order to succeed "professionally." (See Gablik, *Has modernism failed?*, 1984, and see also Edward Rothstein's essay on the failure of the self-conscious "return to romanticism" in music, 1984.)

ON PLAYFULNESS AND CONVERSATIONS

I have cited Karl Barth for the proposition that the Court must speak with authority in order to encourage conversation, and I have in connection with Oakeshott's work suggested that conversations are playful. The two notions are compatible. Recall any good argument you have had with someone and you will probably find that both sides advanced the arguments by the most strenuous insistence of correctness, and in doing so you played with one another. Playfulness maintains the conversationalist's trust that the conversation will not turn hostile. More significant, playfulness communicates that "I might be wrong," and therefore that the conversation should continue. In Oakeshott's words:

> [The excellence of conversation] springs from a tension between seriousness and playfulness. Each voice represents a serious engagement . . . and without this seriousness the conversation would lack impetus. But in its participation in the conversation each voice learns to be playful, learns to understand itself conversationally and to recognize itself as a voice among voices. As with children, who are great conversationalists, the playfulness is serious and the seriousness in the end is only play. (1962, p. 202)

What is the legal analog to play? I suspect that the real tension between constitutional theory and pragmatism involves attitudes toward error. If there are no real right answers, but if creating visions of coherence case after case, performance after performance, suffices to meet the normative needs of communities, then error is inescapable. Accepting the inevitability that one never gets the thing "quite right" encourages the conversations to continue, both among practicing judges and lawyers and among scholars. I have described dozens of immensely impressive scholarly works in this book, and I have reviewed serious criticisms of each one. But no one doubts the greatness of Rawls' performance because Kenneth Arrow (1977), another impressive performer, has shown that it is not possible to arrange Rawls' system into mathematical terms that support Rawls' conclusions.

It may be difficult to imagine a constitutional lawmaking process that is consistently and explicitly playful, but we do know that the legal system contains many structural devices that presume the pervasiveness of error. These include multiple opportunities to appeal, the requirement that judges write justificatory opinions, which inevitably invite critical comment, and the presumption that dissenting opinions convey legally significant ideas. A constitutional opinion is the product of a series of actual conversations that have occurred among the justices, face-to-face in conference and through their exchange of letters and draft opinions. And opinions stimulate conversations among students and practitioners that eventually feed back to the Court. I suspect the quality of constitutional opinions might improve if the justices wrote in more explicitly conversational form. Perhaps Traynor's (and Cardozo's) caution against "pole-vaulting" is the key. How refreshing it would be if the authors of opinions routinely articulated the evidentiary and normative conditions in which the author would have reached the contrary result. How refreshing if, in *Schall v. Martin* (the juvenile pre-trial detention case), Justice Rehnquist had held that "On its face, the length of pretrial detention—a maximum of 17 days—is not likely to produce systematic and substantial injury in fact to the minors involved. Bring us evidence of substantial injury in fact, and we shall take another look." Such a response would both invite and help refine further conversation on the issue. Indeed, the obligation to write in this conversational manner might have forced Justice Rehnquist, given the factual record in *Schall*, to reach a different result, for conversational writing highlights rather than hides the evidence of the goodness of the fit the opinion creates.

My main motive for concluding my book with a discussion of playfulness and conversations is to turn the concept on myself. As I complete this book I am most keenly aware of the things it does not yet seem to have gotten quite right. More conversations are in order. I do wish, with Lohn and Ball (p. 151), to treat argument as a verbal dance. I have no capacity to emulate the conversational dance created by Gabel and Kennedy's "Roll Over Beethoven," but I want to conclude with a few samples of where conversations about aesthetics and jurisprudence might go.

Question: Near the beginning of the book you wrote that the Court does not interpret the Constitution, it creates constitutional meaning. But as the book progressed the distinction between interpretation and creation began to blur. Stanley Fish seemed to say that good literary criticism is both good interpretation and good creation at the same time. You criticized H.L.A. Hart's statement that the courts sometimes do one and sometimes the other because they do both at once. What do you really mean?

Answer: You are right that my meaning appears to shift in the course of the book, but the two positions are not quite opposites, and I do endorse Fish's position. When I wrote initially that the Court does not interpret the Constitution, I meant that the Court has never consistently confined its justifications of its results to the meaning of the text of the document and its political history. It certainly has not approached its task as one of "thick description," in Geertz's terms, of the document. Rather I have suggested that a good constitutional performance seeks a fit among legal elements in the case (the facts on the record and the legal rules the lawyers raise) and the extra-legal elements (social experiences and normative values about which we converse seriously). In performing this way, the Court (or any other artist) does seek to interpret experience, to communicate the existence of a fit among elements that exist beyond his or her purely private experiences. I do not find it helpful to say that the Court interprets "the Constitution" when it does this. And, contrary to Dworkin, I do not believe this process produces right and wrong answers, only better and worse ones. In art there are many possibilities for different good fits or harmonies. I do not claim that the legal process should change its self-definition and operate "artistically." I argue that it always operates in this fashion. The aesthetic element in law allows it to function effectively despite the fact that each of its doctrines inevitably exposes paradoxes and antinomies. The tension between altruism and individualism makes impossible the derivation of demonstrably correct legal answers, but somehow the legal process survives.

Question: But you seem to come down on the side of dignitarian legal doctrine. Don't you therefore end up sitting pointedly on one horn of the dilemma?

Answer: I do indeed. In my defense I can only repeat that I find that dignitarian theories create a more satisfying fit among elements in the jurisprudential conversation as we currently perceive them than do authoritarian theories, of which preservativism is one example. I am especially intrigued by the triangulation on dignitarian theories produced by (a) such natural law approaches as Walter Murphy's, and (b) the current mainstream of constitutional jurisprudence, especially Ely, Choper, Perry, and Dworkin, and (c) the conclusion of Bernstein's post-relativist philosophers (particularly Habermas and Rorty) that affording equal dignity and respect is a necessary condition to meaningful conversation, even if conversation is all that holds communities together.

Question: You have said that an opinion is good if it generates moral conversations, but I don't see why bad opinions don't accomplish the same thing. Haven't you shown that *Chadha* and *Bob Jones* and *Dred Scott* stimulate powerful conversations? If so, why should we care about the goodness of the opinion? Maybe bad opinions are better!

Answer: Perhaps I have overstated the importance of conversations in my theory. My references to conversations really serve as an indicator of the coherence of a message. *Sweatt* teaches us clearly that we must, if we take racial equality seriously, account for subtle political and social differences the educational environment creates. It pushes us away from a crassly empirical definition of equality, hence we can talk about what experience of subtler forms of discrimination might mean. *Chadha*, on the other hand, blurs and confuses its subject. But remember that the good opinion serves primarily to encourage us by its example to believe that our conversations can take any political question seriously. What we really need are examples that moral visions are attainable within a shared framework. The bad opinion does not give us an encouraging model. I know that constitutional law is only one of many models of good and bad conversation. Television programs and class-room teaching probably have a much greater effect on our ability to converse than does the Supreme Court, but the Court is a model. As in teaching and television programming, I would like judicial performers, as far as possible, to provide us with good models.

Question: You seem to propose a major change in the way the justices conceive of themselves. Is it realistic to expect justices to start thinking of themselves as performers or as teachers instead of lawyers?
Answer: Of course not. We will have to content ourselves with whatever values political appointees take to the bench. I propose an evaluative theory more than a prescription. I defend it because I think it explains differences in judicial opinions as they have come to us. If it seems like a prescription, it is only because I believe (and I may be wrong) that an exceptionally high fraction of Burger Court opinions are confused and unpersuasive. Besides, the question forgets James Agee's warning not to "think of it as art." From my perspective all effective performances teach, but I do not think the justices should consciously assume a teaching role any more than should Dustin Hoffman or Glenda Jackson. The justice should perform the role of justice as the best examples from our legal tradition define it. It is playing that or any institutionally defined role well that protects against the dark. To perform anything well is to fight against the falsification and trivialization of the language and the symbols the role represents. Cardozo and Traynor and Dustin Hoffman's *Tootsie* don't try to teach; they try to get a good fit. We are, of course, instructed by their efforts, but that's just the point. They teach because they communicate, and they communicate because they perform persuasively. Or, as Justice Ellen Peters of the Connecticut Supreme Court put it, in an article in the *Yale Law Journal* titled "Reality and the Language of the Law" (1981), law is a continuing dialogue about reality.

Question: By abandoning legalistic standards of consistency with rules, texts and cases, don't you make legal conversations harder to sustain?
Answer: I'm not so sure. Remember that the extent to which constitutional

fits must pay attention to good *legally defined* fits is very much up for grabs in our jurisprudential conversations. I also believe that if the justices attended more seriously to defining and harmonizing in pragmatic fashion the basic elements in a case they would, merely by clarifying the topic of conversation, increase consistency across cases. Traynor and Cardozo, who thought things, not words, had, I think, just this effect, though more in the law of tort than in constitutional law. Please remember in this regard that my argument hinges on the assumption that we share pragmatic ways of thinking and knowing. Roger Traynor (who, incidentally, earned a Ph.D. in political science as well as a law degree), might have been jailed as a political dissident had he lived in modern Iran.

Question: Doesn't the approach you offer in this book almost prove that you can't write a book about it? In other words, if we are a pragmatic bunch and therefore treat constitutional cases as unique events, reacting to each in terms of the fit they create for us, then what can a book like this add?
Answer: A telling point indeed, and in many respects I agree with you. James Boyd White answered the question well when he wrote (1982, p. 421n):

> [T]here are real limits upon what can be achieved in abstract critical discourse. The most precise and interesting expressions of what one means by reading and writing will be found not in general accounts such as the present one, but in work reflecting detailed and active engagements with particular texts, legal or literary.

Let me put the point on which we agree yet another way. I have argued that, from Bork to Ely to Dworkin to Fish and the Critical movement, each scholar seeks to create a good fit within the framework provided by his or her own scholarly community. This book can only highlight that, underlying such diverse approaches, a common commitment to good fits exists. This observation in turn matters if you believe our search for communal goodness depends on good conversations, and that good conversations in turn depend on well-crafted visions of good communities. But once that point is made, I think it is entirely appropriate, as Fish suggested (p. 133), to forget it and get on with the task of creating visions and conversing about them. My criticisms of so many scholars come attached with a guilty suspicion that the Elys and the Rawls and the Murphys and the Dworkins, and maybe even the McDowells, make more useful contributions. I suspect it is more constructive to make peace or love than to write books about how peace or love might be made, and this book may resemble more the latter than the former. Still, I think it useful to sense how we can appreciate the goodness of a constitutional opinion free of the nagging concern that, unless the opinion is conclusively right, it is conclusively wrong. I hope also that each reader finds some encouragement in the conclusion that his or her beliefs need not conform to some standard of "right belief" prescribed by anyone in authority in order to be "good."

Question: You suppose that the whole enterprise of conversing about political goodness, using the Constitution and the Court as essentially empty vessels, can effectively occur without underlying agreements about *any* moral beliefs. Did not Professor Bernstein (chapter six) insist that some basic moral under-standings (even if they are completely culture-bound) are necessary for any conversations to occur, and did he not worry that pluralistic states such as ours would die for failure to sustain such common understandings? Moreover, many of the scholars you cite seem to agree. Cover thinks we must have a "nomos," a normative narrative. Geertz and Berger and Luckmann say com-munities need beliefs and ideologies to survive. You yourself argue that the communities of preservative scholars, on one hand, and Critical scholars, on the other, both exist because they share some common substantive belief, If all this is true, I don't see how a mere series of judicial creations of fits, fits which may contradict each other, can maintain a community. Fits by themselves don't sustain or advance any common myths or ideologies.

Answer: This is, I think, the most important question of all, and I do not have a good answer. I would like to believe that our constitutional conversations actually do rest on a common appreciation of the sort of dignitarian theory that so many different lines of legal and philosophical analysis have led to. On the other hand, I think it is clear that the justices have never agreed on any such theory, and I don't really see much evidence that it matters, just as I don't observe that it matters much whether people who go to church together year after year share, in any serious form, a common theology. Patriotism and friendship seem to unite us much more than ideologies. The best answer I can give for now is, yes, of course we share common myths and ideologies, but these lie below the level of any imaginable constitutional theory. The myth might simply be that we *are* legally constituted. Or perhaps better, that we care, in pragmatic fashion, about fitting norms and policies to raw experience. I think the Court can maintain such myths by performing persuasively, even if, at the level of legal doctrine, all remains tentative. My conclusion may parallel the final words of William of Baskerville at the close of Umberto Eco's *The Name of the Rose*: "*non in commotione Dominus.*" (God is not found in confusion.) I wish the justices took William more to heart.

Still, I only guess, but guessing in one form or another is all the Court, or this book, can do. I hope you are, in your guessing, in good company.

PERMISSIONS

 # TABLE OF CASES

 REFERENCES

Abbey, Lynn (1981): "Essay: Things the Editor Never Told Me," in Robert Asprin, ed., *Shadows of Sanctuary* (New York: Ace Fantasy Books).

Ackerman, Bruce (1980): *Social Justice in the Liberal State* (New Haven: Yale University Press).

Ackerman, Bruce (1984): *Reconstructing American Law* (Cambridge: Harvard University Press).

Agresto, John (1980): "The Limits of Judicial Supremacy: A Proposal for 'Checked Activism' " 14 *Georgia Law Review* 471.

Alexander, Larry (1981): "Liberalism and Neutral Dialogue: Man and Manna in the Liberal State," 28 *U.C.L.A. Law Review* 816.

Alexander, Larry (1983): "Painting Without the Numbers: Noninterpretive Judicial Review," 8 *Dayton Law Review* 447.

Alfange, Dean (1984): "Congressional Regulation of the 'States Qua States': From *National League of Cities* To *EEOC v. Wyoming*," in P. Kurland, G. Casper, and D. Hutchinson, eds., *The Supreme Court Review–1983* (Chicago: University of Chicago Press).

Anderson, Peter (1983): "A Remembrance," 71 *California Law Review* 1066.

Anderson, William (1955): "The Intention of the Framers: A Note on Constitutional Interpretation," 49 *American Political Science Review* 340.

Arendt, Hannah (1963): *On Revolution* (New York: The Viking Press).

Arnold, Thurman (1935): *The Symbols of Government* (New Haven: Yale University Press).

Arrow, Kenneth J. (1977): "Extended Sympathy and the Possibility of Social Choice," 67 *American Economic Review* 219.

Ball, Milner (1975): "The Play's the Thing: An Unscientific Reflection on Courts Under the Rubric of Theater," 28 *Stanford Law Review* 81.

Ball, Milner (1981): "Don't Die Don Quixote," 59 *Texas Law Review* 787.

Ball, Milner (1983): "Book Review," 51 *George Washington Law Review* 311.

Barber, Benjamin (1982): "How Good Must We Be?" *The New Republic*, July 12, p. 37.

Barber, Sotirios (1984): *On What the Constitution Means* (Baltimore: Johns Hopkins University Press).

Bennett, Robert (1984): "Objectivity in Constitutional Law," 132 *University of Pennsylvania Law Review* 445.

Bennett, W. Lance (1979): "Imitation, Ambiguity, and Drama in Political Life," 41 *Journal of Politics* 106.

Bennett, W. Lance, and Martha Feldman (1981): *Reconstructing Reality in the Courtroom: Justice and Judgment in American Culture* (New Brunswick, N.J.: Rutgers University Press).

Bennett, William (1979): "Comment on Celia Kenyon," in J. Roland Pennock and John Chapman, eds., *Nomos XX: Constitutionalism* (New York: New York University Press).

Berger, Peter, and Thomas Luckmann (1966): *The Social Construction of Reality* (New York: Doubleday).

Berger, Raoul (1977): *Government by Judiciary* (Cambridge: Harvard University Press).

Berger, Raoul (1984): "Lawyering vs. Philosophizing: Facts or Fancies," 9 *Dayton Law Review* 171.

Berman, Harold J. (1983): "Religious Foundations of Law in the West: An Historical Perspective," 1 *The Journal of Law and Religion* 3.

Berns, Walter (1976): *The First Amendment and the Future of American Democracy* (New York: Basic Books).

Bernstein, Richard (1983): *Beyond Objectivism and Relativism* (Philadelphia: University of Pennsylvania Press).

Bickel, Alexander (1962): *The Least Dangerous Branch: The Supreme Court at the Bar of Politics* (Indianapolis: Bobbs-Merrill).

Bickel, Alexander (1970): *The Supreme Court and the Idea of Progress* (New York: Harper & Row).

Bickel, Alexander (1975): *The Morality of Consent* (New Haven: Yale University Press).

Bleicher, Joseph (1980): *Contemporary Hermeneutics* (London: Routledge & Kegan Paul).

Bork, Robert (1971): "Neutral Principles and Some First Amendment Problems," 47 *Indiana Law Journal* 1.

Bork, Robert (1979): "Commentary: The Impossibility of Finding Welfare Rights in the Constitution," 1979 *Washington University Law Quarterly* 695.

Brest, Paul, and Sanford Levinson (1983): *Processes of Constitutional Decisionmaking* (Boston: Little, Brown & Co., 2nd ed).

Brest, Paul (1980): "Accommodations of Majoritarianism and Rights of Human Dignity," 53 *Southern California Law Review* 761.

Brest, Paul (1981): "The Fundamental Rights Controversy: The Essential Contradictions of Normative Constitutional Scholarship," 90 *Yale Law Journal* 1063.

Brest, Paul (1982): "Interpretation and Interest," 34 *Stanford Law Review* 765.

Brewer, David (1883): "The Salvation of the Nation—A Strengthened Judiciary," Address before the New York State Bar Association, January 17.

Brummett, Barry (1984): "Consensus Criticism," 49 *Southern Speech Communication Journal* 111.

Canon, Bradley (1982): "A Framework for the Analysis of Judicial Activism," in S. Halpern and C. Lamb, eds., *Supreme Court Activism and Restraint* (Lexington, MA: Lexington Books).

Cardozo, Benjamin (1921): *The Nature of the Judicial Process* (New Haven: Yale University Press).

Carter, Lief (1977): "When Courts Should Make Policy: An Institutional Approach," in John Gardiner, ed., *Public Law and Public Policy* (New York: Praeger).

Carter, Lief (1983): *Administrative Law and Politics* (Boston: Little, Brown & Co.).

Carter, Lief (1984): *Reason in Law*, 2nd ed. (Boston: Little, Brown & Co.).

Cavanaugh, Ralph, and Austin Sarat (1980): "Thinking About Courts: Toward a Jurisprudence of Judicial Competence," 14 *Law and Society Review* 371.

Chayes, Abram (1976): "The Role of the Judge in Public Law Litigation," 89 *Harvard Law Review* 1281.

Choper, Jesse (1974): "The Supreme Court and the Political Branches: Democratic Theory and Practice," 122 *University of Pennsylvania Law Review* 810.

Choper, Jesse (1980): *Judicial Review and the National Political Process: A Functional Reconsideration of the Role of the Supreme Court* (Chicago: University of Chicago Press).

Clark, Charles E. (1963): "A Plea for the Unprincipled Decision," 49 *Virginia Law Review* 660.

Coase, Ronald (1960): "The Problem of Social Cost," 3 *Journal of Law and Economics* 1.

Cohen, Felix (1935): "Transcendental Nonsense and the Functional Approach," 35 *Columbia Law Review* 809.

Cohen, Ronald (1984): "Procedural Justice and Participation," paper delivered at the 1984 annual meeting of the Law and Society Association, Boston, June 8.

Coleman, Jules (1982): "The Normative Basis of Economic Analysis: A Critical Review of Richard Posner's 'The Economics of Justice'," 34 *Stanford Law Review* 1105.

Cover, Robert (1982): "The Framing of Justice Brandeis," *The New Republic*, May 5, p. 17.

Cover, Robert (1983): "Foreword: *Nomos* and Narrative," 97 *Harvard Law Review* 1.

Cox, Archibald (1976): *The Role of the Supreme Court in American Government* (New York: Oxford University Press).

Croasmun, Earl, and Richard Cherwitz, "Beyond Rhetorical Relativism," 68 *Quarterly Journal of Speech* 1 (1982).

Dahl, Robert (1956): *A Preface to Democratic Theory* (Chicago: University of Chicago Press).

Dahl, Robert (1958): "Decision-making in a Democracy: The Supreme Court as a National Policy-Maker," 6 *Journal of Public Law* 294.

Dewey, John (1934): *Art as Experience* (New York: Capricorn Books).

Dolbeare, Kenneth, and Phillip Hammond (1971): *The School Prayer Decisions* (Chicago: University of Chicago Press).

Drew, Elizabeth (1984): "A Political Journal," *The New Yorker*, September 24, p. 81.

Dworkin, Ronald (1978): *Taking Rights Seriously* (Cambridge: Harvard University Press).

Dworkin, Ronald (1978a): "No Right Answer?" 53 *New York University Law Review* 1.

Dworkin, Ronald (1982): "Law as Interpretation," 60 *Texas Law Review* 527.

Dworkin, Ronald (1983): "Please Don't Talk About Objectivity Any More," in William Mitchell, ed., *The Politics of Interpretation* (Chicago: University of Chicago Press).

Eco, Umberto (1983): *The Name of the Rose* (trans. William Weaver) (New York: Harcourt Brace Jovanovich).

Elias, Norbert (1982): "Scientific Establishments," in Elias, Martins, and Whiteley, eds., *Scientific Establishments and Hierarchies* (Boston: D. Reidel Publishing Co.).

Ely, John Hart (1973): "The Wages of Crying Wolf: A Comment on *Roe v. Wade*," 82 *Yale Law Journal* 920.

Ely, John Hart (1980): *Democracy and Distrust: A Theory of Judicial Review* (Cambridge: Harvard University Press).

Ely, John Hart (1983): "Professor Dworkin's External/Personal Preference Distinction," 1983 *Duke Law Journal* 959.

Emerson, Thomas (1980): "First Amendment Doctrine and the Burger Court," 68 *California Law Review* 422.

Fairlie, Henry (1981): "Who Speaks for Values?" *The New Republic*, January 31, p. 17.

Fairlie, Henry (1984): "The Decline of Oratory," *The New Republic*, May 28, p. 15.

Fifoot, C.H.S. (1959): *Judge and Jurist in the Reign of Victoria* (London: Stevens).

Fish, Stanley (1980): *Is There a Text in This Class? The Authority of Interpretive Communities* (Cambridge: Harvard University Press).

Fish, Stanley (1982): "Working on the Chain Gang: Interpretation in Law and Literature," 60 *Texas Law Review* 551.

Fish, Stanley (1983): "Wrong Again," 62 *Texas Law Review* 299.

Fisher, Roger and William Ury (1981): *Getting to Yes: Negotiating Agreement Without Giving in* (New York: Penguin Books).

Fiss, Owen (1979): "Foreword: The Forms of Justice," 93 *Harvard Law Review* 1.

Fiss, Owen (1982): "Objectivity and Interpretation," 34 *Stanford Law Review* 739.

Flathman, Richard (1976): *The Practice of Rights* (Cambridge, England: Cambridge University Press).

Frankfurter, Felix (1939): *Law and Politics* (New York: Harcourt, Brace and Co.).

Freund, Paul (1961): *The Supreme Court of the United States* (Cleveland: Meridian Books).

Freund, Paul (1962): "Social Justice and the Law," in Richard Brandt, ed., *Social Justice* (Englewood Cliffs, N.J.: Prentice-Hall).

Fried, Charles (1981): "The Artificial Reason of the Law or: What Lawyers Know," 60 *Texas Law Review* 35.

Friedmann, Wolfgang (1961): "Legal Philosophy and Judicial Lawmaking," 61 *Columbia Law Review* 821.

Fuller, Lon (1964): *The Morality of Law* (New Haven: Yale University Press).

Gabel, Peter, and Duncan Kennedy (1984): "Roll Over Beethoven," 36 *Stanford Law Review* 1.

Gablik, Suzi (1984): *Has Modernism Failed?* (London: Thames and Hudson).

Gadamer, Hans Georg (1975): *Truth and Method* (New York: Seabury Press, 1975).

Geertz, Clifford (1973): *The Interpretation of Cultures* (New York: Basic Books).

Gilligan, Carol (1982): *In a Different Voice: Psychological Theory and Women's Development* (Cambridge: Harvard University Press).

Goldberg, Arthur (1982): "The Supreme Court Reaches Out and Touches Someone— Fatally," 10 *Hastings Constitutional Law Quarterly* 7.

Golding, Martin (1983): *Legal Reasoning* (New York: Alfred A. Knopf).

Goodman, Nelson (1978): *Ways of Worldmaking* (Indianapolis: Hackett Publishing Co.).

Goodman, Nelson (1984): *Of Mind and Other Matters* (Cambridge: Harvard University Press).

Gopen, George (1984): "Rhyme and Reason: Why the Study of Poetry Is the Best Preparation for the Study of Law," 46 *College English* 333.

Gordon, Robert (1981): "Historicism in Legal Scholarship," 90 *Yale Law Journal* 1017.

Grafstein, Robert (1983): "Taking Dworkin to Hart," 11 *Political Theory* 244.

Greenawalt, Kent (1978): "The Enduring Significance of Neutral Principles," 78 *Columbia Law Review* 982.

Grey, Thomas (1975): "Do We Have an Unwritten Constitution?," 27 *Stanford Law Review* 703.

Grey, Thomas (1978): "Origins of the Unwritten Constitution: Fundamental Law in American Revolutionary Thought," 30 *Stanford Law Review* 843.

Gusfield, Joseph (1981): *The Culture of Public Problems* (Chicago: University of Chicago Press).

Hart, H.L.A. (1979): "Between Utility and Rights," 79 *Columbia Law Review* 828.

Hart, H.L.A. (1983): *Essays in Jurisprudential Philosophy* (Oxford: Clarendon Press).

Haskins, George, and Herbert Johnson (1981): *Foundations of Power: John Marshall, 1801–1815* (New York: Macmillan Publishing Co.).

Hicks, John (1939): "The Foundations of Welfare Economics," 49 *Economic Journal* 696.

Hochschild, Jennifer (1981): *What's Fair?: American Beliefs About Distributive Justice* (Cambridge: Harvard University Press).

Holmes, Oliver Wendell (1881): *The Common Law* (Boston: Little, Brown & Co.).

Horowitz, Donald (1977): *The Courts and Social Policy* (Washington, D.C.: The Brookings Institution).

Horowitz, Donald (1983): "Decreeing Organizational Change: Judicial Supervision of Public Institutions," 1983 *Duke Law Journal* 1265.

Hutchinson, Allan, and Monahan, Patrick (1984): "Law, Politics, and the Critical Legal Scholars: The Unfolding Drama of American Legal Thought," 36 *Stanford Law Review* 199.

Jacobsohn, Gary (1984): "E.T.: The Extra-Textual in Constitutional Interpretation," 1 *Constitutional Commentary* 21.

Kairys, David, ed. (1982): *The Politics of Law: A Progressive Critique* (New York: Pantheon Books).

Kaldor, Nicholas (1939): "Welfare Propositions of Economics and Interpersonal Comparisons of Utility," 49 *Economic Journal* 549.

Karnow, Stanley (1983): *Vietnam: A History* (New York: Viking Press).

Karst, Kenneth (1977): "Foreword, Equal Citizenship" 91 *Harvard Law Review* 1.

Kennedy, Duncan (1976): "Form and Substance in Private Law Adjudication," 89 *Harvard Law Review* 1685.

Kennedy, Duncan (1979): "The Structure of Blackstone's Commentaries," 28 *Buffalo Law Review* 205.

Kommers, Donald (1976): *Judicial Politics in West Germany: A Study of the Federal Constitutional Court* (Beverly Hills, CA: Sage Publications).

Kordig, Carl (1978): "Discovery and Justification," 45 *Philosophy of Science* 110.

Krash, Abe (1984): "The Legacy of William Crosskey," 93 *Yale Law Journal*, 954.

Kuhn, Thomas (1970): *The Structure of Scientific Revolutions* (Chicago: University of Chicago Press).

Kurland, Philip (1978): "The Irrelevance of the Constitution: The Religion Clauses of the First Amendment and the Supreme Court," 24 *Villanova Law Review* 3.

Leedes, Gary (1984): "An Acceptable Meaning of the Constitution," 61 *Wahington University Law Quarterly* 1003.

Levi, Edward (1949): *An Introduction to Legal Reasoning* (Chicago: Unversity of Chicago Press).

Levinson, Sanford (1983): "The Turn Toward Functionalism in Constitutional Theory," 8 *Dayton Law Review* 567.

Lewis, Anthony (1964): *Gideon's Trumpet* (New York: Random House).

Lewis, Felice (1976): *Literature, Obscenity and Law* (Carbondale: Southern Illinois University Press).

Linde, Hans (1984): "E Pluribus: Constitutional Theory and State Courts," 18 *Georgia Law Review* 165.

Lohn, D. Robert, and Ball, Milner (1982): "Legal Advocacy, Performance, and Affection," 16 *Georgia Law Review* 853.

Lupu, Ira (1983): "Constitutional Theory and the Search for the Workable Premise," 8 *Dayton Law Review* 579.

MacCormick, Neil (1978): *Legal Reasoning and Legal Theory* (Oxford: Clarendon Press).

MacIntyre, Alasdair (1981): *After Virtue* (South Bend, Ind.: Notre Dame University Press).

MacKay, Alfred (1982): "Human Motivation: The Inadequacy of Economists' Models," 10 *Hofstra Law Review* 441.

Mansbridge, Jane (1982): "A New Way of Doing Normative Political Philosophy," paper delivered at the annual meeting of the American Political Science Association, Denver, Colorado, September 5.

Mashaw, Jerry (1983): *Bureaucratic Justice* (New Haven: Yale University Press).

McAffee, Thomas (1984): *"Berger vs. The Supreme Court:* The Implications of His Exception-Clause Odyssey," 9 *Dayton Law Review* 219.

McDowell, Gary (1982): *Equity and the Constitution* (Chicago: University of Chicago Press).

McDowell, Gary (1982): "Earl Warren's Good Intentions Weren't Enough," *The Wall Street Journal*, August 26, p. 20.

McDowell, Gary (1983): "The Problem with Amendments," *The Wall Street Journal*, January 26, p. 20.

McKay, Robert B. (1983): "Judicial Review in a Liberal Democracy," in Pennock and Chapman, eds., *Nomos XXV: Liberal Democracy* (New York: New York University Press).

Michelman, Frank (1982): "Ethics, Economics, and the Law of Property," in J. Roland Pennock and John Chapman, eds., *Nomos XXIV: Ethics, Economics, and the Law* (New York: New York University Press).

Miller, Arthur Selwyn (1982): *Toward Increased Judicial Activism: The Political Role of the Supreme Court* (Westport, CT: Greenwood Press).

Mishkin, Paul (1983): "The Uses of Ambivalence: Reflections on the Supreme Court and the Constitutionality of Affirmative Action," 131 *University of Pennsylvania Law Review* 907.

Moore, Barrington (1978): *Injustice: The Social Bases of Obedience and Revolt* (White Plains, N.Y.: M.E. Sharpe).

Moore, Michel (1984): "The Need for a Theory of Legal Theories: Assessing Pragmatic Instrumentalism," 69 *Cornell Law Review* 988.

Muir, William (1967): *Prayer in the Public Schools* (Chicago: University of Chicago Press).

Murphy, Bruce (1982): *The Brandeis/Frankfurter Connection* (New York: Oxford University Press).

Murphy, Walter (1964): *Elements of Judicial Strategy* (Chicago: University of Chicago Press).

Murphy, Walter (1978): "The Art of Constitutional Interpretation: A Preliminary Showing," in M. Judd Harmon, ed., *Essays on the Constitution of the United States* (Port Washington, N.Y.: Kennikat Press).

Murphy, Walter (1980): "An Ordering of Constitutional Values," 53 *Southern California Law Review* 703.

Murphy, Walter, and C. Herman Pritchett (1979): *Courts, Judges, and Politics* (New York: Random House, 3rd ed.).

Murray, James (1982): "The Role of Analogy in Legal Reasoning," 29 *U.C.L.A. Law Review* 833.

Nisbet, Robert (1982): *Prejudices: A Philosophical Dictionary* (Cambridge: Harvard University Press).

Nozick, Robert (1974): *Anarchy, State, and Utopia* (New York: Basic Books).

Nozick, Robert (1981): *Philosophical Explanations* (Cambridge: Belknap Press of Harvard University).

Oakeshott, Michael (1933): *Experience and its Modes* (Cambridge, England: The Univesity Press).

Oakeshott, Michael (1962): "The Voice of Poetry in the Conversation of Mankind," in Oakeshott, *Rationalism in Politics* (New York: Basic Books).

O'Brien, David (1981): *The Public's Right to Know: The Supreme Court and the First Amendment* (New York: Praeger).

Orwin, Clifford (1984): "The Just and the Advantageous in Thucydides: The Case of the Mytilenaian Debate," 78 *American Political Science Review* 485.

Parker, Richard (1979): "The Jurisprudential Uses of John Rawls," in J. Roland Pennock and John Chapman eds., *Nomos XX: Constitutionalism* (New York: New York University Press).

Peltason, Jack (1961): *58 Lonely Men* (Urbana, Ill.: University of Illinois Press).

Pennock, J. Roland, and John Chapman, eds. (1983): *Liberal Democracy* (New York: New York University Press).

Perry, Michael (1982): *The Constitution, the Courts, and Human Rights* (New Haven: Yale University Press).

Peters, Ellen (1981): "Reality and the Language of the Law," 90 *Yale Law Journal* 1193.

Posner, Richard (1977): *Economic Analysis of Law*, 2nd ed. (Boston: Little, Brown & Co.).

Posner, Richard (1981): *The Economics of Justice* (Cambridge: Harvard University Press).

Posner, Richard (1983): "The Meaning of Judicial Self-Restraint," 59 *Indiana Law Journal* 1.

Powell, Thomas Reed (1925): "Constitutional Metaphors," *The New Republic*, February 11, p. 25.

Pritchett, C. Herman (1948): *The Roosevelt Court* (Chicago: Quadrangle Books).

Railton, Peter (1983): "Judicial Review, Elites, and Liberal Democracy," in J. Roland Pennock and John Chapman, eds., *Nomos XXV: Liberal Democracy* (New York: New York University Press).

Rauh, Joseph (1979): "A Personal View of Justice Benjamin Cardozo," 1 *Cardozo Law Review* 5.

Rawls, John (1971): *A Theory of Justice* (Cambridge: Balknap Press of Harvard University).

Riker, William (1984): "The Heresthetics of Constitution-Making," 78 *American Political Science Review* 1.

Rodell, Fred (1939): *Woe unto You, Lawyers!* (New York: Reynal and Hitchcock).

Rorty, Richard (1979): *Philosophy and the Mirror of Nature* (Princeton: Princeton University Press).

Rorty, Richard (1983): "The Pragmatist," *The New Republic*, May 9, p. 32.

Rothenberg, Randall (1983): "Robert Nozick vs. John Rawls," *Esquire Magazine*, March 1983, p. 201.

Rothstein, Edward (1984): "The Return of Romanticism," *The New Republic*, August 27, p. 25.

Rumble, Wilfred (1968): *American Legal Realism* (Ithaca, NY: Cornell University Press).

Sacks, Oliver (1976): *Awakenings* (New York: Random House).

Sacks, Oliver (1984): *A Leg to Stand on* (New York: Summit Books).

Saphire, Richard (1981): "The Search for Legitimacy in Constitutional Theory: What Price Purity?," 42 *Ohio State Law Journal* 335.

Sarat, Austin (1977): "Studying American Legal Culture: An Assessment of Survey Evidence," 11 *Law and Society Review* 427.

Scheiber, Harry (1984): "Public Rights and the Rule of Law in American Legal History," 72 *California Law Review* 217.

Schmidhauser, John (1984): *Constitutional Law in American Politics* (Monterey, CA: Brooks Cole).

Schwartz, Elliott (1983): "Performance in the Midst of Pluralism," in Betty Jean Craige, ed., *Relativism in the Arts* (Athens, GA: University of Georgia Press).

Shaffer, Thomas (1981): *On Being a Christian and a Lawyer* (Provo, UT: Brigham Young University Press).

Shapiro, Martin (1964): *Law and Politics in the Supreme Court* (New York: The Free Press).

Shapiro, Martin (1965): "Stability and Change in Judicial Decision-Making: Incrementalism or Stare Decisis," 2 *Law in Transition Quarterly* 134.

Shapiro, Martin (1981): *Courts: A Comparative and Political Analysis* (Chicago: Univerity of Chicago Press).

Shapiro, Martin (1983): "Fathers and Sons: The Court, the Commentators, and the Search for Values," in Vincent Blasi, ed., *The Burger Court: The Counter-Revolution that Wasn't* (New Haven: Yale University Press).

Shechner, Mark (1982): "Three Honest Men," *The New Republic*, February 17, p. 32.

Shklar, Judith (1964): *Legalism* (Cambridge: Harvard University Press).

Shneidman, Edwin, ed. (1981): *Endeavors in Psychology: Selections from the Personology of Henry A. Murray* (New York: Harper & Row).

Smolla, Rodney (1982): "The Reemergence of the Right-Privilege Distinction in Constitutional Law: The Price of Protesting too Much," 35 *Stanford Law Review* 69.

Soifer, Aviam (1981): "Complacency and Constitutional Law," 42 *Ohio State Law Journal* 383.

Strauss, Peter (1983): "Was There a Baby in the Bathwater? A Comment on the Supreme Court's Legislative Veto Decision," 1983 *Duke Law Journal* 789.

Summers, Robert (1982): *Instrumentalism and American Legal Theory* (Ithaca, NY: Cornell University Press).

Terrell, Timothy (1984): "Flatlaw: An Essay on the Dimensions of Legal Reasoning and the Development of Fundamental Normative Principles," 72 *California Law Review* 288.

Thayer, James Bradley (1983): "The Origin and Scope of the American Doctrine of Constitutional Law," 7 *Harvard Law Review* 129.

Thibaut, John, and Laurens Walker (1975): *Procedural Justice: A Psychological Analysis* (Hillsdale, NJ: L. Erlbaum Associates).

Tribe, Laurence (1978): *American Constitutional Law* (Mineola, NY: Foundation Press).

Tribe, Laurence (1980): "The Puzzling Persistence of Process-Based Constitutional Theories," 89 *Yale Law Journal* 1063.

Tushnet, Mark (1979): "Truth, Justice, and the American Way," 57 *Texas Law Review* 1307.

Tusnhet, Mark (1980): "Darkness on the Edge of Town: The Contributions of John Hart Ely to Constitutional Theory," 89 *Yale Law Journal* 1037.

Tushnet, Mark (1981): "The Dilemmas of Liberal Constitutionalism," 42 *Ohio State Law Journal* 411.

Tushnet, Mark (1981a): "Legal Scholarship: Its Causes and Cure," 90 *Yale Law Journal* 1205.

Tushnet, Mark (1983): "Following the Rules Laid Down: A Critique of Interpretivism and Neutral Principles," 96 *Harvard Law Review* 781.

Tushnet, Mark (1984): "Critical Legal Studies and Constitutional Law: An Essay in Deconstruction," 36 *Stanford Law Review* 623.

Tushnet, Mark (1984a): "The Optimist's Tale," 132 *University of Pennsylvania Law Review* 1257.

Twain, Mark (1916): *The Mysterious Stranger* (New York: Harpers).

Tyler, Tom (1984): "The Role of Perceived Injustice in Defendants' Evaluation of Their Courtroom Experience," 18 *Law and Society Review* 51.

Unger, Roberto Mangabeira (1983): "The Critical Legal Studies Movement," 96 *Harvard Law Review* 563.

Van Alstyne, William (1983): "Interpreting *This* Constitution," 35 *University of Florida Law Review* 209.

Walzer, Michael (1983): *Spheres of Justice: A Defense of Pluralism and Equality* (New York: Basic Books).

Wechsler, Herbert (1959): "Toward Neutral Principles of Constitutional Law," 73 *Harvard Law Review* 1.

Weisberg, Richard (1982): "How Judges Speak: Some Lessons on Adjudication in *Billy Budd, Sailor*, with an Application to Justice Rehnquist," 57 *New York University Law Review* 1.

Weisberg, Robert (1984): "Deregulating Death," in Kurland, Casper and Hutchinson, eds., *The Supreme Court Review—1983* (Chicago: University of Chicago Press).

White, G. Edward (1982): *Earl Warren: A Public Life* (New York: Oxford University Press).

White, G. Edward (1984): "The Working Life of the Marshall Court, 1815–1835," 70 *University of Virginia Law Review* 1.

White, James (1982): "Law as Language: Reading Law and Reading Literature," 60 *Texas Law Review* 415.

Winch, Peter (1958): *The Idea of a Social Science and its Relation to Philosophy* (New York: Humanities Press).

Wolfe, Christopher (1981): "A Theory of U.S. Constitutional History," 42 *Journal of Politics* 292.

Wolff, Robert (1977): *Understanding Rawls: A Reconstruction and Critique of "A Theory of Justice"* (Princeton: Princeton University Press).

Wolin, Sheldon (1960): *Politics and Vision* (Boston: Little, Brown & Co.).

Woodward, Bob and Scott Armstrong (1979): *The Brethren: Inside the Supreme Court* (New York: Simon and Schuster).

 INDEX

"Caine Mutiny Court-Martial," 152–153
Cambridge, Godfrey, 88
Canon, Bradley, 82
Cardozo, Benjamin 10, 12, 39, 52,
    55, 120, 156, 168, 182–184, 186,
    191, 192
Carolene Products footnote, 86–89, 139
Carter, Lief, xvii, 26, 53, 91, 119n, 155n,
    172
"Casablanca," 129, 138
Cavanaugh, Ralph, 90–91
Chapman, John, 30
Chayes, Abram, 90–92, 96
"Chicago School" of jurisprudence, 41–
    42
Choper, Jesse, 31, 83–86, 90, 95, 101,
    134, 162, 192
Christie, Agatha, 122–123
Clark, Charles E., 77
Coase, Ronald, 109
Cohen, Felix, 97
Cohen, Morris, 72
Cohen, Ronald, 57
Coleman, Jules, 110
Commonwealth Edison v. Montana, 84–
    85
Communities
    defined, 15–16
    political and academic communities
        contrasted, 15–16, 66
Constitution
    mythical nature of, 64–65
    normative nature of, 3–5
Constitutional history
    conflicting doctrinal patterns through-
        out, 21–25
    political patterns throughout, 25–29
Constitutional jurisprudence
    conflicting theories of, 29–39
Constitutional law
    modern patterns of in other countries,
        56
    public ignorance of, 17–18
    recent developments in, 18–21
Corwin, Edward, 55
Courts
    advantages of as policymakers, 91–92
    shortcomings of as policymakers, 90
Cover, Robert, 32, 139–143, 147, 157, 195
    "Nomos and Narrative" described,
        139–143
Cox, Archibald, 31

"Critical Legal Studies" movement
    generally, xv, xvii, 8, 98–101
    aesthetic character of, 130–133
    and hermeneutics, 128
    nihilism in, 130–131
    playfulness in, 129
    and pragmatism, 127, 130
Croasmun, Earl,
    and Richard Cherwitz on aesthetics in
        rhetoric, 188
Crosskey, William, 53
Cuomo, Mario, 52n, 169

Dahl, Robert, 30, 97
Dauenhauer, Bernard, xviii
DeVries, Peter, 104
Dewey, John, 9, 107, 109, 112, 135, 144,
    187
Dickens, Charles, 36
    "David Copperfield," 117–120, 122,
        145
Dignitarian theory
    conflict with interpretivism, 56–57
    Dworkin and, 116–117
    Murphy and, 123–127
    Rawls and, 112–116
    research support for, 57
    triangulation on, 134, 192
Disch, Thomas, 40
Dolbeare, Kenneth, 17
Douglas, William O., 113, 125, 180
Drew, Elizabeth, 170
Dworkin, Ronald, xv, xvii, 11, 55, 113,
    116–129, 134, 145, 152n, 192
    critique of, 119–123
    internal/external preference distinc-
        tion, 119–121
    and literary criticism, 121–123
    policy/principle distinction, 117
    and positivism, 118

Easterbrook, Frank, 42
Eco, Umberto, 195
Elias, Norbert, 13
Ely, John Hart, xvii, 86–90, 92, 94–95,
    99, 101, 103, 119–121, 129, 134, 149,
    192
Emerson, Thomas, 28
Engle v. Issac, 177–178

Fairlie, Henry, 66, 170–171
Fairman, Charles, 53
Fifoot, C.H.S., 33–34

 # ABOUT THE AUTHOR

Lief Carter holds a law degree from Harvard and a Ph.D. from the University of California, Berkeley. His doctoral dissertation won the American Political Science Association's Corwin Award in 1973. Since 1973 he has taught legal process, jurisprudence, constitutional law and administrative law at the University of Georgia. He has published books and articles in each of these fields. In 1984 he received Georgia's highest award for excellence in teaching. Professor Carter is an amateur musician. His current research focuses on the interactions between politics and music, both serious and popular. He lives in Athens, Georgia, with his wife, three children, and several animals.

Pergamon Government and Politics Series

Series Editors:
Richard A. Brody, Norman J. Ornstein, Paul E. Peterson,
Nelson W. Polsby, Martin M. Shapiro